'Phil Cool – the frankly unbelievably talented impressionist – was the biggest and funniest face on television for much of the 1980s...'
– LANCASHIRE POST

'I watched every Phil Cool show with pure joyful amazement. His blend of dry beautifully-observed wit one moment and then ingenious, shape-shifting facial contortions the next was glorious. Anticipation of what Phil was going to create was palpable – a jaw-dropping treat of hilarity and amazement...'
– JON CULSHAW

'As a fellow impressionist, I have nothing but admiration and respect for Phil; a true inspiration and virtuoso of vocal and facial dexterity...'
– JOHN THOMSON

'He did this Aquaphibian and scrunched his face up. I remember actually weeping with laughter. I had never seen anything as funny as that...'
– STEPHEN MERCHANT

'Phil is a joy to behold. But, most of all, that face..! It's remarkable...'
– JASPER CARROTT

STAND-UP CHAMELEON

PHIL COOL

Scratching Shed Publishing Ltd

Copyright © Phil Martin 2024
All rights reserved
The moral right of the author has been asserted
First published by Scratching Shed Publishing Ltd in 2024
Registered in England & Wales No. 6588772.
Registered office:
47 Street Lane, Leeds, West Yorkshire. LS8 1AP
www.scratchingshedpublishing.co.uk
ISBN: 978-1068618949

Cover image: Phil Cool © Phil Martin
Back cover images: © Phil Martin

No part of this book may be reproduced or transmitted in any form or by any other means without the written permission of the publisher, except by a reviewer who wishes to quote brief passages in connection with a review written for insertion in a magazine, newspaper or broadcast

Every effort has been made to obtain the necessary permissions with reference to copyright material, both illustrative and quoted. We apologise for any omissions in this respect and will be pleased to make the appropriate acknowledgements in any future edition.

A catalogue record for this book is available from the British Library.

Typeset in Minion Pro and Futura
Printed and bound in the United Kingdom by

Printed and bound in the UK
by CPI Group (UK) Ltd, Croydon, CR0 4YY

For my family

CONTENTS

Foreword ix
Curtain-up xiii

The Tale 1
There are Some Cruel Bastards Out There 32
The Tale Continues 39
COOL 42
The Tale Continues 49
Comedy Out of Tragedy 58
The Tale Continues 65
Killing Time on Tour 69
The Tale Continues 77
Getting Spotted 83
The Tale Continues 87
Phil O'Sophicool 93
The Tale Continues 96
Hecklers, Drunks and Other Interruptions 99
The Tale Continues 106
Tales of Nutty Bits – Not Naughty Bits 112
The Tale Continues 116

Contents

It's a Funny Business, Comedy. Sometimes 120
The Tale Continues 131
A Winter's Tale 137
The Tale Continues 143
A Rant 152
The Tale Continues 156
Fringe Benefits – Making It in Scotland 159
The Tale Continues 171
Wales 178
The Tale Continues 181
Gone Fishing... in Ireland 194
The Tale Continues 202
Death on the Ocean Wave 209
The Tale Concludeth 218

Encore 225

Foreword

* by Bev Bevan *

I first saw Phil Cool at a comedy club in Kings Heath, Birmingham, during the early-1980s. Like most musicians, I love my comedy and Phil was clearly very special indeed.

I had never seen anyone like him before, with his unique talent for mimicking and that amazing rubber face of his. I told my good friend Jasper Carrott about him and he then began booking Phil at The Boggery, his folk comedy club in Solihull. Jasper was much impressed too and went on to take an active part in furthering Phil's career on television.

After which, it wasn't long before the rest of the country also discovered Phil. I'm convinced there is still residual love for him up and down the land.

In more recent times Phil, sadly, decided to retire from comedy and we lost contact. But then, during the lockdown years, my wife Joy and I put a show together on social media called 'Quill Connect' and we asked Phil to take part. He was nervous after his long lay-off, but his performance was of course hilarious and he became the star of the series.

Foreword

I am so happy to see that he has now put his life story in print – the wider world of entertainment has missed him. I'm sure fans of comedy – and music – will absolutely lap up his hugely entertaining book. I know I did.

I'm very happy to say that our friendship with Phil and his wife and son is now rekindled. We look forward to seeing them all again – and sharing a lot more laughter – soon.

Bev Bevan,
The Move, Black Sabbath, ELO, Quill.
July 2024

A Note from the Author

I just don't hope that you will ever find none of this book even slightly grammatically incorrect. If you do then dont be two sure it's perhaps you that cant ever appreciate a good reed. I hope as well that my pooer skooling doesn't impare you enjoying this autobiographical biography that I just wrote. Also it must be sad that although this hook is all my own fork I admit to having used vice recognition software.

Curtain-up

Dust. It has its own smell you know; there amid the dark and dimly-lit recesses of any theatre beyond a certain age. Not unpleasant like the stuff that accumulates in old attics, but welcoming.

Bits of dead skin, hair, soil particles and whatnot that have settled backstage and in the wings down the years, coating those forlorn old boards with what for me was always a very distinctive presence.

When disturbed, specks swirl in the lights and on the air and it was then that I'd feel anointed. This will be my special hour, the dust seemed to whisper, its aroma and presence as I waited out these last 'eternal' minutes adding to a state of nervous excitement. Then, in common with countless other entertainers who have stood behind these curtains down the years, the moment comes to walk out in front of over 1,600 people, all of whom feel they know me, having bought a share in Phil Cool for the price of a ticket.

Running through my opening lines in my head, the dust now becomes peripheral as I focus on the job in hand. The noise of cross-conversation from the auditorium merges into a solitary hum, as many voices become one. One big animal – friendly, I hope.

No, it is going to be fine. The people out there, bless them, have

Stand-up Chameleon

paid good money. They've made the effort to leave home for a while just to see me and, for now, I am theirs and grateful for it. My last minute over, the house music stops, the house lights dim and an expectant hush falls over the audience.

One last deep breath, a look to the heavens and then away I go, out into the spotlight. It has taken me eleven years as a professional to get here, from the wilderness of obscurity to the Leeds Grand.

And at last, it feels like I am home.

The journey has not been easy. In fact, it has been a long hard slog. But now, here I am, the kid from class 3C at St Augustine's Secondary Modern School, Chorley, not so far removed as might be assumed from those early days of mayhem and disruption.

Phil Cool Died Here
And Lived To Tell The Tale

The Tale

Generally, I was a shy 14-year-old, by no means the class clown. Yet every now and then a compulsion would rise in me to try something completely crazy – just for the hell of it.

Like the day, in 1962, when I was looking in the mirror at home and experimenting with facial expressions, contorting my face into Charles Laughton's Quasimodo. It was frightening!

Was I wearing some revolutionary new make-up? No, nothing like that. There were no props, elastic bands or fingers pulling flesh either. This was just my face, naturally flexible and able to transform in an instant from relaxed neutrality to a gargoyle of epic proportions. Behold! I could talk through these crumpled features too if I tried.

'Wow! This'll go well,' I thought and tried it first on Neil Woods, the kid I sat next to in class. It sent him into hysterics, only just managing to control himself as our form teacher walked into the room. I'd planted an image in his mind that, throughout the lesson, he fought to subdue, stifling his laughter.

This teacher – a bloke in his 40s nicknamed 'Phlegmy' because he would cough up globules of the stuff, surreptitiously deposit it in a bit of paper and walk, casually, over to a first floor window in the

Stand-up Chameleon

pretence of looking at the views before dropping it nonchalantly out every couple of minutes or so, despite everyone being aware of what he was up to. As the lesson progressed, Phlegmy turned his back on us at one point, writing on the blackboard. Here was the ideal time to give Woods another blast of Quasimodo and this time it nearly knocked him backwards off his chair. Laughter erupted. He had started and wasn't going to finish which, of course, got the rest of the class at it too. Not at me but at Woods, hysterically out of control.

Phlegmy spun around. 'Woods!' he spat. 'Come here and tell us all what you find so amusing. I am sure we can all share in the joke.'

And so our classmate walked out to the front, desperately trying to keep the lid on as he stood facing the other pupils at their desks.

'Well?' crackled Phlegmy, fishing for more paper. 'Let's hear it.'

'It's Martin, sir,' said the crimson faced boy, pointing at me, because Martin is my real surname. 'He keeps... he keeps...'

'Spit it out, Woods...'

'He keeps doing this face, sir,' he said, his Chorley accent by now having taken on a somewhat queer tone owing to repressed mirth.

Setting off for another admiring view of the felt roof below, sir too now sounded weird, a bit like a human concertina. 'Martin!' he bellowed. 'To the front of the class!'

I walked out, deadpan, not saying a word.

'Now. Why is Woods laughing?"

'I'm not sure sir,' I replied, straight-faced.

'Not sure, boy? *Not sure*?' His phlegm threatened to go volcanic. 'I'll ask you one more time, Woods. What is it that you find so very amusing about Martin's face?'

By this point, the co-accused and I stood either side of Phlegmy at the front of the class and so, as the teacher addressed Woods, I saw my chance. Everyone in the classroom save Phlegmy, who had his back to me, sat eyes front, the ideal opportunity to give them my Quasimodo. At which, instantly, everyone exploded into hysterics. Phlegmy spun around furiously, but my face now held an innocent 'Search me, I don't know what's going on' expression. Four times I managed to repeat the floor show before everything culminated in

The Tale

six strokes of the cane across the hands of Woods and I. But, it was worth it! I had discovered something. Something that would set me apart from everyone else. I had a talent. I could make people laugh without uttering a single word. And from that day to this I have been exploiting that ability – mercilessly.

※

St Augustine's Catholic All Boys Secondary Modern was one of those schools you left thicker than when you enrolled.

I always reasoned it was 'All Boys' simply to accustom its lads to a jail environment. There was an air of anarchy about the place that was only kept in check by the brutality of certain teachers, the most dreaded of whom was the Neanderthal who taught pottery, and also took us for French and Religious Studies. Six foot four with a stoop that meant his knuckles practically scraped the corridor floors, he had a choice of nicknames: 'Fester' or 'Fink'. To me, he was Fester as it rhymed with his surname. He invariably wore brown sandals and socks that squeaked loudly when he walked, which for us was most fortunate. That distinctive squeak meant you knew he was coming well before he appeared – a warning it was time to scarper.

Falling foul of this beast was most unpleasant if, for any reason, he deemed you had fallen short of expectations. Not scrubbing the table clean enough after pottery class, for instance, or not being able to recite word perfect and from memory the banal catechism questions and answers that make up Catholic dogma. Or even if you simply looked at him the wrong way, or he caught you 'loitering' (he was fanatical about that). He would take you by the scruff of the neck, force you over a table and lay into you with a strap. It was unnerving being in the same room. He wore reflective – what I called 'twinkly' – glasses so you never knew where the bastard was looking. Tucked into his trousers was a white nylon shirt through which a string vest could faintly be seen, but when he pressed against any clay-soiled surface he'd be left with a bold clay imprint of said vest on the outside of his shirt; and keeping everything in check was that red leather belt.

Stand-up Chameleon

The bloke unnerved me. He made my life and that of my classmates hell but, through him, I discovered another talent I possessed – and one that I have been able to use ever since to great advantage.

By way of revenge, I wrote a poem that became so popular with the boys they learnt it, recited it and even sang it to the tune of the Burl Ives song 'Mr Froggie Went A-Courtin' on the bus home. I had become a hero and realised that my face wasn't the only thing that could make people laugh, my words could too. Here it is:

Fester's Poem

I was working late in the craftroom one night
When my eyes beheld a horrible sight
A clay covered hand crawled out of a pot,
His twinkly glasses were covered not
He grabbed his strap off the dirty front bench
Grabbed my right arm and gave it a wrench.
You could plainly see his stringy vest,
he said 'next time laddie it's six of the best.'
As the clay on his forehead started to melt
He looked down at his pretty red belt,
Then furiously distinguished a clay splashed candle
Then listening I heard the squeak of a sandal
Then I heard the crack of a knee
My only alternative was that to flee.
I jumped out onto the window sill
And entered the den of the kiln.
Twas in this weird room came out a great boom!
And to my surprise his twinkly glasses were smashed in his eyes.
His clay covered face was no longer brown
But as black as death with an ugly frown.
Behold Fester is dead as there is a crack
Right through his pot head.
Little brown demons arose from the clay
And ceremoniously dancing I heard them say
Whilst advancing faster and faster
'Mr ****** is surely our master
Oh we know he is not very learned'

The Tale

Then looking in the big pot said 'who stole our Bernard ?'
Mr ******'s picture was on the front page
It showed his dead body embalmed in a cage.
They lowered his coffin into a sea of white clay
Mr ****** won't be heard of until the last day.
Hurray! Hurray! Hurray!

(P.Martin, age 12)

Our headmaster at this Academy of Ignorance was known to us all as 'The Boss'. He was a decent enough bloke.

Every morning during assembly, he would address the boys from the stage of the school hall. 'It's come to my notice' was his favourite phrase. It was always: 'It's come to my notice that a number of boys are going around the school ... swearing, or not wearing the correct uniform or whatever.' As the speech was delivered his jowls would wobble and he would get worked up, go red-faced. The Boss was my first impression, therefore, with a script. I performed it to some of the lads. Not only did I enjoy doing that, I must have realised – at a subconscious level perhaps – that mimicry meant easy laughs.

The Boss was the last member of school staff I spoke to on the day I left St Augustine's. I was fifteen at a time when the Beatles were in between 'Love Me Do' and 'Please Please Me'. Minutes before the final bell, the Boss stopped me outside his office, smiled and feigning interest said: 'It's your last day today, isn't it, Philip?'

'Yes, sir,' I replied.

'What job are you going into?'

'I thought maybe I'd be an electrician, sir,' I said, having been told by several people that it was a good trade to be in.

His reply was a farewell and career lesson rolled in to one. 'No, Philip. You'll never be an electrician. You've got to be good at maths.'

'Well, thanks a lot for your encouragement,' I thought and, with that, left the wretched place to go on and eventually become ... an electrician. It has been a trait of mine throughout my life that when anyone has said I couldn't do a thing it made me extra-determined to prove I could. Without that, I'd have got nowhere. And it is why,

Stand-up Chameleon

in an odd sort of way, I can look back on those bleak days at school and see how much I owe to the place. Despite their best attempts to destroy all hope and ambition, it was there that I learnt those (to me anyway) massive life skills, making people laugh with my rubber face or use of words and, ultimately, my ability to mimic. But all of that would have been useless, professionally, if I wasn't also instilled with determination. Learnt not to give in when all around you say it's useless. Learnt to believe in myself and have the courage of my convictions. As I write and reflect on my schooling, I'm actually very thankful to St Augustine's and feel I ought to convey the appreciation I feel towards the establishment. That is, until I realised the council had already done it for me. The place was demolished years back.

※

Upon leaving St Augustine's, I did a lot of hanging around and got under my parents' feet. The first job I took was at a cotton mill just around the corner as I didn't really know what else to do.

My mother and sister had both worked there in the past, been well-liked and left in good circumstances, so I was pretty sure I'd be employed there if I asked. It was what you might call a dead-end job though, in the warehouse, and paid just under four quid a week but with as much fluff as you could eat. My function was to lift huge rollers of cloth off a table and couple the roller to a machine that would then strip the cloth off the roller and fold it into yards. While this went on, I had to stand at the machine and guide the cloth over by laying my hands on it. This ensured even and straight folds at the other end. It was quite scary at first because it made one hell of a clattering sound. After that was completed I would walk around the machine and lift off the folded cloth with both arms underneath it – a bit like a human fork-lift truck. Then I had to walk thirty yards over to a table where the cut-lookers examined the cloth for faults and oil stains. When this was finished I'd repeat the whole process.

So, I thought to myself, this is my reward for staring out of the window for four years and daydreaming for seven hours a day at St

The Tale

Augustine's is it? Slaving in a dark satanic mill, the only light relief being getting teased, embarrassed and aroused by some of the great looking women. The tedium soon became unbearable.

Another roller ... another stack of cloth ... over and over again.

Once, during this dire evolution into a cabbage, I allowed a wave of madness to take me over. Suddenly, I refused to do any more of this crap, stopped and wandered off to the mill lodge to watch the small carp and goldfish for an hour. Upon my return, the rollers had built up and the women I worked with were not pleased. Neither was the foreman, Gilbert, a dead ringer for Toulouse-Lautrec, only smaller. I felt even worse now having made the girls cry and having little Gilbert constantly scowling up at me.

My eventual rescue from this mundane existence came in the form of my mother, who asked the owner of an electrical contractor in Chorley town centre if he would take me on as an apprentice. He agreed and my nine months of vegetable gestation came to an end.

※

One day, I was singing to myself in the bathroom.

> Look at her turn her nose up,
> She makes my face go red,
> Drivin by with that other guy,
> It's all gone to her head...

A tune had come simultaneously with the words and so the process continued – more words, more tune. By the time I'd finished making my bed, I thought I'd written a pretty good song. Today, on reflection, I think it *would* have been a great song – but only if I'd given it a different tune and a different set of lyrics.

What it did have was the twee and simplistic stamp of a naïve young kid, but it was a start and it was mine. Consequently, I went out and bought myself a Grundig reel-to-reel tape recorder. It had a lid and a handle and looked like a small suitcase, so rather than feeling self-conscious carrying it around I felt at ease because no-

Stand-up Chameleon

one would have known what it really was. I felt smug too because nobody I knew had one of these. I was charged with excitement in anticipation of using it, all the way back to the council house where I lived with my mother. I must have been about 17 at the time as my father was no longer with us at this early stage of my development.

Dad died on 4 January 1965. We never did find out whether that was at Leyland Motors itself, where he worked, or in the ambulance taking him to Chorley Hospital. We were told he'd collapsed during dinner break, got to his feet again and made his way to the medical centre, looking pale and dreadful. He had damaged his face too from the fall. The staff there told him to wait for the works ambulance to return from another call-out. Sometime between sitting down to wait and arriving at the hospital he passed away.

Heart failure. At fifty-four. Smoking twenty a day, sometimes Embassy filter tips, sometimes Consulate menthol flavour.

Perhaps it was mixing the two that killed him.

I often wonder what my dad would have made of my new found musicianship. He had been a good harmonica player. Just before we lost him he had been really pleased that I had started training as an electrician. 'All you'll ever need, Spud,' he once said, 'is a few little screwdrivers and a pair of pliers.'

Of course he was wrong. You need chisels, bolsters, star drills, a hacksaw, tenon saw, umpteen types of screwdriver, a lump hammer, claw hammer, pin hammer, penknife, torch, snips pliers, long nose pliers and a hundred and one other things whose names I've long forgotten. All of these I bought over time and carried around in an old toolbox I'd been given until, one day, I thought I'd treat myself to one of those new jobs with little sections that pull out. Big it was, metallic blue-painted steel. I cleaned all my tools and placed them lovingly in their new home, along with a few more tools to fill it out. I put everything in its appropriate place and closed the lid, it had no lock as yet, and the very next day took a bus to work. It was a double decker – no doors at the back, just a pole for people to grab onto in those days. Under the stairs was a space for prams, luggage and the like, which is where I stored my precious new toolbox.

The Tale

The bus set off and, after a hundred yards or so, the driver swung it around a hard right at a junction. Meanwhile, I had made my way upstairs. All of a sudden there came this almighty bang, clatter, smash and a screeching of brakes before the bus shuddered to an abrupt halt. I peered out of my window expecting to witness the wreckage of a vehicle, a bollard in smithereens or something. But no. Instead, there were tools in the road. Lots of tools and a shiny blue toolbox stood upright on its end. The damn thing had slid across the floor, an unwitting victim of centrifugal force.

While I swiftly gathered up the debris the bus driver waited in stony silence, a painfully embarrassing experience as I was holding up the traffic and my fellow passengers were peering at me through their windows. This was an clearly an omen. As it turned out I wasn't ultimately suited for a career in the building trade. Nevertheless, I did end up sticking it out for just over ten years.

The first four of those – aged 16-20 – were spent at the Chorley Town Centre Electrical Contracting Firm. Four years doesn't seem a long time nowadays, but back then it felt like an eternity.

At school I hadn't been very keen on Fester, it's true, but the boss of this company was an even nastier piece of work. In my entire life I have only once truly hated a fellow human being. Him. To say that the firm had a climate of fear would be an understatement.

Everybody who worked there was frightened stiff of the man. He had white hair and was in his late-fifties, I suppose. He would arrive like a whirlwind in your midst and scream (he had a horrible voice) at you if unsatisfied with what you were doing, which was the norm. I kept out of his way for the first few days, but after that he assigned me to re-filling shelves. I'd have to make a list of which items were needed, go upstairs and along a corridor to the back door (the shop was on a hill), come out on another level to the outside stores, grab all the accessories, stick them in a cardboard box and run back down to the shop and stock it up ready for when customers came in to buy a lampholder, plug, fuse or whatever. Sounds simple doesn't it?

Well, it wasn't for a 16-year-old! At that age, a boy's brain doesn't work too well and I used to get everything mixed up. The two-amp

Stand-up Chameleon

plug tops would end up in the five-amp plug top section and the one-gang, two-way switches would end up in the two-gang, one-way switch compartment. And all the time this white-haired maniac would hover over me. A customer might ask for a switched brass lampholder. The boss would then go to put his hand on one, only to discover it wasn't there, at which would erupt into a furious rage and start hurling abuse. It was excruciatingly embarrassing and the more verbal punishment he dished out, the more mistakes I made. This lasted a few months until it was decided that I should go out on a wiring job and 'help' the electricians while trying to learn their trade.

The incident that stands out above all others while I worked there does so because it almost got me killed. I was with an electrician named Jim, a Glaswegian. On meeting him, I couldn't tell a word he said – neither could anyone else. But I stuck with it and eventually became his interpreter. One day, we were wiring a nice big detached Victorian house in a posh part of town. The job was almost finished, only a bit of tidying up to do, so Jim was told to start another one elsewhere. Before he went, he briefed me on what was left – just a few trivial things ... bit of plastering beneath the stairs where the fuse boxes and meters were ... some cables coming through the ceiling would have to be sunk into the wall plaster. For this latter job, a hole would have to be 'chased out' with a bolster chisel. The cables should then be pressed into the wall and secured by metal capping. Finally, the wall needed to be plastered flush, so the cables couldn't be seen. It ought to have been easy enough.

Jim said goodbye and disappeared. I was now alone in the house. It was a big place and a lovely home. The owners, a couple in their forties, were out at work but a coal fire burned steadily in the hearth.

I decided to do the worst job first, the sinking of the cables, so took up my lumphammer and chisel. Surveying the wall, I picked my target area carefully, placed the chisel in contact with it, drew back the hammer, aimed and struck, not too hard, nor too soft. The chisel went clean through the aging plaster – and clean through the gas pipe that lay concealed within.

Now at that time the gas in use was coal gas, a horribly smelly

The Tale

substance that was deadly poisonous and popular among those with suicidal intent. Which is something I didn't have at that time.

The force of the gas coming out of my carefully chosen and executed hole was startling as it hit me full in the face.

'God, what am I going to do?' I yelped, in a complete state of panic. 'I can't just stand here with this deadly poison blowing in my face.' I was astute for my age when it came to life and death situations. 'I know, I'll find the gas meter and switch it off!' Despite their best attempts, St Augustine's hadn't sucked all the intelligence from my head, but where do you start looking for such a thing? Round the back of the house perhaps? In the outhouse? Under the sink? Maybe in a cupboard? I searched everywhere but found no gas meter and was soon running about like a headless chicken. I could feel the icy tentacles of death wrap themselves around my windpipe and became convinced that the gas was going to kill me. Then I had a brainwave. I would flatten the burst pipe! *Eureka*! I took a giant deep breath and went back under the stairs. Firstly, I knocked off more plaster, so I could expose the pipe better before flattening it but, believe me, this isn't as easy a task as it sounds with poisonous gas blasting you in the mush – the terrible smell, sinister hissing noise and necessity of having to continually step back ten paces to take a breath. Worse, I was failing dismally. I knew I'd soon be overcome by the noxious fumes and would keel over limp and lifeless if I didn't change tactics.

So, I retreated and decided to phone the shop, tell them what had happened and get them to send Jim back. I found the house phone and started dialling. Of course, this took an age in itself. We forget, with our modern mobiles, how slow dialling a number used to be. You would stick your finger in the dial, turn the disc, let it slowly revolve back and then dial the next number. And the next. And the next etc. It felt like a lifetime before I got through. But finally a girl answered and I told her of my plight, urging her, begging her, to send someone quickly. I sensed her own panic as she appreciated the gravity of my situation. She promised to send someone and I put the phone back on its hook. Then an awful thought hit me like a thunderbolt. The fire! The fire was still burning, the house filling up

Stand-up Chameleon

with gas – I was going to be blown to smithereens. I must put it out! I went into the washhouse, found a bucket, filled it as quickly as I could with water, ran back to the living room of this lovely home and threw the lot on the flames. Instantly, steam, soot and cinders erupted all over the hearth and onto the rug, but the fire blazed on.

Three buckets later, it still refused to die, spluttering defiantly as all around it gallons of black water covered the once pristine carpet.

Still, though, the hiss of escaping gas filled my ears. I had another brainwave – fear certainly makes your brain work quicker. Mix some plaster and plug the hole with it. I leapt into action, sweat pouring over me, tears rolling down my face as I faced my own imminent departure from this world. I took great dollops of plaster and thrust it into the hole that I had made only for it to come hurling straight right back at me, hitting me in the face. The more of it I tried to stick into the pipe the more I got covered in the stuff. It was my final desperate attempt to save the situation and I was close to giving up. Covered from head to foot in a weird composition of wet and sooty sand and gypsum I again took up the phone and rang the office.

The same girl answered. 'Jim is on the way,' she told me. 'He will be with you shortly.' I put the phone down, which was also now covered in plaster – every hole in the dial was completely encrusted. I glanced into the living room and to my complete horror saw the fire raging vigorously, behind me the coal-gas dragon was blowing wildly. It would now only be a matter of time...

'I don't want to die,' I thought and caught the sound of my own whimper. Next moment, I was walking out resolutely into the street thinking 'If the house goes up, I ain't going with it. I'd sooner face the mother of all bollockings, which I'm bound to get after this."

As I strode into the middle of the road, I saw Jim in the distance walking at what seemed like a snail's pace in my direction.

'Jim!' I screeched. 'Get a move on, quick!! The house is going to blow up!!!'

Jim broke into a trot, entered the house and then, without a hint of panic, calmly asked: 'Why did'na ye turn it off, Phil?' Standing right in the gas jet stream, I could have nutted him there and then.

The Tale

'I couldn't find the meter,' I replied with a tremor in my voice.

'Ye dozy wee f------ ye, it's right under ye nose,' he said, pointing at said meter under the stairs. 'Give me yer pliers, Phil.' I passed him the tool and with that he turned the gas off.

I never did get to finish off that particular job. It seemed that when the owners of the house returned and saw the mess they took the decision to finish the job themselves with the strict instruction that the young lad who had made it could not come anywhere near their place ever again.

*

The shop, stores and yard of this Electrical Contracting Firm were in Chorley town centre which, for those unfamiliar with the place, can be found about twenty miles north west of Manchester, not far from Bolton, Blackburn, Wigan and Preston.

Our shop front was in Market Street, but the tradesmen and lads used a back entrance through an alleyway off West Street. The boss also owned a house in West Street that was pretty much derelict and was used as an extra store and brew room. Occasionally, I'd take my Grundig reel-to-reel to work and do impressions of the boss and the foreman, a Londoner with a great voice I could imitate easily. He also had a moustache that made him look like a cross between Groucho Marx and Hitler. I would do these ridiculous scripts for the lads and they would all listen to them at dinnertime and crack up laughing. The foreman, generally horrible to everyone, completely changed in character when the boss was on holiday. He would then be really pleasant. Which proved to me that when the boss was away the climate of fear evaporated. This foreman was also obsessed with grommets – those little rubber things that fit into electrical boxes to protect a flex or a cable when it enters the box through the hole. 'Always make sure you put your grommets in, Philip,' he would say. There was many a script about grommets in my recordings.

There in that room in West Street, I would also sing one or two of the songs I had written. At the time, The Searchers had 'Needles

Stand-up Chameleon

and Pins' in the charts and, I think, The Beatles had 'From Me To You'. I would listen to this stuff on the radio and wonder at how great it would be to be a songwriter. Just to write songs for other people and remain unknown yourself, getting some mug to get up on stage or on TV and sing them while you stayed at home waiting for the cheques to shoot through the letterbox and land on the mat. Also at this time, I would look in the music papers for the addresses of likely London agents that might be interested in new songs for their artists. So there I was, a naïve kid writing corny songs and singing them unaccompanied into a recorder before sending them off to all these addresses, excited in anticipation of a reply. I was totally unaware that these little spools of tape would go straight into a London skip.

'Perhaps', I thought, 'if I were to get an instrument and learn how to play it, I might stand a better chance.' Was it more naivety? Nevertheless the next thing that went on to my shopping list was to be the key that opened the door to many a friendship.

A guitar.

Guitars are definitely my favourite objects. Especially acoustic guitars, whether nylon-stringed, Spanish classical type, or big steel-stringed jumbos. Not only are they beautiful to look at, with their sexy curves, they can hold you in fascination by their smell. A blend of the exotic woods of the instrument's bare interior with the varnish that finishes off the outside surfaces, it hits the spot in an area of the brain where dreams are born. Guitars leave you suspended in some other world and all this before you've picked the thing up to play it. Once you do, if its a real 'honey' it can send you off on a trip to magical places. Even if it's not perfect by construction or material, it will still sing for you and make you smile.

I waited long enough for the acoustic guitars I would describe as the best I've ever had. A 'Martin HD28' and a 'Fylde (Ken Nicol Signature)' take that honour, both big-bodied steel-string beauties. The 'Martin' I've had for around twenty-five years now, the 'Fylde' around fourteen years. That latter guitar inspired a tribute song to it I wrote called 'Ode To My Fylde Guitar'. I sing it in a Jake Thackray -style voice, with the opening line: 'Thar a little lump a wood that

The Tale

keeps me sane.' Yes, I talk to them now, no apologies. The guitars preceding the Fylde were the Martin HD28 and before that a 'John Hullah', which was made for me by John, a well-known guitar maker, in 1986. It served me well but ended up badly-broken, irreparable. I'd leant it up against the wall in the lounge. 'Fool,' said Bev, my wife. 'Don't leave it there. It will get damaged.' I'd meant to move it, but it slipped my mind. Joe, our son, had friends coming round and asked if I knew any party games. 'Yes,' I replied. 'I'll go to the pub and you lot have got to guess what time I'm gonna come back.' When I did return, it had been smashed, of course. One of Joe's mates had tripped and ploughed into it with the force of a rugby tackle. The insurance money went towards buying the 'Fylde' at least, and I can still see the 'Hullah' intact if I want to because it featured in the third BBC series of *Cool It*, which I have on disc at home.

Prior to that I had couple of Italian EKOs, the first of which I sold. The other was donated to an auction raising money for the family of Tim Parry, the 12-year-old boy killed by an IRA explosion in 1993 in Warrington. That was the one I played on the first and second series of *Cool It*. And before them I had a Hagstrom, a great looking classic Swedish guitar stained in a style they called sunburst. That was what I had in the 1970s when the American singer Melanie, who I fancied at the time, had a hit with 'Brand New Key', the song about the roller skates. I was naïve enough to stick a photo of her in the round hole on the back so, when you looked inside, there she was gazing out with that sultry sexy look she had. What was I like, for God's sake? I wouldn't be surprised if it's out there somewhere still, collecting dust in somebody's loft. Poor old Melanie, who I've just noticed died in January 2024, staring out into space at no one.

Before that, I played another Hagstrom. This one had a built-in pick-up and two knobs on its face. I never did plug it into anything. Bigger than the Melanie guitar, it was a darker shade of sunburst; in fact I recall seeing John Lennon with something similar. Mine was destroyed in a fire which took out a whole row of transit camp billets at Pembroke power station, one of which I was occupying while working as an electrician in 1971. I claimed on the insurance for

Stand-up Chameleon

that as well. All that was left of it in the ashes was six strings and the machine heads.

Next guitar, going back, was a nylon-stringed Spanish-type I picked up in 1966, a beauty and easy to play. I had to trade it in for the Hagstrom, though, when I realised something bigger and louder was required to suit my changing needs. All of which brings me to the guitar I would class as my first (my big sister did get me one as a kid, but I don't really count that as I never played it), bought for four quid in 1965 from a guy who ran a music stall on Chorley market. After getting the thing home and examining it, I concluded that it wasn't even worth the pound I'd put down in advance of the monthly installments. But still, it was a start.

During the short time I had this 'guitar' I worked out from a book how to play a couple of chords, or to be more accurate 'part' chords, 'C' and 'G'. With these I managed to write several songs, although with very simplistic tunes. Imagine the opening bars of the *Steptoe and Son* theme tune going on for three-and-a-half minutes and you will have an idea of what they sounded like. What I really needed was someone who could teach me to play.

About a mile from us there lived a guy who also used to go to St Augustine's. I'd never really spoken to him. If we passed in the street we might exchange a quick 'hello', but that was all. He was known as Cloggy Woods, because that was what he wore on his feet. Being a bricklayer which might explain that; you obviously need good foot protection when handling bricks. Many a time I'd be waiting for the bus to take me the mile-and-a-half to the electrical shop and Cloggy would be walking down Harpers Lane, feet clattering and clanking. He'd nod as he reached the bus stop and go on, on his way to work. Somehow I heard he had a guitar and so one day, as I waited in town for the homeward bus, instead of just saying 'hello' I stopped him and explained how I'd bought a guitar to accompany my songs but was struggling to play it and getting nowhere. I'd heard he had one, so would he mind giving me a bit of coaching and advice.

'Sure I can,' said Cloggy. 'Come round to my house after tea with your guitar and we'll see what happens.'

The Tale

Later, I demonstrated my skill, or lack of it, on an instrument worth less than it own weight in firewood. Lets just say this was the only guitar that never sang, for me it was a real 'dog'.

Cloggy didn't laugh, but perhaps saw a glimmer of talent in my playing of this two-chord song, responding with a smile. 'What do you think, Owen?' I asked, Owen being his real name. I wasn't for calling him Cloggy; that was reserved for his workmates.

'Well, you strum okay,' he replied, 'but you need to know loads of different chords and learn a few well-known songs.'

Owen was a Dylan and Donovan fan and asked if I'd heard them. I told him I was familiar with singles like 'Subterranean Homesick Blues' and 'Catch the Wind'. Owen took a draw on his roll-up and blowing a cloud of Old Holborn into the air said: 'You ought to listen to these guys and learn a few of their songs, as they are easy to play. Like this...' Reaching for his guitar (a much better built thing than I was struggling on) and poised over the strings while positioning himself on a chair in the parlour of his parents' terraced house, he then began to play 'Mr. Tambourine Man', his high-pitched voice launching the first line as his fingers danced and picked away. Upon finishing the song he waited for a moment, in silence, which left an echo of it slowly decaying in my mind.

I didn't speak for a while. It would have been difficult with my jaw still on the floor. 'How did you learn tha – tha – that?'

'Finger style?' asked Owen, nonchalantly. 'Oh, it's just something I developed myself. You just listen and learn, keep experimenting like. If you keep at it, it just comes.'

After that encouragement, Owen showed me how to position my left hand to make chord formation easier. There was also a bit of coaching on finger style and, eventually, he introduced me to that great combination of sound you can get by simultaneously playing a mouth organ in a neck bracket. With his help, I was soon well on my way to learning to play and enjoying it.

It was shortly after this that I upgraded my guitar, getting rid of the four-quid market one. In fact, I sold it back to the guy I bought it from, for a pound. One of the few people who ever forgot my face.

Stand-up Chameleon

Following which I went straight to a proper music shop and snapped up the nylon-stringed Spanish one.

Owen and I went on for a few years together, playing at parties and in pubs, sometimes singing a Beatles song together in harmony, just for the love of it. We never made any money. We would also frequent local folk clubs and have a laugh at the type who filled these places, bearded blokes with chunky roll neck woollen sweaters, often sucking on a pipe. 'Plain clothes morris dancers,' we called them.

Occasionally Owen, more often than me, would get up to do a song, he being more advanced than I was. Besides, I was scared to death of getting up there in front of people who had actually paid to get in the place. There was a group called The Blue Water Folk, who Owen and me would gravitate towards because they were from the town and gigged around the Chorley area. We thought they were great, probably because we both fancied the blonde lead singer, Rita, although she was married to the guitarist.

We also ventured out on the bus to Preston, where a great cellar bar club, The Schooner, had two resident groups. One, the Cobblers, did traditional Lancashire stuff. The others, known as The Arkansas Travellers, were more interesting and made me wonder if there was a duo in Arkansas called The Preston Travellers. They were great, doing stuff from blues to bluegrass, one on guitar, the other banjo. They were in a different league to Owen and me, but as we visited the place every week we'd soak up their influence and leave inspired.

Owen liked one of my two-chord wonders, 'Weary Welcome,' and sang it while auditioning at Granada studios, Manchester. This was a competition for singer songwriters announced on a local TV show, *Firstimers*, that Owen followed up and entered in 1968. Shown in the afternoon, the programme was produced by Johnnie Hamp, a big name in television back then and responsible for such hits as *The Comedians* and *The Wheeltappers and Shunters Social Club*. He also had – or would go on to have – a hand in the first TV appearances of The Beatles, Burt Bacharach, Woody Allen, Cannon and Ball and Lisa Stansfield, so a handy man to impress. Owen sang and played 'Weary Welcome' for him and I remember Hamp being tickled pink

The Tale

by the lyrics. Looking back they were terrible but he must have made allowances for this poor soul singing his heart out with plinkety-plonkety two-chord accompaniment.

> *Next door's cat sitting on the wall in the same place,*
> *fancy that, I been away a week, it's the same face.*
> *Ma and Pa sittin' at home with their feet on the fireplace,*
> *I walk through the door, put my case on the floor,*
> *same expression on their face. Well I must be out of my mind,*
> *I must be out of my mind, well I must be so cause not a week*
> *ago I left the girl I loved behind... etc. etc, etc*

However, when the song ended Johnnie Hamp was so up for it and complimentary I thought Owen was home and dry. No chance. An act from Barnsley called Foggy Dew-O won (there were two of them) and I've been wary of talent competitions of any kind since. Years later, my manager would be baffled as to why I refused point blank to audition for *New Faces*, the *Britain's Got Talent* of its day. The reason is, I have always had a credibility line in my head and talent shows fall on the wrong side of it; not to mention the stigma attached to the damn things and the suspicion that every one of them is fixed in some way.

Still, that said, our day out at Granada Studios all those years ago was worth it and created a bit of excitement for two young dreamers. After a few more years, Owen gave up singing and playing in public while I continued to struggle by on my own. He left home one day, headed south with a tent, rucksack and guitar. Settling in Kent, after 'tramping it' for a while, he found a job, got wed and sired two kids before, many years later, getting a divorce. Even then he seldom returned north except for quick family visits. While married he lived in Gillingham and then alone in Whitstable. Occasionally, I would visit him on my travels, but by then he had packed in singing and playing. He did though still lay bricks.

Sadly, he passed away in November 2023. I still miss my first guitar guru very much indeed.

Stand-up Chameleon

※

Throughout the late-1960s and early-1970s I'd sit on a hard chair in our kitchen and the record songs I'd written on my Grundig.

The kitchen walls were bare brick, painted over with cream gloss paint, so the room had an echo to it which made recordings sound a lot better. Soon, I was also playing the usual Dylan and Donovan tunes. Paul Simon and the easier Beatles ones too. That wasn't many with Lennon and McCartney whose writing could be very complex, full of unusual chords that always left me scratching my head. My mother would walk in from the front room, where she'd be watching TV and relaxing, listen to what I was playing and then make some constructive criticism like 'Is it worth it?' – meaning she believed I was going nowhere. She had a point. I mean, I wasn't very good at this time, although had she lived until my break in the 1980s with *Cool It* she would have had the answer to her question. She did give me *some* encouragement though and meant well in her way. When I told her I was uncomfortable performing in the old pub spot I did she'd say: 'When you're up there playing in front of people imagine you're playing in the kitchen and it won't be overwhelming for you.'

You see, the spotlight was always a difficult place for me because I was on the shy side, self-conscious, having a morbid fear of making a fool of myself. I only managed to go through with it time after time for some reason I cannot explain.

Another mate of mine, Mick – also an electrician – frequented many a pub in Chorley and one night we ended up in the Imperial Hotel, still standing to this day. There was a band on that night from Preston called the Lune Street Gas Band, who didn't win, but came second on *Opportunity Knocks* in July 1971. Their singer, Bob Johnson, was doing his own songs and some really unusual stuff too; they were terrific. After they'd finished and the drinkers had supped the last drop of ale from their pint pots and reluctantly vacated the place, the landlord locked the doors and pulled a few more pints for the band. He must have thought Mick and I were with them and so

The Tale

we had fortunately got locked in too. We all stood at the bar having a laugh and I started to do some impressions. Burt Lancaster would be in conversation with Kirk Douglas about who had the nicest set of toothy pegs. John Wayne, though, was the one that made Bob crack up most, especially the line: 'Okay mister, just get on yer Honda 50 and get the hell outta here.' Then I'd do the Duke's unique silly walk. When the fun and laughter subsided Bob said: 'You ought to get up on stage and do that stuff, instead of just fooling around at the bar. If you want, we'll have you do a gig with us sometime.' This seemed a good idea to me, because Bob and his band were doing what I considered to be the right kind of stuff. They had that credibility about them and were all brilliant musicians.

Time moved on and after a year or so trying out comedy material and songs in the breaks between their sets, I was still struggling with putting together what you might call a decent half-hour show. The main problem being that Bob's gigs came every month or so and by the time the next one came around I had gone rusty again.

All this changed when Bob and his band (having now changed their name to Bush Country) got a regular spot every Monday night at The New Ship Inn, which was also in Preston. It had a really good rectangular room at the side which held about 150 people and had a raised stage at one end. It was here that I finally began to improve, not exactly in leaps and bounds, more a steadily evolving sort of way, as I gained more confidence and faced my stage fright. Once a week for a whole year was just what I needed, allowing me to experiment with ideas I thought were funny and sing one or two songs too.

And so, by the back end of 1974 I became known as 'him with the short hair' in the town, because everyone had long hair but me. It wasn't through choice. I did try growing it, but it's not the kind of hair that, when long, lies down under its own weight. Its awkward curly stuff that grows upwards and keeps on going. Have a look at the photograph of me with my mother, *overleaf*, standing side by side at a wedding when it was at its longest. I dig it out every now and then to remind myself just how horrendous it was, perched there in a column on top of my head...

Stand-up Chameleon

Me at a wedding with my mother and my hair

So anyway, before long 'him with the short hair' was doing quite well for himself and getting plenty of laughs at the Ship, introducing something new into the act every week. The audience consisted of people from the local music scene, bands and solo performers, who would come every week to listen to Bush Country and get me into the bargain, all for fifty pence. Wow! There were plenty of student types and a few middle-aged hippies hanging out, all with long hair of course. As such, it was a laid back scene and there was never any trouble. At 9.30-ish every Monday night, I'd walk up to the mic with my guitar and bag of props and do my thing.

The size of this bag expanded every week as people would bring

The Tale

me a new toy to adapt into a routine ready for the following Monday. One guy brought me a pith helmet that I still have to this day. The next week, I incorporated it into a rather rude sketch about Cliff Richard, which involved a wooden coat hanger clasped tight in my crotch upon which I hung said item. I can't remember the script but that pith helmet apparently suspended in mid-air above my fly hole is still a fond memory for myself and no doubt those who remember being there on those crazy nights.

I also had a fake joint, or reefer – the audience had the real ones. Really, it was just a pencil wrapped in paper I worked into a Mick Jagger routine. If you are familiar with the Stones' cover of Chuck Berry's 'Reelin' and Rockin'' – and the version they did of 'Tell Me (You're Comin' Back to Me)', which starts with the line 'I want your love again' – then you might think it's funny. It certainly was at the time. What I did was put on my Jagger wig, do a few Jagger facials, a few Mick moves, and say [Jagger voice]: 'Gimme a minute, I'm just gonna have a blow,' then produce the fake joint. Around its middle it had an elastic band and was blackened at one end. 'Gotta light up first, excuse me,' I'd say, as Mick again, then do a Jagger turn away from the audience and pretend to light it with a match, obscured from them, before turning back to face them again and take a draw on the 'unlit' end while pretending to hold the smoke in my lungs while doing all kinds of Jagger-style grimaces. Then I'd turn the joint half a revolution in my fingers so that the blackened 'lit' end was now closest to my pouted rubbery lips. I'd go to take another draw, pretend to get burned by the lit end and cry out 'Aaaargh', which could be taken for an 'I', then '...want your love again', which is how Mick sounds on the record. Repeating this, I'd get a second laugh.

Meanwhile, unknown to the crowd, while turned away from them I'd wound the 'joint' around my finger through an elastic band, like a mini aeroplane propeller. Keeping it clamped between my fingers so it didn't spin, I'd pretend to take another drag on the unlit end and then 'discover' a bit of substance on my lower lip, which I mimed picking off and examining. 'Ere,' I'd say, looking at it in bemusement. 'What's a nice dope like you doing in a joint like this?',

Stand-up Chameleon

then go straight into 'Reelin' and Rockin' – first line: 'I said the joint was a rockin', goin' round and round...' It was then that I'd let the fake joint loose in my fingers so it spun at speed on the elastic band and finish with: 'Ere, this aint half strong stuff!' A roomful of musicians and hippies loved this kind of humour, of course. Not only could they totally understand it, they completely related to it as well.

There every Monday in that humid smoked-filled venue I would feel my way through bits that I'd maybe only half-thought through. A piece, maybe, that didn't have a proper ending yet but which I'd do anyway because it was funny enough along the way. I'd just keep on busking it, tweaking and adding bits every week in the hope that somehow an ending would finally present itself out of the blue. This was very much the case with my underwater routine, which required miming slow-motion-type swimming with my whole body.

Anyone who was around in the 1960s and early 1970s might recall a husband and wife underwater exploration team called Hans and Lotte Hass. They were on television all the time, pre-Jacques Cousteau. Hans, an Austrian, was from Vienna and had the accent to go with it, making for great comedy I thought. The first line would go: 'Lotte and I have discovered this rare Coral reef, where muff divers come to dive for the muff,' I'd say as I did my undersea strokes, 'a rare tropical sponge, honest!' Swaying and turning in imaginary underwater currents, I'd go on, in a silly accent: 'Lotte and I frolic with a couple of groupers,' while miming the movement and patting the imaginary fish. 'Lotte almost drowned three times, whilst I swallowed a gobful of water,' and so on. For a while, this skit had a poor ending but I felt it was worth doing anyway. And how could this long-haired heaving mass in the Ship know that, ten years later, it would be a highlight of the first series of *Cool It*, after the associate producer and myself between us thrashed out the perfect ending?

Another winner with that Monday crowd was my Rolf Harris. Back then, Rolf was so widely known and had so many wonderful eccentricities that he was pure gold for a performer like me. Yet perfecting my 'Rolf' didn't happen over night, it too came more in stages. At this time, I was still working as an electrician, but now at

The Tale

a firm in Bamber Bridge, near Preston, wiring houses and no longer filling them with gas. Along with my workmate and friend Dennis, I'd beaver away on piece-work, trying to make as much money as I could. And while I chipped away at the breeze blocks with hammer and chisel, or sank switch and socket boxes into the walls, I'd do it all in Rolf's voice, singing 'Tie me Kangaroo Down, Sport' but with the words 'Strap me Kangaroo down, Jock' and then 'Comb me quiff when I'm stiff, Cliff. Comb me quiff when I'm stiff. It won't take more than a jiff, Cliff. Comb me quiff when I'm stiff.'

I could hear Dennis laughing in the other room as he was pulling cables through the holes I'd made in the wooden joists with my auger drill bit, so knew I had the voice off pretty good. It took a while though for it to dawn on me that I might be able to look like Rolf as well. One night, just before setting off to the Ship, I thought I'd make an improvised beard so picked up a roll of black insulation tape and scissors and headed for the bathroom. I already had a pair of glasses I used for Alan Whicker and Jack Benny impressions, black frames with no lenses, so grabbed those as well. Standing there, in front of the mirror, I cut bits of tape from the coil and stuck them on to my face where Rolf's beard and 'tash would be. I then slowly lifted the specs to my face to complete this identikit picture and, to my real astonishment, Rolf was staring back. I spoke and did a few Rolf-isms wallowing in laughter and delight at my own reflection. And why not? I knew this was going to knock 'em dead at the Ship.

Later, I would make a properly robust beard and moustache fashioned from Sellotape and my own hair, collected from the barber shop floor after he'd finished giving me a trim. I never told him what it was for, as he handed it to me in a brown paper bag, but replied 'How did you guess?' when he suggested I had a pet mouse and used it to make nests. The look was completed by cutting off tiny bits of sticky tape and fixing them onto my chin and up the sides of my face to meet up with my own hair next to my ears. When I'd got enough and they were criss-crossing each other, literally hundreds of them, I'd peel the thing off and have an exact mold of my chin and jawline up the side of my face. I had an instinctive inkling that the moustache

Stand-up Chameleon

would look more realistic if it was split in two, one bit on the right over my top lip and one on the left. They would then, I figured, move independently as I adopted expressions and be more convincing. The hair would then be painstakingly glued, tuft by tuft, to the outside of the mold with ordinary glue, then trimmed when it dried. I fixed this to my face with spirit gum on the inside of the mold at first. However, the gum began to irritate my skin so I reverted to strapping a thin round piece of black elastic to the beard's sideburns that went over the top of my head and held it on. My jaw was now free to move in any direction without hindrance. The 'tashes I stuck on with toupée tape that caused no itching. Was it worth it? Years later, Rolf himself would certainly think so..

That outfit went on to be part of my act for forty years or more, to say it was robust is an understatement. In fact, at one point I was set on having them mounted in a glass case when I retired.

However, that was then. I doubt anyone was more surprised than myself when, following the Jimmy Savile scandal in 2013, Rolf was arrested during Operation Yewtree investigations.

I was sorrowful for his wife after all the things he dragged her through. And Bindy, of course.

I met them both and they were very nice people, as was Rolf, or so it seemed. As surprised as I was, though, and I'm not just being wise after the event, he *was* always telling dirty jokes, which I always found peculiar. I don't like those. It got to the point where I had to tell him to stop doing it. We'd gone out for a curry, but even then I just thought 'he's a bloke, isn't he? Loads of blokes I know tell them.'

I was also invited to his 70th birthday party, full of celebrities ... Beatles producer George Martin ... Esther Rantzen. I sat next to Jon Culshaw. So everybody was of the same opinion – a decent guy. He's been respected all those years, family seemingly proud of him, then shame and a tarnished reputation because he couldn't control his worst impulses.

※

The Tale

All that, of course, was a long way in the future at the Ship Inn, where the audience, as I say, was made up of musicians and bands, or groups as they were then called. One night, members of Rainbow Cottage, a soft rock group from Wigan, were in. They saw me do my stuff and later mentioned me to their agent. Word got back to me that they were about to do a charity gig in their home town and if I were to come along I'd be welcome to do a short set. If their agent liked what he saw he might get me paid work.

So I gave it a go, but this agent wasn't too impressed by my failure to win over what was a very conventional audience, certainly no Ship crowd. However he was willing to take a gamble in a few places because he thought I had potential. So he sent me to various venues, not too far afield at first as I told him I was scared of getting stranded in my rickety black Morris Minor saloon miles from home. It was one of those with indicator wings that stick out from the side panels and retract when switched off. It wasn't going to be easy, this new apprenticeship I'd embarked upon. There were no tradesmen to pass down their skills. I would have to watch, listen, observe and learn alone, while assuming the role of tradesman myself, both disciple and master in a quest for comedic enlightenment.

What had I got myself into? I'd soon find out. A baptism of not so much fire, but hostility. I may as well have been from Mars going by some of the audience reaction, they just didn't get it – or me. I don't blame them. When you analysis it, people think they know what they like but in the end they only like what they know. We are all bound by our own conditioning. I would have several disastrous gigs in a row, feel quite down about it, and my agent would get stick over the phone about how bad his act – Phil Martin – was, which only compounded my depression. Then at the dark midnight hour of woe – sunrise! An audience would suddenly connect and lift my spirits, going out of their way to come over after a show and bestow all manner of compliments and praise. But why only sometimes and not all times? I would then theorise about audience reaction, still do. If I'd ever found an answer I would be a multi-millionaire now.

Why is one group of people responsive and positive, while others

Stand-up Chameleon

are totally opposite? I reckoned a certain set of conditions had to be in place for the perfect gig. For a start, the audience had to be up for it. Paying to get in? All the better, as they would at least be listening so as to get their money's worth. Rooms should be dark. If the audience can't be seen they aren't self-conscious and so more likely to let rip in bursts of hysterics. The stage needs to be raised so they can see the performer fully, not just waist up. Lighting must be of good quality and shine from the correct angle or a performer's face can be obscured by shadows. If I'm doing Clint Eastwood, say, the last thing I need is for my face to be just a vague nebulous blob. It helps too if there's some kind of warm-up person or decent compère, who can get a crowd in the mood. I was once introduced by an idiot at a club in Swinton, near Manchester, who went on stage before me and announced the death of a dearly loved committee member. Then he gave a long and rambling sorrowful speech about "our departed friend" with a request at the end that the audience (by now sobbing into handkerchiefs) should stand, heads bowed, and join him in a two-minute silence. That done, he looked down at the smudged ink on his sweaty palm and read: 'And now, Phil Coot.'

The best chance of a good gig is in a room shaped so as to allow everyone to see the stage. L-shaped venues are no good, with half the audience around the corner having a good chin wag. For comedy – and you may think this far-fetched – room temperature is also vital for both audience and comic. Cooler rooms, yes. Boiling hot rooms, definitely no. It drains the energy and cooks their brains.

Unfortunately, when sent to a venue by an agency, unless you've already played the place you never know what you are up against until you get there and make do with what you have at your disposal. A good sound system is also crucial. There's no use trying to emulate the voice of Terry Wogan or Sean Connery with a crackly PA – and don't say 'take your own.' In comedy, you never know when you might have to run for your life at the drop of a hat.

Preferably with the money.

I officially went into the profession in 1976, having earlier that year been dithering on the brink of transition from sparkie to stand-

The Tale

up. The decider came when I made more in one night than I had in a whole day on the tools. I obviously can't tell you about every gig that landed in my diary since then otherwise this book would be the length of *War and Peace* and about as funny. But they came, went, and I slowly got better at performing, my material steadily more sophisticated. The guitar was eventually only used for comic effect with the serious songwriting side almost dormant – I say 'almost' because it re-emerged recently. From then on, comedy dominated.

Before long, I realised that the ultimate aim of my career should be to leave these godforsaken bear pits and follow the path of comics I admired most. Billy Connolly, Jasper Carrott and Mike Harding were who I had in mind, and lesser known ones who never quite made it as big but were equally brilliant, like Tony Capstick and Bolton pair Bob Williamson and Bernard Wrigley. In other words, the ones who didn't tell jokes so much as a good tale. Plus these guys weren't playing in clubs but in theatres, which when you think about it are places built for the job. Proper sound and lighting ... seats all facing the right way ... no disruptions etc ... etc.

One night, a seismic shift in my style came after playing in some strange venue, I can't remember where. It must have been 1977 or thereabouts and when it was over I packed up quickly, vacated the dressing room and walked through the crowd towards the exit. Back then my show was one impression after another mainly, punctuated with observations of those I was about to mimic. When I got to the table at which my girlfriend had sat during the show, suitcase and guitar in hand, I was ready to go. As we went to get her coat she told me she'd heard a couple in front of her make a comment. 'This guy's impressions are brilliant,' they had apparently said, 'but he'd be much better off if he had more personality about him.'

This stayed with me. I dwelt upon it and knew I had to change tack. Now, I'd seen the aforementioned Mike Harding perform at folk clubs, liked his style, and knew he'd graduated to big theatres as his popularity grew. Mike would write a funny song and precede it with a story. This yarn would be packed with gags and observations and get loads of laughs. He would then end with a song relevant to

Stand-up Chameleon

his tale that rounded the whole thing off. If I could do something like this, I realised, I wouldn't be just a 'talking head', going from one impression to another, it would give my act a new dimension. Maybe doing this would loosen me up, I'd develop more of a rapport with the audience, life would be easier and I'd have a higher success rate.

But who – or what – could I spin such a story around?

My Morris Minor Traveller, of course, with its wooden panelling on the sides and back. Mine was a real pile, always going wrong and painted green, the wood on it rotting and home to fungi. My mother warned me not to buy it. 'Bad luck,' she said. Still, if I hadn't bought it I definitely wouldn't have come up with 'The Deadwood Morris', a parody of 'The Deadwood Stage' from the Doris Day musical *Calamity Jane*. After writing and learning the song by heart, I started on a monologue to set it up, quite a long one too, full of quirky ideas.

To cut a long story even longer, I'd led the audience to believe I'd acquired the car because I felt confident driving it after a skinful of ale, convinced the cops would never flag me down because only little old ladies, vicars and spotty geek students drove such vehicles. They are the face of innocence, owned only by fine upstanding pillars of the community. Little round headlamps for eyes. Chubby cheeks for mudguards. That friendly radiator grill for a mouth. By now I would be doing an impression of a Morris Minor with my face.

I would tell the crowd about a gig I'd done recently in Liverpool when, on my way home and after downing a few jars, to my horror I'd been flagged down by a young copper. A mere piglet who seconds earlier had been sheltering in a shop doorway while devouring a bag of pork scratchings, the nearest thing to cannibalism. I'd imitate him munching away and instructing me to wind the window down. 'Ere,' says this copper authoritatively, 'now it all makes sense you've only got one light working because you're a dummy, son. That's what you are. A dummy...' At which, still in the car, I'd resume my own identity and do an impression of a ventriloquist's dummy, head going up and down, eyebrows rising and falling, one eye closed, and replied in a puppet-like voice, without pronouncing my 'm', 'b' or 'p's properly: 'Alright, if you say I'm a dummy, I must be a dummy. I didn't always

The Tale

used to be a dummy, you know. I used to be a policeman, but I'm goin' straight now.' Monologue finished, I would round it all off with 'The Deadwood Morris Song'...

> *Oh, the Deadwood Morris is travellin' down the road*
> *With a clapped-out 1,000 engine pullin' my load*
> *What's that funny noise? Needless to say*
> *Big ends away, big ends away, big ends away...*

This routine stood me in good stead for a long time. Because it worked so well, it made me relax on stage more and made my life that little bit easier, leading to other comic songs and monologues.

At its best gig, the Deadwood Morris song had audiences singing along. At the worst, a prime middle-aged couple took to the dance floor of some idiot working men's club and engaged in a 'quick step', totally missing the humour and hijacking all the attention from me on stage. Never mind. I carried on regardless.

There are Some Cruel Bastards Out There

Birkdale is the next place along the west coast from Southport and a 'well sought after area.' So, driving towards it in my not-so-trusty Morris Minor, I only had butterflies in my stomach rather than the usual pterodactyls crashing around in there.

Birkdale, after all, famous for its royal golf links, was just as pleasant a place as its neighbour. The address was in my diary – Birkdale Labour Club, on Such and Such Street. It was the 'Labour Club' bit I hadn't reckoned on, never having previously played one. Nor was this going to be any old Labour club in some crumbling inner-city slum zone.

This was *Birkdale* Labour Club.

I would probably get away with it. I mean, I would most likely get a few laughs, get paid and maybe learn a thing or two. It would all be part of the evolutionary process of my new approach to comedy. I had gone down a storm in several shows prior to this and even had the confidence to slip in a straight song or two with my EKO guitar for accompaniment – usually Paul Simon's 'Homeward Bound' or Don McLean's 'Vincent'. I had even received some friendly comments of praise that were still having an effect on me.

At the time, the perceived wisdom of other comics in the business was that you must have music (aka dots), which you'd hand to the organist and drummer well before the show and discuss it with them.

Cruel Bastards

You should also look smart – wear a well-cut suit or tuxedo with nice shiny shoes and walk on to the stage accompanied by music. Then, you would open with a song while everyone accustomed themselves to the sight of you and hopefully 'warm' to you. Then you would tell a few jokes, it didn't really matter whether they were jokes that had 'done the rounds', as long as they were well delivered and funny.

I didn't bother with any of this nonsense.

I was going to be different even if it meant a few painful gigs – 'suffering for your art', I think, is the phrase.

As this was very early in my career, my act wasn't exactly 'together' yet. It was at the experimental stage and I was 'busking it' most of the time. Every show came out different to the last. I considered the actual courage of getting up on stage just as important as what you did when you were on it. It was a barrier thing and I just had to go through it.

Stage fright is so difficult to overcome. Ask anyone who has to make a speech at short notice in public. But it has to be beaten and this was the only way for me to do it.

It is probably even worse for a late-starter, which I certainly was – 26 years old before I turned professional. The ten years prior to that I had lived in the real world of the 'eight-to-five' job, so when many of my contemporaries would have been learning the business, I was just playing at it with the odd paid stint. In 1976, I'd grasped the nettle and gone pro, but knew there was a world of difference between fooling around for friends at parties or down the pub and a proper show for a paying audience, who wanted value. This would be demanding and bring with it responsibility. The prospect filled me with dread and was the reason for my putting it off for so long. But the longer I did that, the more self-conscious and inhibited I became.

The stage fright got worse. It's hard to describe, but waiting to go on stage in those days felt like having a horrible disease in every fibre of the body. The only cure was laughter (on a good night) or the end of the show (on a bad one). It comes down to confidence in the end. I suppose each paid gig a comedian does when starting out chips away a little bit more self-consciousness. The ultimate comedian, I suppose, ends up with no inhibitions at all. Think Billy Connolly or Eddie Izzard and you might understand what I am getting at.

As my girlfriend and I finally drew up alongside the venue in my clapped out Morris I felt another flutter in my guts. The aroma of stale ale wafted out to greet us from the club doors and evaporated into

Stand-up Chameleon

the warm July early evening. Ah! The uncertainty. Would the crowd be receptive to my humour? Would we be on the same wavelength? Would they understand what was funny about my routine of Max Bygraves and Frankie Vaughan doing a duet of The Beatles' 'I Am the Walrus', which ended with 'Max' singing 'goo goo ka choo, goo goo ka choo'? Others had. I'd had people crying with laughter at it. But there were no gags – just the song. Would they appreciate my Alan Whicker impression, reporting from Yates's Wine Lodge totally drunk on Aussie white wine? I did it by leaning from side to side at a steep angle while my Whicker spectacles dangled off the end of my nose. Not delivering gags as such but just commenting on the place...

'*Whicker's World*' this week takes you to Yates's Wine Lodge (*wobble, wobble*), where, if the Amoroso sherry doesn't get you the Amontillado will! (*hick!*) Here at Yates's Wine Lodge, where a little old gentleman has collapsed in the doorway so many times that the management have found it in their hearts to provide him with an overcoat with 'Welcome' written on the back... (*hick! Wobble, wobble*)" etc.

It had worked before, people had howled, and I hoped it was going to work tonight. Well, I only had one act. 'They'll either like it or not,' I said to myself. 'We'll soon find out'.

More butterflies, as we walked into the place. The ambience of pungent beer-soaked carpets immediately made me ill at ease. I wasn't sure where I belonged, but I was sure it wasn't here. A few punters lingering from the afternoon were in the concert room and I could hear more in a games room too. I didn't like the look or sound of them at all. They weren't 'my kind of people'. I questioned my girlfriend as to the best course of action. Should I install myself in the dressing room, seek out the committee and make myself known, or run out into the road and throw myself beneath the first available car?

'Don't be daft, you'll be alright,' she replied, with her lips. The reply from her eyes was entirely different. 'Goodbye,' they said, 'it's been nice knowing you.'

Hours later, I was peeking out of the dressing room curtains. The place was full. Foolishly, I had agreed to do three twenty-minute spots but it was clear to me that for the audience awaiting me I barely had enough material for one. I scoured the room. They were hunched over their tables playing bingo with religious fervour, passionately checking their numbers and then furtively glancing at their neighbours' cards. Occasionally a blood-curdling scream would erupt: 'Line!' or "House!'.

Cruel Bastards

Stand-up Chameleon

I would describe this audience as elderly, but it would be a severe understatement. Elderly means old. This lot weren't old, they were ancient. Dinosaurs. Antiquities with pulses. A pterodactyl swooped in my stomach at the sight of them all. Nevertheless I had to go through with it even if all dignity and self-esteem were going to be annihilated.

'Psych yourself up man, go out there and smile,' I said to myself. 'Mention something about Southport's expanse of sand and no sea in sight for miles'. Another pterodactyl. No! I'm lying! A whole bleeding flock of them battled with each other in my poor solar plexus.

'Wasn't *Lawrence of Arabia* shot in Southport? Oh shit, it's not funny enough'. After a deep breath I decided I would just stick with the plan. I would open up with the Eamonn Andrews routine – walking on with his red *This Is Your Life* book, ready, unfazed and calmly unprepared for what lay ahead on the dressing room table, on its cover a discoloured patch where my sweaty palm had worn it away while clutching it at the opening of most of the shows I'd done before.

Then, from a microphone at the side of the stage, the compère's voice suddenly bellowed out in a decidedly unfriendly tone. He was heralding in either my doom or my victory for a new style of comedy.

My girlfriend had taken her seat – craftily well positioned for a quick escape to the sanctuary of the car. Seconds away and my sweaty palm gripped the book, pressing it into my chest like the comfort blanket it had become. 'Ladies and gentlemen, welcome on stage Phil Martin,' the compère announced, before adding with more enthusiasm: 'Oh, yeah, and the pies have arrived...'

At that, the pterodactyls stopped and my survival instinct took over. I walked up onto the stage – a box-like affair in the middle of the room, which meant there were people to the back of me, at the bar and at the sides (who would just see me in profile).

This wasn't good. It made it feel as though the audience had been split into three – some in front, some on each side. An impressionist needs everyone to get the visual humour simultaneously, otherwise you tend to try to appeal to the ones on your left, thereby turning your back on the people on your right and catching the ones at the front inbetween.

The band had been instructed not to play me on and so I was given strange looks. There were whisperings. People shrugged at this peculiar creature in jeans and denim jacket over a Yates's Wine Lodge T-shirt.

I hid my nerves and began my routine, getting the instant reaction

Cruel Bastards

every comic dreads. Deathly silence. Cold stares. Antagonising looks that say 'you think this is funny ?'

When things don't go according to plan on stage it's a weird feeling. If you deliver what you consider to be your best line or gag and don't get the laugh you expected, but are instead met with stoney-faced silence, you think 'Oh Jeez, if they didn't find that funny or understand it, there's no way they're going to understand what's coming up next'.

Panic begins to set in. The mouth goes dry and your tongue sticks to the roof of your mouth. You can't talk properly, let alone do an accurate impression. Embarrassment turns into a soul destroying thing and obliterates any speck of dignity left. This was one of those times. Wretched. I can't remember exactly what material I used or tried to use. I only know it scored a zero on the clap-o-meter. My twenty minutes lasted ten or so. My composure disintegrated as I went from bad to worse. The Labour Club members began to murmur among themselves and mock the poor deluded critter who had walked in on them on this summer's night only to orchestrate his own crucifixion.

Through the glue-like froth of my dried-up mouth I managed to splutter an exit line, a quick 'We'll take a break now' or simply 'Thanks! Bye!' But just as I was about to get my head down and make towards the dressing room I was joined on stage by a committee member who addressed the audience: 'We can't let him come back on ladies and gentlemen, now can we? Not after such a rubbish performance. He's got to go, so I'm getting rid of him.' There was a ripple of applause from the back and I thought I heard a cheer. Then turning to me, but not looking at me, he said: 'Pack your stuff and go!'

By this time my girlfriend was nowhere to be seen. A silence hung over the room, broken by the odd whisper and snigger. I began to pack up my props, stuffing them haphazardly into my old suitcase. Wigs, glasses, beard, mouth organ and its holder and all the other various oddities just got flung in there. I couldn't wait to get out of the place.

Now, what made this particular gig so bad was that there was only one way out. To exit, the artiste (namely me) had to walk all the way down the centre aisle of the concert room to the main door, which was at the opposite end of the room to the stage. Without any further exchange of words with anyone I grabbed my guitar and prop case and began the long walk through the middle of the crowd, towards the door (come to think of it, this very moment could have inspired the Shakespearean-style poem I wrote and performed in the second *Cool*

Stand-up Chameleon

It series years later, with the apt title 'Feeding Caviar To Pigs'). I don't remember if I lowered my head and put on a sprint while walking the gauntlet, but if I could look back into the past I'd probably see myself moving slowly with my head up in an expressionless show of defiance. It had never happened before and hasn't happened since, but I received the ultimate show of disapproval from an audience to an artiste. The slow hand clap! It seemed as though their displeasure was turning into pleasure as their clapping got louder while I walked further and further down the aisle. I never looked directly into their faces, but sensed they were smiling and savouring this pathetic spectacle.

I reached the car, with its smiley Morris Minor face, only to find my girlfriend standing by it looking as though she had just witnessed a murder. 'Did you see any of that?' I asked.

'Oh yes,' she replied, stoney-faced. 'I went and locked myself in a cubicle in the ladies. I overheard two women who had walked in there talking about you, saying how dreadful you were and laughing.' I said nothing and let her continue. 'I thought they'd gone but when I came out they were still there and recognised me as being with you. So they blushed and then ran out giggling.'

I loaded up and we would have driven off there and then, but – wait for it – I couldn't! What I've omitted to mention is that I still had an amplifier and speakers, microphone stand, leads and other bits and pieces to pack up and – because no-one was going to help me carry them out – I had to go back in and out twice more.

This resulted in two more long walks down the aisle and two more slow hand claps to endure. By the last one, this merciless rabble was really enjoying itself. 'One day,' I thought. 'One day, my time will come and when it does I hope they remember this face of mine and how they helped to shape it.'

The Tale Continues...

A character who would periodically bring a little colour into my life was a guy referred to by his peers as Psychedelic Sid. His real name was Michael Cavanagh and he was from Brinscall, near Chorley.

For some reason, in the early 1960s, the kids in that village gave each other alternative Christian names. George would be Fred. John would be Sam. Michael was Sid. They would travel to St Augustine's on the early bus, Brinscall being about six miles away. Sid was in my class, 2C. We were both good at art and he had a penchant for drawing dogfights between British and German aeroplanes in World War One, the twin-winged type with machine guns and a single propellor. I would go off into my own world too, in my case featuring Spanish Galleons rolling on rough seas, sails proud in the wind.

One day, our schooldays long over, I bumped into Sid on the bus into Chorley town centre. By now his hair was long and he wore a groovy floral-patterned shirt, cords and sandals. He also carried a guitar case and despite his dishevelled look was smiley and very 'up'. We spoke briefly and it was obvious that he was taking the 'hippy' route through life. His manner of speaking was a giveaway too. 'Hi, man,' he said. 'Notice anything different about me, man?' Everything

Stand-up Chameleon

was ending in 'man', hence him now being known as 'Psychedelic' Sid, as I was to discover, either by himself for kudos or by others who were humouring him. I took this new persona in my stride, but what did strike me as amusing was the fact that he had a huge shiner that stood out like a ... well, black eye. I had to ask him about it.

'Oh, it's just something I picked up at a festival at the weekend, man,' he said. 'I was trying to persuade this chick that I could do her some good and her boyfriend [he pointed to the purple bruise] gave me this, man. Ha ha! When I got home I told my dad what happened and he said: "What did you give him back?" I said: "A flower." Ha ha! I'm getting off at the next stop. See you, man.'

Sid went on to be a good guitarist eventually and I bumped into him several times in future years. In fact, he showed me another kind of finger-picking, which helped me very much. I saw Sid play in a few bands too, and with his movements and with his *far out, too much*-speak he could well have been the inspiration for those hippies in *The Muppets*. I was invited to his wedding in Pleasington, which was bizarre. His wife wore a white wedding dress in church, but the virginal theme was diminished somewhat by a huge belly poking out, her late-stage pregnancy very much in defiance of convention back then. As for the groom, he wore a snakeskin-patterned suit made of curtain material. The best man was a really good keyboard player and as the bride made her entrance he played Pink Floyd's 'A Saucerful Of Secrets' on the church organ, filling the entire hallowed space with its trippy sound and coming to a timely stop as she got to the end of the aisle. There at the altar rails, waiting to begin the ceremony, stood the humble vicar, knees visibly trembling against the underside of his cassock. Adding to the surrealism, the distinct aroma of a joint came in on a draught of air from the porch, having been smoked there moments before. The vicar somehow unglued his tongue from his palate and got through the ceremony before Sid and his lovely bride posed on the church steps as cameras snapped the happy hippy couple. In fact one caught the groom raising a joint in celebration, captured for the wedding album. Gifts included a bubble pipe and an ounce of hashish.

The Tale Continues...

Needless to say the marriage didn't last. Sid and his wife in fact went on to have two kids, twins I think, but my old classmate went from one crazy scene to another, formed many an amateur band and eventually burnt himself out. Not unlike his semi-namesake Syd Barrett, whose last Pink Floyd album *A Saucerful Of Secrets* was, he took drugs of every description and in his case drank a lot of booze, especially cider. He once told me that his doctor had warned him to stop drinking the stuff because his brain was turning into an apple core, to which he replied: 'I've still got a few pips left, man. I'm saving 'em for the four- minute warning.'

In short, Sid became a local celebrity, so I thought it worthwhile to do an impression of him on the local music scene. It always went down a storm; people love humour they can relate to first hand and I copied Sid's look to a tee. Long wig ... bandana on forehead ... I made a Van Dyke beard and tash and threw in as many 'Sid-isms' as I could muster and got his voice just right too, playing and singing a few of his songs. Sid went along with it to a certain extent, but I'm sure he thought the whole thing undermined his status as a serious musician. In fact, he once said: 'What do you keep taking the piss out of me for, man?' Mainly, though, he tolerated it and even joined me on stage a couple of times when I was 'doing' him, to join in the chorus of a parody I'd written to the tune of Lee Marvin's 'Wandering Star' – only in our case 'I was born under a Brinscall bar.'

'Joints were made for rollin ... rucks were made to pack ... when somebody says this time of year that Ambleside's good for the craic...' and many other such lines. With him up there too, it was as though the audience were watching and listening to Sid in stereo.

Great fun at the time, that has to have been one of my favourite routines ever, even allowing for the wider fame still to come. But, alas, after being very ill for eighteen months, poor Sid sadly died in February 2013. I went to the funeral service to pay my last respects, a far more sombre affair than the wedding had been.

I will always be grateful to him for nudging me one stage further with my finger-picking.

COOL

In 1980, I was asked by my manager in Wigan if I wanted to do a show for Yorkshire Television. It would feature a variety of bands, artists and comedians and be called *Rock with Laughter*. Naturally, I immediately said 'yes' and an audition was set up for me to meet the producer and director at Allinsons Theatre Club in Litherland, near Bootle.

They liked what they saw – an ordinary-looking short-haired bloke wearing denims and a Yates's Wine Lodge T-shirt doing impressions, pulling daft faces, sharing observations and telling stories about his experiences with a guitar strung around his neck. They would be in touch with my agent, they said, to seal the deal.

In those days, it was essential to be a member of Equity, the actors' union, if you were going to be part of a TV series. I wasn't one, so my manager said we would have to apply immediately. One week later, after sending in my application, we had a reply along the lines of: 'We cannot accept the stage name Phil Martin as it is already registered to a member from Manchester. Please choose another one.'

Naturally, I could understand the objection because identical names are bound to cause confusion. And I knew this to be so because it had happened to a friend of mine who recommended me to a mate of his. 'You must go and see this Phil Martin guy,' he'd said, 'who is very funny, does amazing impressions and has the ability to do facial aerobics.'

COOL

The guy he told saw the name 'Phil Martin' advertised in the local press, appearing at a nearby venue, and duly went to see him. He went in, chose his seat carefully, and prepared for an onslaught of hysterics. The artiste came on stage with a guitar slung over his shoulder – that would be fine; our mutual pal had said I sung the occasional song.

Anyway, Phil Martin began his set with '(Is This the Way to) Amarillo'. The friend awaited laughs. And waited. 'Sweet Caroline' commenced. The friend began to squirm in frustration and irritation, annoyed at wasting his evening, totally unamused. When the act started to strum the opening chords to the Thunderclap Newman song, 'Something in the Air', it was the last straw. The guy stormed out, furious. Phil Martin, in his opinion, was definitely *not* the funniest man he had seen. Nor were his facial aerobics anything to write home about!

Fast forward, therefore, to the meeting I had my manager, where it was decided I needed a middle name in order to differentiate me from this 'other' Phil Martin. He told me of a comedian called Mike Douglas who'd had the same problem. He solved the issue by adding 'Stand' to his name – becoming Mike 'Stand' Douglas. So we should do likewise.

There was a lot of laughter in that Wigan office as various people offered suggestions – daft stuff like 'Face', 'Hip' and 'Mental' were in the running. Until, after much more similar brainstorming, my manager suddenly said: 'Hang on, there's a word I've heard you use onstage every time I see you.'

'What's that then?' I asked.

He scratched his bald head and said: 'I've forgotten, but I'll know it when I hear it.'

With that, the telephone rang. There were several staff in the room with us and one of them, Owen Hughes, answered the call. On the other end of the line was Little Roy, another act the agency had on its books. When Owen said who it was my manager said to ask Little Roy if *he* had any suggestions for my middle name and he immediately came back with 'Loon'. As in, Phil 'Loon' Martin.

'Hang on,' I said. 'I don't want to be thought of as a complete idiot. I want to at least retain a bit of cool.'

'That's it, that's the word, "Cool!" You say it all the time on stage.'

I wasn't exactly taken with the idea to begin with, but reluctantly agreed to go along with it.

So off went another Equity application and it seemed an age before they replied. During the wait we had taken it for granted that it would

Stand-up Chameleon

be accepted, so I was billed Phil 'Cool' Martin at several gigs. What's more, the date for the *Rock with Laughter* series was fast approaching so when Equity did reply it threw a spanner in the works. 'Sorry,' they said, 'our member Phil Martin in Manchester still isn't happy and refuses to allow any combination of his name to be used by another act. He suggests you use your initials.' That would have meant I'd be known as PJ Martin, because my middle name is Joseph, which didn't seem too bad. It had already worked for PJ Proby after all.

Yet again, we debated the various options available to me until my manager suggested we drop my real surname altogether and just go with 'Phil Cool'. So we did. After a third application, Equity sent back my membership card and I did *Rock with Laughter* as planned.

Curiously, for years afterwards Equity addressed their mail to me Phil 'Cod' Martin. I assume it was some administrative error; when they had put me on their files as Phil 'Cool' Martin, perhaps a typing error or misreading of poor hand-writing converted the 'o' and 'l' into a 'd'.

Between 1980 and 1985 – the years before my first BBCTV series – I was billed, introduced and referred to in general by many variations of 'Cool'. I spoke to one couple who had come to see me only because they had been intrigued by my name – on that occasion I was billed in the brochure as 'Phil Coon'. I also remember arriving at a venue in Wythenshawe and seeing my name up in lights – as 'Phil Tool'.

The trouble I found with having 'Cool' as a surname is that it is easy for people to mis-hear it over the phone. Consequently, I have also been 'Phil Cook', 'Phil Coil' and even 'Phil Stool'. There are probably even more versions that have escaped my attention.

Even today I am still not totally comfortable with it, although it wasn't too bad when I became a father and found myself named 'Daddy Cool' by the press. Now, however, my youngest daughter has three children of her own – 'Granddaddy Cool' just doesn't cut it, does it? Nevertheless, 'Cool' has served me well and when I've told people in the business of my real name they've always grimaced and agreed that 'Phil Cool' is a far better stage name.

So off I went, back into the murky world of venues with a new name and after a bit more TV exposure on *Rock with Laughter* my fee went up slightly. The newspaper reviews however were not good. The one I particularly remember went: 'This show has turned a load of nobodys into a load of non-entities.' It didn't bother me. This was all experience.

COOL

One good thing from being on the show was that I got to meet the brilliant impressionist and great musician Terry Webster (ex-Rockin' Berries front man), who became a good friend. We still keep in touch and occasionally meet up.

In those days, the venues could be anything from military bases to nightclubs, political clubs, social clubs and an occasional folk club, which is what I wanted to play all the time but never quite managed, as most folk club organisers were purist and didn't want to embrace this alien from the unclean world of mainstream showbiz.

I also did a lot of private functions. Whenever I had 'private function' written in my diary I would never know what I would be in for.

It could be the time of my life with a great bunch of people who were with my comedy from the outset and intent on making the most of their evening. Alternatively, it could mean that I would have every ounce of dignity drained from my soul.

I was also frequently booked for strip show events – as the support, I hasten to add, not the main act. For some strange reason I always fared well at those. More often than not the organisers would try to fabricate an air of respectability by calling it 'A Gentleman's Evening' or similar, perhaps a more accurate term would have been 'Pig Nights'! Of course now I wouldn't be seen dead working this sort of 'do', but not only did I need the money, back then, audiences were so 'up for it' that nine times out of ten I'd go down a storm. In those early years, I would take on a strip show gig without hesitation.

The first time I worked with strippers was at a nightclub/disco out in the wilds of Lancashire, near a little town called Ribchester in the Ribble Valley. The 'crowd' (yes that word is just right), mainly consisted of blokes of all ages and a few women who were waiting for the show to finish so they could get 'pulled' afterwards at the disco.

There were never any fights or trouble of any kind and as I played this place I gained in confidence and was able to work out new material in my 45-minute spot. I always felt sorry for the strippers and said so. I can't explain why. No-one was forcing them to do this, but then as one stripper once told me: 'If nurses got a proper wage, we wouldn't be having this conversation.' These 'exotic dancers', as they were sometimes called, came in all shapes and sizes and backgrounds. Some were absolutely gorgeous and great movers, others obviously ill-suited to this strange career – they would have been more suited to stripping wallpaper.

Stand-up Chameleon

You could always tell the ones who were new on the scene – the poor things would be trembling beforehand, as they went through their dance movements. I really felt for them.

One girl was cross-eyed. *Very* cross-eyed, which I thought may have been both to her advantage and disadvantage. On the one hand, she probably didn't get much work. However, when she did, her crossed-eyes wouldn't see the drooling hunks of tosstesterone (no, I haven't made a spelling mistake) in the sweaty atmosphere of this dimly-lit twilight world. Once, she invited an over-excited punter to unclip and take off her bra. As he did so he breached her trust and slipped his hands around the front, inside her bra cups, and squeezed. I swear that for a second I saw her eyes straighten up.

Sometimes my agent would send me straight into the jaws of hell. One of these occasions was when I was booked for an afternoon show at a working men's club in Yorkshire. As my girlfriend and I turned up at this place the sun was shining, it was a hot summer day. She decided not to come in for the show, but just to get herself several drinks and then go back out to sunbathe on a nice grassy piece of secluded land adjacent to the club. How nice it would have been for me to do that too! But no, I had a show to perform.

Me doing 'Rock with Laughter' for Yorkshire TV – eventually

COOL

Three strippers were due to appear on the bill with me, but they were late. Very late. A spokesperson for the rabble that sat awaiting their arrival told me to get everything ready for when they eventually got there. I was to act as compère, introducing the girls, but was under strict instructions not to do my show until they'd done their routines. Time went on and still no sign of them. No phone call, nothing. I paced up and down in the dressing room, walked out on stage several times to check the microphone level and my props for the tenth time. All out of nervousness, I suppose. Each time I stepped out I sensed the audience's growing impatience; it got to the point of being downright ugly. I seemed to be waiting for hours and eventually resolved to go on and do my stint anyway. I edged up to the microphone to address the potential lynch mob when I noticed the girls breezing through the doors with seemingly not a care in the world.

'They've arrived', I spluttered.'We will have them on in ten minutes'. Then I fled off-stage.

In that interim period a few more gallons of ale must have slid down many necks, turning this audience into a dangerously unpredictable and unexploded human bomb. It hurled verbal abuse, fag packets and beer mats at me as I returned to meet their gaze.

'Right, lads' ... *duck* ... 'at last' ... *side-step* ... 'welcome on stage the fabulous ... *ouch* ... a missile cut me short as it bounced off my head.

I gave up and stomped off as the first girl came on to a rapturous outpouring of lust-laden animal noises.

The curtains on the windows were open, which allowed sunlight to penetrate the room and therefore resulted in a bright and totally inappropriate setting for a comedy show. That said, however, had the curtains been drawn and I had the best lighting rig ever devised, it would have made no difference before this unruly bunch of drunks.

Having been well and truly groped, the three girls finished their acts, jumped straight back in their car and disappeared. My time had come. I absolutely knew it was going to be a painful experience but wasn't really prepared for what lay before me. I shuffled to the mic and tried to start my routine. A beermat spun through the air on its way to greet my cheek. A roar of amused approval met the collision. I opened my mouth to speak and closed it again, unsure of how exactly to break into this crowd. It was going to be futile. Nay! Impossible.

Several individuals, encouraged by the herd, then climbed up on stage and decided to do a show of their own, improvising their way

Stand-up Chameleon

through some booze-fuelled antics involving props I'd left on the table at the centre of the stage. One put on my battered Indiana Jones-type trilby, did a dance and fell over. Another had my Alan Whicker specs on while his mate was bashing himself on the head with my *This is Your Life* book. I stood in the wings watching this going on, thinking that I'd just let them get on with it, they were sure to wear themselves out eventually, which they did, finishing off the afternoon by talking between themselves and a sort of calm reasserted itself in the room.

If I recall correctly, I did get paid for my efforts. I had, after all, been there to do my show as contracted. Physically prevented from doing so was the explanation I gave to my agent.

I often wonder what happened to some of the strippers working those dreadful places all those years ago. Are they now in a specialised care home for retired exotic dancers? Do they tell tales about the time they worked with this really strange comedian who didn't quite connect with people and who was either very brave or very stupid?

There were two I worked with several times. and I remember the first time we met. I didn't know it was a 'strip do' until I arrived and saw on poster on the wall:

Gentleman's Evening
Featuring 'Baby Jane' and the delectable 'Zoe'
Plus comedian Phil Mule
All tickets £6

I thought: 'There's going to be a lot of people disappointed tonight!'

Interestingly, Baby Jane made the Sunday papers once because she'd had her breasts insured for £12,000. A publicity stunt, of course. £12,000, though! That's an indication of how long ago this was. When I saw it I thought: 'Wow! £7,000 for the left one, £5,000 for the right one.' Joking, of course. As I recall, they were both perfect.

My agent continued to put me in all of these rough places and I would get slightly disheartened when I had several bad ones in a row, but then out of the blue would come a great gig and my spirits would be lifted by people saying they'd never seen anyone like me before. But, years would pass before I got those kinds of comments every time.

The Tale Continues...

Another good thing to come out of those six episodes of *Rock with Laughter* in June 1980 was that the agency in Wigan was contacted by a comedian hero of mine from the Birmingham area.

It made my day. I was in some town or other doing a week away from home and called the office from a red telephone box. Owen Hughes answered and, after we had exchanged hellos and such, said: 'Guess what? Jasper Carrott has been in touch. He's seen you on *Rock with Laughter* and wonders if you'd like to meet for a chat.'

An opportunity was arranged for my wife and me to go see him perform at the Manchester Apollo. It was a great show, the first time I'd seen him live, and after the three thousand-strong audience left the auditorium we remained and were called up on stage, before meeting Jasper in his dressing room. After a beer, a sandwich and a laugh, we thanked him and walked back to the empty stage. Jasper came with us to say 'so long' and, as we stood looking out upon those thousands of empty seats, in awe of the enormity of the place I asked: 'How can you bridge that chasm between you and all those people?'

'One day, Phil, you'll see,' he said. 'You'll be doing it yourself. It will come I'm telling you.' At which we left the stage, waved goodbye

Stand-up Chameleon

and made our departure. Jasper kept in touch and from then on was to have a huge influence upon me on many different levels. My five-year contract with my Wigan manager still had four years to go and the quality of gigs he was getting me wasn't improving. I'd a feeling they never would, but I had signed for five years and that was that.

I then had the idea of starting a place I could go to every week and work on new material. If I were to make a success of that, it would provide some relief from the mundane gigs the Wigan agency found me while allowing me to try new stuff out. I could have a guest or guest band on as well and get to meet new people in the business. Any money taken on the door would go to the guest artists; I would be content with having the artistic freedom to do what I liked, when I liked. I knew there were comedy clubs in London, like the Comedy Store in Soho, where Alexei Sayle, Rik Mayall, Ade Edmondson and other alternative comics worked, so why not up north?

Fox Lane Cricket Club in Leyland, Lancashire, had run many a folk night over the years and been really successful. I'd seen various acts there and so paid the place another visit. Its manager, Chris Maddison, listened to my proposal. 'Lets do it,' he said, happy with extra bar takings. I decided to call it 'Laughingas' (interviewers wrote it up in print later as 'Laughing Gas') and got in touch with Bernard Wrigley who, as I say, is a real comedy hero of mine. When he agreed to be my first guest I was excited, raring to go. Then I started to think of a poster design and remembered a cute trick one promoter had used after getting me a gig at a college when another act had let him down. He'd done an advert that read: 'Freddie Starr is great, but so is Phil Martin.' The use of Freddie Starr's name to draw attention to mine was downright cheeky, but clever. So I had a go myself – as you can see if you turn your head ever so slightly to the right.

After which, I put an ad in Leyland's local paper. That one took the shape of a clown who had a sandwich board bearing the details: 'Bernard Wrigley the 'Bolton Bullfrog', plus Phil Cool, the 'satirical miracle,' etc etc. For some deluded reason, I kept the entrance fee at £1.00, no matter who the special guest was going to be.

Our third headline act was Jasper. He kindly agreed to do the gig

The Tale Continues...

for nothing, to put the Laughingas on the map. That Monday night we had to shoehorn the punters in at a quid a time, the tickets having gone on sale the previous Monday as bait to pull people in then too, to see a local comedian called Roger Westbrook. The trouble was, I hadn't taken human nature into account and its fixation with fame. People came to Roger's gig, paid a pound, picked up a Jasper Carrott ticket for another pound and then walked out again with no interest in the poor fella. I ought to have seen it coming, but I'm too trusting.

Laughingas at Fox Lane ran for about three years, with a lot of good acts passing through. Somebody else who dropped in from time to time was the bloke who dreamt up that Freddie Starr ad. He's always had his finger on the pulse and is very good at what he does. You might have seen his name in the Sunday papers at the head of all the shows he promotes these days and in the not too distant past: 'Phil McIntyre presents Ben Elton, Victoria Wood, or whoever.' Phil came to several nights and grew infatuated with the Psychedelic Sid character I did every week. But when I suggested introducing him to the real Sid he said, 'No, thanks. It'll ruin the image I have of him and spoil the fun for me. I'd sooner watch your characterisation.'

In those days, Phil promoted the shows of an old comedian and raconteur called Blaster Bates who, bizarrely, was also an explosives and demolition expert, plus bands like AC/DC, Alberto y Lost Trios

Stand-up Chameleon

Paranoias and many others. One night, he said he was bringing over a Canadian duo, two brothers called McLean and McLean, well known in Canada for colourful language in their comedy songs, their biggest hit being 'Dolly Parton's Tits'. He said he was going to put them on the college circuit, convinced their style would prove popular here. One of them played guitar, the other banjo, and their humour was outrageous. He asked whether I would be interested in supporting them. If I opened the show billed as 'Psychedelic Sid', did my ten-minute routine and then went off and returned as Phil Cool for forty minutes, while McLean and McLean did the main slot, it would make for a cracking show. I didn't need to think about it much. My manager in Wigan would have to be cut into the deal but he would approve, I was sure, because he'd be having his work done for him. So it was agreed. Phil got back in touch with McLean and McLean and set the wheels in motion.

A few days passed and I happened to be gigging in the Midlands. While there, I was invited to a party at Jasper's neighbours' house. The place was full, no celebrities, mainly more of Jasper's neighbours and friends. When I arrived I followed the music and let myself in, squeezed through the crowds and spotted Jasper across the room. He clocked me and I returned a flash of my Quasimodo face. He laughed and called me over, introducing me to a few people. We all chatted, then he told me to mingle and we would chat again later.

Towards the end of the night, as I was preparing to leave, Jasper revealed some good news, barely able to keep the lid on his delight. 'I've just landed a thirteen-show series with the BBC,' he said, 'and it's going to be live.' This was the series that was to become *Carrott's Lib*. 'I've told the producers I want you as a guest on it and I'm ninety per cent sure they'll agree to it. I'll give you more details when I've got them.' I congratulated him and left the party elated, thinking 'Wow! This could be my big break.' Of course, things are never that simple. A week passed and Jasper and I spoke on the phone. He gave me the dates when *Carrott's Lib* was to be shot. They clashed exactly with the McLean and McLean tour.

Clearly, I had to choose one or the other.

The Tale Continues...

'Jasper,' I said down the line and with a wearisome weight on his name. 'I've got a problem. I *really* want to do your show with you but I've already promised Phil McIntyre I'll do a tour of colleges and universities for him, with two guys from Canada called McLean and McLean. The dates are the same, so I've got to do one or the other.'

'Look Phil,' Jasper said, firmly. 'You've got to think what will be better for your career – thirteen appearances on primetime TV or going on tour with two guys nobody here knows from Adam around beer-filled student halls.' He had a point. A good one too. 'Phil,' he went on, 'you'd be crazy to turn this down. It could make you a star. The other won't but it's up to you.' I felt hollow after the conversation because it all pointed to me getting back to Phil to explain. And if there is one thing I absolutely hate it is going back on my word.

But anyway, I did tell Phil of my dilemma. He understood and said he'd make alternative arrangements with McLean and McLean but was still annoyed about all the groundwork he had put in. At least he hadn't had the posters printed yet. He cancelled the tour.

Before I could be on *Carrott's Lib*, though, I had to be approved by its producer, Paul Jackson, and director, Geoff Posner. These guys wanted to see me in action, pronto, but my diary hadn't one decent place in it where I might stand a chance of pulling off a good show. On my behalf, my agency in Wigan invited them to come all the way up north to a hole that called itself Chadderton Reform Club, in Oldham. I'd done it in the past and not gone down well. But anyway, the night was soon upon us and Jackson and Posner sat watching from the middle table in a forlorn and threequarter empty room.

I felt I'd lost it and it turned out I was right.

They didn't like what they saw. It wasn't right for the type of show they were making, they said, although in hindsight I'm guessing I wasn't politically correct enough, Jackson widely credited as the man who brought alternative comedy to television. When I gave Jasper the news, he said: 'Well, that just goes to show how much notice they take of me then.'

So that was that. I'd lost the McLean and McLean tour, ruffled Phil McIntyre, and then lost *Carrott's Lib* too.

Stand-up Chameleon

※

The sea of comedy has its rough waters. Had I been a surfer, I'd have been washed up and left for dead. However, it also has its periods of calm. I clawed my way back through the foam and waited. As the wave I yearned to surf eluded me I resided in a low trough, unaware that soon I would be re-elevated to the crest of a tsunami that would take me to the promised land – theatres. Well, it maybe wasn't quite as dramatic as that, but you get the picture.

'Has that Chris Tarrant got in touch yet?' Mike Harding would ask, when we happened to bump into each other every blue moon. 'I keep telling him he should have you on his show.'

Mike had seen me do a short open mic spot at Band On The Wall in Manchester in 1978, after I'd gone there alone one night and asked if I could play. The owner and I had a mutual friend, a saxophonist called Harold Salisbury. On mentioning his name the bolts slid off the door and I was allowed in. Mike had been full of praise for my material that night and must have kept me in his memory.

His insistence on badgering Tarrant with my name every time he saw him was eventually effective, because around four years after that brief Manchester spot my agent rang. 'Chris Tarrant wants to come to a show of yours and check you out for a programme he's doing,' he said. It was to be a follow-up to *OTT* – short for 'over the top' – which had itself been a late-night adult version of the popular and zany Saturday morning kids' show *Tiswas*. In the end, *OTT* had only managed one series featuring Lenny Henry, Alexei Sayle, Bob Carolgees and Spit the Dog, Helen Atkinson Wood (replacing Sally James) and John Gorman. Critics hated it. This new show, *Saturday Stayback*, would also be produced by Central TV in Birmingham. 'Should I tell him you are up for it?' asked my agent.

The night Tarrant saw me was nasty and the venue even nastier – some bombed-out half-derelict social club in the backstreets of Toxteth or Kirby, I can't remember which. It was the only date Chris

The Tale Continues...

could manage, so we met and the night ran its course. I sensed Chris was anxious to leave as soon as he could; he wasn't the only one. There was a certain ambience about the place... otherwise known as menace. 'Ya!' said Chris, after seeing me strut my stuff to a wall of indifference. 'You're different Cool, you'll do. I'll give you a chance. You're on the show. Turn up at Central TV, we'll go through a few scripts together and I'll explain the concept. Our people will be in touch with the details. Bye.'

I hardly had time to thank him as he was escorted to the exit by his companions. As Chris made his re-entry into the rainy winter night and walked over a Liverpudlian wasteland of broken bricks and bottles to his car, I waved and went back inside to grab my gear, spirits lifted a little as I tried to imagine where this would all lead.

Chris recruited a host of artists and scriptwriters to work on a show whose name came from a Midlands term meaning to carry on drinking in a pub after licensing hours. Bob Carolgees and Helen Atkinson Wood made the transition from *OTT*, and Tony Slattery came on board too. A guy called Kevin Seisay and myself were the resident performers. We had guest bands too like Thin Lizzy, Suzi Quatro and Chas and Dave. Guest comedians included Jim Bowen, Frank Carson and even Bernard Manning. It was a real mixed bag of people doing their party pieces, plus actors performing sketches. The pub, a real one, was also full of the general public who provided applause, laughter and reaction. All in all it was a mess, but different.

Not so different as to become a hit though. There were only six episodes in all, broadcast in January and February 1983. Early in the series Chris allowed me to be in a few sketches but I always struggled to remember my lines, which annoyed him to the extent he stopped me doing them. He did let me to do a few of my own routines and songs, however, with which I was more comfortable. One was a Mick Jagger impression with a Rolling Stones-style song I'd written called 'It's Hard Being A Stone', a sarcastic jibe at Jagger that went:

It's hard to being a stone,
Especially for man that's fully grown,

Stand-up Chameleon

> It's hard being a stone,
> You've gotta work yer fingers to the bone,
> You gotta sweat blood,
> You gotta shed tears and you've gotta bring a single out every six years,
> It's hard, so hard, so hard.

The middle went:

> Too much dope, not enough soap.
> When you're the prince of pop,
> You hardly need a crop,
> Life is just a joke, you smoke, and take in coke,
> When you're riding high at the top...

After more verses, the song ended with my face moving closer and closer to a second camera before, in the final fade-out, my 'Jagger' lips pressed a big sloppy kiss against glass in glorious close-up.

I also did a Pope John Paul II routine in which the Catholic church was likened to a locomotive in which the Pope was the train driver and the cardinals stoked the boiler. The bishops, meanwhile, were inspectors and the priests ticket collectors through the stations and tunnels of life as the Devil kept changing the points. I remember being allowed to sing a parody I'd written of Andy Fairweather Low's 'Wide Eyed and Legless', too, called 'Premenstrual Tension'.

I was amazed by Tony Slattery in particular and his phenomenal ability to do these long and crazy scripts without faltering, all while keeping a straight face. It must have been the result of his rigorous Cambridge Footlights training, I figured. Yet, as the weeks went on, my on-screen appearances grew fewer and fewer, my contribution soon down to a quick Quasimodo here or Rolf Harris there. My Rolf bit would consist of a few lines of 'Tie Me Kangaroo Down Sport' or 'Sun Arise' while Bob Carolgees 'assassinated' him with a gun or electric drill. Don't ask me why, it wasn't my idea. Maybe they knew something I didn't. By this time I was more or less just doing what I

The Tale Continues...

was told. Even so, looking back it was all quite an adventure and a bit of fun. At least I was getting my face on the box and I'll be forever grateful to Chris Tarrant for giving me the opportunity.

The director of *Stayback* was Peter Harris, who had a great track record of hits including *The Muppet Show*. Our meeting on the show would prove significant in my career direction as we will soon see.

✸

Around the time of doing *Stayback* in Birmingham I was also asked to perform at a folk club Jasper Carrott and his friend Les Ward had started way back in February 1969, in Solihull. They called it The Boggery and by now it was run by Les alone, whom I must have met at Jasper's Apollo gig in Manchester. Its compère was Malc Stent, a very funny bloke who would drive the crowd wild.

The first time I played it was when Jasper put us in touch after seeing me on *Rock with Laughter* in 1980. I'd just bought my first new car, a denim blue Austin Maxi, of which more anon. I was quite chuffed with the thing and able to afford it because my income had grown as a result of being on TV. I'd rolled up in it at The Boggery when Jasper was there and, on seeing it and with me raving on about never having had one before, he said: 'And its all because of comedy Phil, all because of comedy!' with a philosophical lilt. John Starkie, his manager, was around too from management company Starward.

After I'd played The Boggery a few times to that brilliant audience and loved every minute of it, Les Ward and I became firm friends. Les died in October 2013, aged 75, after collapsing at East Midlands Airport, just before he was to catch a flight to Corfu. It really upset me. He was a great bloke, we got along really well. He would book me for shows regularly and get me the odd gig elsewhere in the area. While it was on, we'd meet up at the Birmingham pub *Stayback* was shot in and discuss the future. I told him that my contract with the Wigan manager was due to run until July 1984 and hinted at being taken on by Starward, when the time was right.

His response was: 'Well, we'll see what transpires.'

Comedy Out of Tragedy

It was 1978. I had not long moved from my mother's house to a rented flat on the outskirts of Chorley, in a place called Astley Village. I lived there with my then wife and our four month old daughter. Occasionally I would ask my mother if she'd like to come over — I felt for her being alone, my dad by then having died thirteen years before. Nearly always she would say 'yes' so I would go to collect her. I always felt she was glad to get out of the house and we were pleased to have her around to see us and her new granddaughter.

My mother, Clara, was then 69 years old and considering her stories over the years must have had a hard life. Her own mother died in 1910, when my mum was two years old, the youngest of four children. Mary, the eldest, was her favourite sibling, being kind and protecting her from the dreaded Ada, the middle girl, who my mother said was cruel and a bully. I met them both when I was very young and, looking back, can see her assessment was spot on. The other child, the second born, was Joe. I can't recall meeting or hearing any stories about him.

Following their mother's death, these four were brought up by their grandmother and, partially, their father Arthur, a miner who suffered from all the ailments associated with that job. He'd work in atrocious conditions and, according to my ma, come home with an evil cough if he had worked that day in a dry and dusty part of the mine known as the 'dry bones'. Another day he might work ankle deep in water, which brought health problems of its own. On returning from the pit, black with coal, he would have a bath in the main room of the house in front of the fire – sounds like a Michael Palin *Ripping Yarns* sketch, I know, but this really was the 'lifestyle' of the poor – in a galvanised metal tub.

One of the stories my ma told me of him was that he was one of just eight survivors from an entire battalion in World War One. He was only a little fellow and this, my mother joked, was the secret of his survival. 'The bullets would fly over him,' she'd say. Arthur would also cut his comrades' hair in the trenches, which helped to hold him together mentally while he and his pals faced an agonising wait for a call to action in the muddy fields of northern France.

Another tale of my mother's that made me shudder was about the time when she was six and had cataracts. To cure this condition way back in 1914, the eyes (she said) had to be taken out of the head and (wait for it) ... scraped. I'm sure there must have been a less severe medical term for that procedure, but my mother could tell a good tale and knew how to get the right effect. 'My eyes,' she'd say, 'were never the same again.' Well, they wouldn't be, would they, if you'd had them yanked out and 'scraped'. Consequentially, according to her, there were blank spots in her field of vision. In fact, she had lovely eyes; they were my favourite coloured ones, green. It's true, though, that her vision was never too good, wearing spectacles from an early age.

My mother's ability to make friends quickly came naturally. Bright and attractive, she had a special warmth to her and, going by early photos, was quite vivacious with styled black hair, those laughing green eyes and the nicest, broadest, smile in the world.

She married my father, Thomas, at St Mary's Church in Chorley and they had two children before the Second World War broke out. First Rita and then James, two years between them; in 1939 they would have been six and four respectively. My father was slightly too old to be sent to the front so was kept back and became part of the home guard. He was stationed at various coastal regions and also in the hills around Britain. While he was away, my ma, poor soul, had to let Rita and James be taken care of by neighbours and relatives when she fell ill with tuberculosis (TB). The local Catholic priest, Father Caldwell, kindly used church funds to pay for her treatment and care at an isolation hospital in Grange-over-Sands, which back then was in Westmorland and is nowadays part of Cumbria, on Morecambe Bay. One day while

Stand-up Chameleon

she was there my dad got leave from his post in the hills, where he manned the Bofors guns fired at Nazi planes before they could bomb British aircraft factories in Halifax. As his train pulled into the little station at Grange-over-Sands, she recalled, she could hear his army boots hit the platform and his footsteps getting louder as she sat in the waiting room. 'I knew it was him,' she'd say. 'I could tell by his walk.' If you're imagining *Brief Encounter*, you wouldn't be far wrong... they only had a short while together before he had to return to his post and she had to get back to hospital to rest. Happily, by the time the war was over the TB was no more and my dad returned safely too.

Everyone rejoiced as life went back to normal – and I made them even more cheerful by being born in 1948. At this time, we all lived at lucky number seven, Milton Terrace, a council house but a happy home made all the better by ma's keen sense of humour. She loved to hold court and had a talent for keeping people entranced before doubling them up into fits of laughter. Maybe that's where I got my calling.

I'd lived at Milton Terrace for twenty-eight years and now here I was, just over a year after moving out, collecting her again to bring her to my new home in Astley village for tea.

On this particular day, I remember her making a special fuss of our baby, Jenny, before coming into the kitchen to help. We would be having Lancashire Hotpot, a simple dish of meat and potatoes mainly, and she was going to show us a few cooking tips – one of which was how to 'brown' the meat. We followed her instructions and, once it was ready, sat down to dine. I can even remember how the meal was finished off – with Italian ice cream for dessert and then a cup of tea.

During this time in her life my mother suffered from angina, whose symptoms are pains in the chest due to heart problems. Sufferers get them when walking up a hill, say, or doing something strenuous.

On this night she had seemed fine, apart from struggling slightly in climbing the outside stair leading up to our flat. She was happy, having a relaxing time and sharing a fair few laughs. Then, it turned ten o'clock and she said: 'I'm really tired tonight, Philip. Would you take me home now?' She then added: 'I'd be grateful if you could spare me some milk and a few vegetables to take back, as it would save me a trip out to the shops tomorrow.' So, I gave her half a bottle, a few carrots in a bag, and we were ready. Mum took a last peak at my daughter, tucked up in her room in bed, and then said her goodbye to my wife as I helped her on with her winter coat.

Comedy Out of Tragedy

Opening the door, I could see nothing but grey, dense fog outside, the kind you could almost lean on and not fall over. This was January, after all, with its relentless chill that gets through to a person's marrow. Friday the 13th of January at that. Not good. 'I will just have to drive very slowly and keep my wits about me,' I thought, while cautiously edging down the steps to the car, unable to see more than a few feet ahead. Eventually, I helped my mother into my old red Vauxhall Viva – just one of the many such mechanical death traps across British roads in the 1970s. I kept my fingers crossed, silently swearing I'd get rid of the damn thing soon. My mother held onto her items and off we slowly rolled into the dark, dank Lancashire night.

We didn't see any other traffic at the first junction as the Viva crawled slowly out of the estate road, just exchanged a few words as it crept up to something like 10mph. You couldn't go any faster in this stuff. I knew the road well. The junction into Euxton Lane was coming up soon and, sure enough, I saw the outline of it form before my eyes through the mist. As the car drew to a halt I asked my mother some vague question or other. She didn't answer in words, instead making a peculiar noise I have since heard people refer to as the 'death rattle'. I looked over. Her head had flopped back, to one side. Panic and terror took hold. I stamped on the brake and pulled the car over.

I was too shocked to cry, my thought processes scrambled, but even so acutely aware I was on a junction in dense fog and a danger to other motorists. Stranded with my poor mother (I didn't know for sure then that she was dead) in a fog the likes of which I'd never seen. On Friday the 13th. It was the stuff of nightmares, happening for real. The loving soul who had cared for me for twenty-nine years had gone. I don't remember the exact words I cried that night, but do still have a hollow pang of indescribable melancholy eating away somewhere deep inside.

In despair yet fighting to stay in some sort of control, I knew that I must get her to hospital. The nearest was at the top of a hill further along the lane we were about to turn into; we would have had to pass it on the way to her house. I pulled out into the foggy abyss, my mind in panic mode, and instantly stalled the engine. It fired up again after a third turn on the starter and so, at last, I blindly eased the old Vauxhall out and, leaving caution to fate, stepped on the accelerator. Its lights didn't penetrate far into the wall of grey swirling in wild weird patterns, but just managed to illuminate the white lines in the centre of the road.

As I straightened the car after the turn my mother tipped sideways

Stand-up Chameleon

in the passenger seat, her head landing on my shoulder. Tears were now ready to flow but couldn't, emotion suppressed by the enormity of the unfolding horror. I was constantly talking to her, begging her to be alright. I tried to go faster but the car would not respond properly. In my panic and confusion I had applied the handbrake. Realising this, I crunched it off again while, at the same time, trying to tip my mother back into the passenger seat, the wheels now turning properly.

Then, in desperation, I thought I should maybe pull over and stop, to see if I could revive her. I'd had no resuscitation training whatsoever but nevertheless stopped several times to try mouth to mouth, shake her gently and press her breastbone. Pathetic, futile efforts of course. I felt sure she had already gone but clung desperately to a faint hope that she might still come round.

At that time, in order to get to the hospital you had to turn left at the top of Euxton Lane, when the hospital was actually to the right, the traffic system having been altered. There was a roundabout but you couldn't use it, instead having to go to the next one, drive all the way around it and come back on yourself. I can't recall whether I did just that or just said 'sod it' and turned right anyway in my haste. Nor do I remember passing or seeing any vehicle en route. On arrival, I left my mother in the car outside and ran into the emergency department for help, suddenly aware of how quiet the place was.

I shouted and rang a bell at the reception desk. Eventually a porter appeared. He listened kindly while I blabbered uncontrollably and said I should use the phone to contact relatives or whoever. On going to the car he took one look at my mother, who was clearly dead by now, and said he would have to remove her from the vehicle, explaining that all the staff went home after 5.00pm. Anyone needing treatment after then you had to go the ten miles to Preston Royal Hospital. Basically he was telling me the place was closed.

I took one last look at her, said my goodbyes, went inside and called my sister. When we spoke I managed to compose myself, not quite the absolute wreck on the phone that I'd been driving up Euxton Lane. My sister was naturally devastated, saying she would arrange to meet the priest from St Joseph's, my mother's church, at the hospital and ask him to administer the last sacraments. She would tell our brother too. I put down the receiver. The whole thing felt surreal, it was as though everything had gone into slow motion. I walked back to the car, its door still wide open, and stood there alone in the fog beneath the

Comedy Out of Tragedy

halo of a hospital light. Only now would the tears flow, now I'd done all I could do. Tears flowed then and throughout the days to come, but that night I got drunk, real drunk, and for a short while got some relief.

The funeral of Clara, my lovely mother, took place a week later on a day that had another surprise for us weather-wise; the cemetery in which she was laid to rest covered in a shroud of fresh white snow.

To this day I still dream of her, a reoccurring dream that comes only once in a while. In it, she's still alive and I've left home in the car, yet the whole thing is set in a different place, not Milton Terrace but somewhere elusive that I can't seem to find. A different town even. In the dream, we never actually meet, but almost do. I get close to her, but we don't speak and she only half recognises me when I attempt to make contact. Then she turns and gets on with this isolated lonely 'life' of hers. The dream fades and I wake up sad with the feeling of having forsaken and abandoned her.

I was contacted by a lady who had heard of my 'experience'. She had fronted a protest for years about the opening hours of the hospital and asked if I was willing to speak to a local newspaper reporter as this would help her cause, should they run the story.

They *did* run the story and the headline went something like – 'Man Arrives at Chorley Hospital with Heart Attack Victim Only To Find it Closed!' – only not in so many words.

Time heals, they say, and time did pass. The only way I knew to help heal the psychological scars of this tragedy was through comedy and I wanted a bit of revenge into the bargain.

The early closing time of our local hospital made for good comedy – at least I thought so. Macabre, I know, but if you didn't laugh you'd go nuts. Sure enough, I started knocking a piece together on stage, busking it night after night. I tried to give it a sarcastic bite too. It came by way of an impression of the local television evening show *Granada Reports*' newsreader of the time, Bob Smithies, and went down a storm when I performed it at gigs. It went like this:

Bob Smithies: Good evening. Last night the entire Chorley Hospital emergency staff slipped on a banana skin and had to

Stand-up Chameleon

be rushed to Preston Royal Infirmary. Nevertheless he's been propped up in bed with two young nurses, given a big bowl of fruit, a colour television set, a supply of baccy, a crate of ale and a pile of girlie magazines. His condition late last night was said to be – 'quite comfortable'.

In the same hospital in Chorley an unmarried woman has just given birth to trastards, two of which had to be put into incubators, but owing to the lack of equipment and government cuts at Chorley Hospital, the other poor little trastard had to make do with a pie warmer. His condition late last night was said to be quite crispy. When I asked an area health authority spokesman why this was allowed to happen he said: 'Mind your own business, Smithies, or I'll put you in **cking hospital.' I said: 'I'm not bothered, so long as it's not Chorley **cking Hospital.'

The *Granada Reports* programme had other presenters on it besides avuncular Bob. There was Pattie Caldwell and Tony Wilson, who went on to be big national names, David Jones and a few others I have now forgotten. In 1979, I impersonated nearly all of them. My agent at that time made a phone call to a friend who worked as a presenter on another Granada show called *What's On*, explaining how I took the piss out of these *Granada Reports* presenters and asking if they'd have me on it. Granada sent a researcher to check me out while I was doing a night at Wigan rugby league club – always a favourite gig of mine because I never failed there (Wiganers, ah, bless 'em!). This researcher reported back with a verdict on this peculiar lanky Chorley comedian she had just watched and before I knew it I was on *What's On* doing my Bob Smithies Chorley Hospital routine.

They wouldn't let me say 'trastards' (TV producers always like to meddle), but still. It was my first ever television appearance.

Strange how life unfolds, eh?

The Tale Continues...

So, remember that line out of my Deadwood Morris song about cops never pulling classic Morris Minor Travellers up at night because they only belong to vicars and little old ladies? Well, apparently that is not the case with metallic-blue Austin Maxis driven at 03.00am.

Tootling along the A6 from Horwich to Chorley, mine was the only car on the road except for the transit van that lay ready to pounce – and pounce it, or rather the piglet driving the thing, did.

Thanks to said arresting officer, I was banged up overnight for scoring 180 on the breathometer, which resulted in a £150 fine and twelve-month ban, starting November 1982. Boy, did I suffer for my sins. When I couldn't find a driver to take me to gigs I had to get the bus, which meant the inconvenience of changing coaches several times and lugging my guitar and suitcase everywhere. It was so bad. Mainly though, I managed to persuade family, friends and friends of friends to drive me up and down the country. My nephew drove me to a show at a university in Liverpool one night that turned out to be the gig from hell. The Hoorah Henry who booked me was an arrogant slimeball who treated me with contempt. He'd booked too many acts, all performing simultaneously in different classrooms. I

Stand-up Chameleon

argued to appear on a proper raised stage under lights and such but was ordered by this character to make do with the junction of two corridors, an acoustic nightmare. My PA system kept howling with feedback, the audience, standing, put off by this and wandering off, only a few people seated on the floor listening to the end. Hooray Henry was infuriated by that; I only got paid after a huge argument I realised I could never win. In the end I resorted to humbling myself in the hope that his aggressiveness might burn itself out and I'd get my cheque, which is what happened. My poor nephew who'd hung around after the show to witness all this nonsense must have been wondering whether the £10 I was paying him to drive was worth it.

On the way home, I said: 'Sorry about that, Peter. It was a one off. They are not all that bad.' Sensing this was the last time he would want the job, I added: 'You may not always be available so, just in case you can't take me one night, have you any friends who might want to?' To which Peter replied: 'I have a mate who can drive. I'll give you his address and phone number. I'm sure he'll do it.'

Shortly afterwards I had a corporate gig in Byfleet, Surrey, and didn't ask Peter this time, instead recruiting his pal over the phone. Soon, my wife was driving over with me to pick him up in the Maxi and then bring him back to our house, where she would get out and he would jump in the front to take over. Now if you, reader, heard the nickname of your new chauffeur was 'Skippy', you'd probably sense something out of place immediately, perhaps cancel the gig or get someone else to take the wheel. Well not me, I'm stupid. My gullibility knows no bounds. Having said goodbye to my wife, we duly set off down the M6 with all six foot two of my new driver, half-boy, half-praying mantis, examining the controls, having eventually slipped the Maxi's admittedly awkward gearbox into first and rolling away. Skippy, whose real name I never did find out, didn't say much and had a strangeness about him. I tried to start a conversation, but my questions were answered with 'yes' or 'no' or a grunt, then silence until I spoke again. In the end I gave up and remained silent myself.

The engine sang away happily as we headed south, but no sooner had we passed Charnock Richard services than something began to

The Tale Continues...

become apparent: Skippy was either drugged up to the eyeballs, tired or both. Worse than that, he was wandering. We would stray onto the hard shoulder slightly, then he would over-correct his steering and slowly leave the slow lane for the central lane, over-correct again and wander back to the hard shoulder. I remained silent and, in any case, something even worse was about to show itself.

What he would do is this. Instead of pulling out to overtake early, he would leave it to the very last second then swerve past the vehicle and cut back in immediately. This was particularly unnerving when he did it with trucks. He'd speed up to the back of one, I'd feel myself stifling a cry of 'Oh, shit! We're dead this time', and then he'd snatch the wheel and miss the back end by a couple of feet. My inner horror grew as I realised I would have to endure this torture all the way to Surrey. So here I was, on the road, a man who in his respect for the law had accepted his punishment and done the right thing by hiring a driver but who was now a hazard of epic proportions. Furthermore because of said law I couldn't do the intelligent thing: i.e. tell Skippy to pull over and let me take the wheel. A ridiculous predicament to be in. I had to sit impotently and put my life literally in his hands because that was legal, whereas if I, a seasoned driver with never an accident to my name, were to take charge that would be illegal. From then on, I could only put an end to this self-inflicted mental scourging by setting myself the challenge of engaging Skippy in conversation. I failed to do so, but on reaching our destination, at least, I had succeeded in remaining sane. The gig over and done, my driver and I headed back up north and somewhere near Watford I did manage to extract a bit of info from Skippy about his family that didn't amount to much and fizzled out by the time we reached the M6. Skippy seemed still to be high on something, the car wandering all over the road again and missing the backs of trucks at the very last second by under two feet. By the time we were halfway up all conversation had ceased, heart once again in my mouth. Had I been driving, I would likely have been drowsy by now. And with someone I trusted totally at the wheel, maybe fast asleep. Not so with Skippy. I kept giving him a sneaky glance to check he was awake. My nerves

Stand-up Chameleon

were tingling, my survival mechanism on red alert. We came to a coned area and the lane we were in was directed across to another, because motorway maintenance was in progress. Skippy followed the temporary signs. This new lane had cones on one side of it and, on the other, the sort of tall white and orange plastic dividers that plug into cat's eyes and stand erect. Ten seconds was all it took, ten seconds at most, in which I relaxed my vigilant watch over my driver and he dropped off to sleep. I only realised this, though, when those cylindrical lane dividers went flying in all directions as the Maxi ploughed into them. Some hit the windscreen, others flew over the top of the car. I got the perspective of a ball in a bowling alley, just as the skittles take a hit. 'Skippy' I shouted, grabbing the wheel and putting us back on track. 'Wake up!' I howled, which, to be fair, he did. He also apologised for the bloody great dents in the Maxi as we examined it at the next services, while promising to stay awake for the rest of the journey and get me home in one piece.

Drinking and driving is a stupid and uncaring thing to do, so being banned for twelve months was well deserved and probably the most inconvenient thing ever to happen to me at a time in my career when I really needed to be able to get around. In retrospect, though, I can say that being breathalysed was a blessing in disguise. Needless to say I've never ever driven under the influence of alcohol again.

It was a lesson well learned and I wasn't going to make the same mistake twice. I know some people do, but they didn't have Skippy.

Killing Time on Tour

If being in the entertainment business doesn't bring fame and fortune, at least it will make a person well-travelled. That's what showbusiness is really, a whole load of travelling, a lot of hanging around and a bit of doing the show.

I always used to think: 'Wouldn't it be great if I could just, by magic, arrive on stage and do my two hours and then, by the same magic, arrive home.' But then again, were this to be so, you would miss out on all the strange things that can happen on the road. It's true, travelling can be a pain, what with checking into hotels and negotiating ludicrous traffic systems in unfamiliar towns and cities. Yet I have sighed many a sigh of pleasure at sights beheld on more scenic journeys through our glorious countryside. I also feel lucky and privileged to have been free, not tied to any workshop or office desk. Nor have I been confined by the walls of a factory. Instead, I've had enough time and space to walk the many coastal paths close to seaside towns I've played at. In twenty-eight years of touring I must have played most theatres in the land.

I must also say, though, that many seaside town theatres these days look forsaken. In fact, the towns themselves seem slightly more forlorn than when last I was there. Ghost towns even. Whole streets of shops boarded up; litter blowing down the road like tumbleweed. The kiosk of the fortune teller is open for business, yet there is no one there to

Stand-up Chameleon

have their fortune told. The wind howls through the rusty crumbling buildings and there they sit, in their kiosks, waiting. You can't help but think: 'If you really can see into the future you'd know no-one is going to turn up today for a reading and so wouldn't have bothered coming into work,.' But no, there they sit, in eternal hope of custom. Is palmist just another word for wanker? It makes you wonder.

Some towns have, over a decade or two, been selected to have works of art bestowed upon them (for a price), in order to brighten up everyone's lives. Some great hulk of rusty metal or twisted tangled maze of stainless steel suddenly appears in the middle of a roundabout, or by the side of a road. Sculptures of famous people associated with the town also appear in the oddest places, right in the middle of the town square maybe. Cast in bronze, they often have not the remotest resemblance to the person they are intended to represent. If thieves can clean out a whole town of manhole covers, why don't they do everyone a favour and pilfer these monstrosities as well? Someone did once, it made the headline in a local paper. I wrote to the council saying it was their own fault – putting it where people could see it. I didn't post it though, what would have been the point? Modern artists take everyone for a ride. They exploit gullibility and good luck to them, I say. If people are so stupid, why not take em' for all they've got?

The Angel of the North? Now, I wish someone would nick that. Wouldn't it be wonderful if someone did, altering its wings so they hinged halfway, adapted them with electronics and hydraulics and reintroduced it to the public, only this time in Piccadilly Circus, London, directing traffic. But no, it's just rusting away on a hilltop by the A1.

A roundabout on a bypass near Barnstaple has these great massive Devonian slate slabs sticking out of it. Are they supposed to look like they've fallen from the sky? We know they haven't! It must have cost a fortune to have them stuck into the earth by an army of men and machines. Wouldn't the council have been wiser to plant some flowers on the damn roundabout? How about a floral clock? A digital one – now that would be impressive – or even the old-fashioned type with two fingers and a one-to-twelve face, way more pleasing to the eye. But no, another beauty spot pandering to the ego of modern artists.

As for that sixty-foot copper woman creation of Damien Hirst in Ilfracombe? Well, if the good people of that lovely town insist on having this wretched thing standing in their midst, they'd do well to acquire some six-foot women coppers as well. If one of them should foil the

Killing Time on Tour

attempts of scrap metal thieves stealing the damn thing, they might enjoy this headline in their morning paper: 'Sixty-foot copper woman nickers nicked by six-foot woman copper.'

If ever I go into an exhibition and find one room solely for modern art I won't even bother to walk in. The only way I could be persuaded otherwise is if Hirst and Tracey Emin were in there, suspended in a tank of formaldehyde and preserved to be ogled at forever. I would probably even pay to see that.

Museums, cinemas and coastal walks kill an hour here or there while waiting for the showtime. As, of course, does grabbing a bite to eat. Sadly, no decent eating place is ever open at 4.00pm when I need to eat (meals need time to 'drop' before shows), only greasy spoons in which everything on their walls and ceiling, including light switches, is ten per cent bigger than it normally would be, covered in so many layers of gloss paint. This might also include the mummified bluebottle on the indoor windowsill trapped for ever in its tobacco-stained cream sarcophagus. As a rule, I tended to let the sound engineer try the food first – if he didn't crumple up in pain or be sick, or most importantly fail to survive the experience, I'd have some of what he had. By now I'm accustomed to the permanent smell of tallow that hangs heavy in the air and hardly notice it. What I do notice, though, is the 'food' still repeating on me, during the show, three and a half hours later.

Occasionally, we would break from the norm and try something a bit more adventurous to help the time go by.

A pony trek in the Brecon Beacons comes to mind, when I had a support act as well as a sound engineer in the early days of my new found fame, trying out new material in small Welsh theatres. I'd never ridden a horse beforehand, why would I? I am nervous of the beasts, they are unpredictable. Fortunately these were placid and just plodded over rugged terrain following the leader on a route they take day after day. My support act was a duo called themselves Little Aeroplane, later changed to Nothing By Chance, Keith Donnelly and Gilly Darbey. Keith wrote the songs, Gilly sang them beautifully. The songs were brilliant too. Many had their roots in folk and could be anything from a gentle love song to an up tempo tune with an edge of protest to it. Keith was and still is a really funny guy, having paid his dues in folk clubs and colleges. I still see him occasionally. His must be the best warm-up act ever. He connects with audiences immediately, having them participate in a variety of crazy songs and routines he's dreamt up. Gilly went her

Stand-up Chameleon

own way eventually, emigrating to New Zealand in 2004. Keith now works alone and occasionally with a French-born singer named Flossie Malavialle. But anyway, there we were, meandering up the slopes of a Welsh hill, Keith, Gilly, sound engineer John Brown, my tour manager Steve Hutt and I on the backs of these horses. We came to a wood they just plodded through, although when passing under the bough of a tree the rider would have to bend and weave to avoid being knocked off. Keith was following up the rear and, after a while, we heard a cry behind us, not seeking help, more a yell of surprise followed by muffled curses and noises of exasperation in a thick Geordie accent. Looking around we saw Keith had been torn from the saddle by several small branches that now held him suspended horizontally and hanging onto clumps of foliage, one leg dangling free. His horse, meanwhile, plodded on totally unfazed by the absence of its furious rider.

I don't know if he did it deliberately to get laughs (here was a man who'd dive through thin ice into a hotel's open-air pool in the depths of winter) or whether it was a genuine mishap. Whatever, it sent us all into hysterics. Keith, with some assistance from the lady leader of the trek, re-mounted and we were soon off again, aglow with the memory of Keith in the tree. We then came out of the woods and onto a vast stretch of moorland when the leader, unknown to me, took a partial consensus on whether we should break into a gallop or not. She got a 'yes' from those upfront and so off they went, with the horses of Keith and myself following suit. Before long, I decided this was the first and last time I'd ever ride a horse – I say 'ride', 'hanging on' would be more like it, for my very life. Even though we were on a level stretch of land there were rocks protruding everywhere as hooves thundered over earth and my chance of survival depended on clinging desperately to that great hairy creature. The danger and seriousness of it all made the comic aspect stronger; if you've ever wondered if it's possible to be frightened and laugh simultaneously I can assure you it is.

By the time the leader brought her horse to a near stop, which was probably two minutes, I was in agony from laughing so much and trying not to fall off and break my spine. God, I was sore. My ribs ached, I laughed every laugh I could muster and had nothing left in there. What almost made me fall was seeing Keith coming up alongside me on his galloping bag of dog meat, guffawing in sympathy and then falling off himself with more Geordie complaints as he hit the clumps of harsh moorland grass. 'Ah just missed crackin' me flippin' 'ead on a bloomin'

Killing Time on Tour

rock, like,' he said when he caught us up again. This would all have been in 1987 and I can say I have laughed hard many times since, but never with such intensity. I was exhausted for the show that night.

While killing time wandering through British towns over the years I have also noticed an increase in the number of new age-style therapy places. Their owners give them names that potential clients in their gullibility will hopefully find alluring. You might see a sign that says something like 'The Aquarius Centre' or 'The Gaia Holistic Suite' or maybe 'The Golden Aura', 'The Pentangle Healing Place' or one-word ones like 'Mind' or 'Peace' or 'Sanctuary'. What I find amusing, other than the fact of their existence, is how some are located upstairs – entered by a flight of steps between a gunsmith or butcher's shop, or over a betting shop adjacent to a scrapyard maybe. The client obviously goes in to enjoy such treats as aromatherapy, has a cuppa something or other while surrounded by fragrant candles with soothing music emanating from the ether. Naked except for a towel no doubt, they are then invited in a whisper from the masseur to lie on the surface of a massage table before being given a right good going over by tender oily hands. One problem, though. The soundproofing doesn't work too well, however, and the noise of betting shop TVs blend in.

> '...and coming up to the final furlong it's Tiger Feet taking the lead from Steel Grey ... breathe in ... and ... you're drifting away ... Tiger Feet is pulling away from Steel Grey falling back into second place ... on the outside Merlin's Pride is gaining ground ... and ... breath ... out ... Now on the final straight it's neck and neck between Steel Grey and Merlin's Pride for second place, Tiger Feet is falling back with yards to go Merlin's Pride now pulling away from Steel Grey and gaining ground on Tiger Feet ... breathe in ... It's going to be a photo finish as Tiger Feet has it by a nose ... it's all over and the crowd here at Aintree is going wild ... and ... breathe ... out ... there now, relaxed?'

I've only ever been to one such place myself, in Chipping Norton, in the Cotswolds. I was playing the little theatre there. Ronnie Barker had retired to this lovely town and ran an antique shop. I was told by the theatre manageress he was coming to the show that night and so looked forward to meeting him. My tour manager Steve was with me that day and said, or rather suggested (he was always suggesting, it was he who suggested the Welsh pony trek) that we kill an hour or so by

Stand-up Chameleon

going to a holistic centre just a short way from the theatre. I agreed. I was always agreeing with Steve's suggestions, he had a way of making you do that. So off we went down the little streets of Chipping Norton, around the corner, down the hill a bit and found the place.

I can't remember its name, a pleasant lady ran it. She would have to be nice in a holistic establishment and wholesome too. We met her in the reception of a building that had a proper Cotswolds look, rustic sandstone, orange-coloured lichens clamped to its walls like limpets, roofs semi-carpeted with moss of the same colour. She explained in a kindly manner that there we had two options. One – try the flotation tank and experience the weightlessness of floating in brine in the dark in silence. This she highly recommended; the client undergoes a shift from 'being' to 'non-being', she said, 'as all the senses are deprived of stimuli. You can't see, hear or feel and there's nothing to smell or taste,' she concluded reassuringly with a smile. 'That sounds different,' I said, glancing at Steve as he interjected with: 'Go on, what else is there here then?' 'Aromatherapy massage which, like the flotation tank session, lasts an hour and you choose from a selection of oils. I'll massage you from head to toe and you'll feel totally refreshed and relaxed.' She then pointed to a list of exotic oils. 'So, what is it to be?'

'I fancy the massage,' Steve and I said, simultaneously. 'Oh no,' said Angel Knuckles, hands on hips. 'You can't both have the massage; one of you will have to go in the tank.' 'So, we don't have an option as such then?' 'Yes, either the massage or the flotation experience.' 'But not both of us?' 'One of you can have the massage and one of you can have the tank; you decide between you.' Following a few seconds of giddy dialogue, Steve suggested he should have the massage while I should be more adventurous and go in the tank. I agreed.

Steve was instructed by Angel Knuckles to go and strip off in a room she pointed to with a nimble finger. 'Shower first and then cover up with a towel. I'll be right with you after I've taken your friend to the flotation room.' I followed her along a corridor and we entered the very place where I was to cease to exist for an hour and half. She had extended the time as a gesture of goodwill as it was our first visit to her 'temple'. 'Listen carefully and follow what I say precisely,' she said, as I looked into the pool of brine that awaited me.

'First have a shower, then put on a pair of these goggles,' she said, gesturing to several pairs hanging on hooks. 'Then step gently into the tank. The water is so saturated in salt it's impossible to sink, you float

Killing Time on Tour

high up on the surface, so you can remain totally motionless and just lie as though suspended in space. Once you are in,' she continued, 'before you settle down, pull this dangling cord and the light will go out. You will be in total darkness with no sound, but just stretch yourself out in the water and float away into nothingness.' 'Well, that'll be different then,' I said, jokingly, as I undid my first shirt button. 'I'll leave you now,' she said, all serious as she moved towards the door. 'I'll be back for you when your time is up. You won't realise an hour and a half has passed. Time doesn't exist anyway, and neither will you in the tank.' She then turned back toward me and said, as I struggled with my last shirt button, 'Oh, the most important thing to remember, and I'm telling you this last so you definitely won't forget, is if you have any cuts scratches or grazes the salt will get into them and be very painful. So, you see that big tub of petroleum jelly on the bench there?' I nodded. 'Well, rub a thick finger full of that into any abrasions or such. In just in the same way goggles prevent salt going into your eyes, the petroleum jelly will stop it getting into any cuts.' On this stern caution she then left and closed the door. 'Well,' I thought to myself as I showered, 'I've no cuts so it's just the goggles, then. Oh yeah, and my trunks (always in my bag lest the hotel had a pool) just in case the fire alarm goes off and I have to get out quick.'

Two minutes later, I'm wearing goggles, trunks and standing in three feet of brine, my hand on the pull switch. Lights out, lie back, float. Chill out, unwind. And it was true, after a while I *did* feel that I was just a 'mind', with no points of reference that could explain such a thing as a body. It was as though I was a spirit cast adrift in nothingness. Every so often though, in a timespan I'm not sure of, I would feel my big toe touch the side of the tank and the minute collision would send me off again in the opposite direction. I figured this out because after what felt like ages my head would gently touch the tank side. Apart from that I was body-less. All thoughts, including those of Steve next door being soothed and caressed by Angel Knuckles, were beginning to cease. I was becoming no-one, nowhere. I'd almost vanished. Being that I wasn't supposed to exist, I couldn't quite pinpoint the source of the feeling. It got worse and worse though and then went from unpleasant to unbearable. I'd have to abort the float and get out of the brine, take off my goggles, switch on the light and investigate the problem.

Have you ever had one of those 'stepmother's blessings?' That's what they call them up north, where I'm from, but other parts of the

Stand-up Chameleon

country may give them different names. You'll know what I mean when I say a torn piece of flesh, only tiny, hardly worth mentioning in normal circumstances. Yes, those little slivers that come about after worrying a nail, more so on thumbs than fingers. In my case, thumb, and it was becoming the mother of all throbs. So I ascended out of this merciless solution, removed my goggles and, on doing so, brine ran into my eyes. The silence was broken by the 'F' word shouted at eighty decibels as both eyes started to sting. Tortured by pain, I lunged for the light switch. The light came on but I couldn't see so good and fumbled my way over to the shower, slipping as I went and almost putting my back out. That caused me to scream venomous profane bile into the air, which must have been heard by the theatre staff. I tried to get the brine out of my eyes and washed my thumb too with soap, but it kept on hurting. I thought it a bit late to stick a dollop of petroleum jelly on, but did so anyway, hoping the pain might now subside. With eyes still stinging and thumb still throbbing I eased my goggles on again and got back in the tank, switched off the light and floated. As I lay there buoyant, high in the salty water trying to relax, the pain in my eyes became less severe, but the 'stepmother's blessing' didn't. It just got worse and worse.

So here I was, having paid for this sense deprivation therapy, not with the feeling of being 'no-one nowhere', but of being a disembodied thumb somewhere, and that 'somewhere' being a lukewarm tank of chemicals at a funny farm in Chipping Norton, the Cotswolds.

I could stand no more and showered quickly. When I arrived back in reception (early), with clothes back on, Steve was still receiving his treatment. I could hear little moans of ecstasy in the aromatherapy room. Still, it passed an hour or so.

That night Ronnie Barker and his wife came to the theatre. The show went well and, afterwards, Ronnie treated me to a few drinks and a laugh or two at the bar, by which time my thumb was back to normal. Going to the pictures is safer but, still, you live and learn.

The Tale Continues...

In the early-1980s, a guy called Steve Taylor came to a concert of mine at a pub in Horwich, which had a big concert room upstairs that the landlord let me use. I knew the gig would sell out because I was well known and liked in the town, five or so miles from Bolton, having played regularly there at a cellar bar called Nibblers.

I'd stuck a few posters up to promote it – those saying 'not Casper Jarrott' and 'not Billy Connery' you read about twenty-odd pages back – and Steve spotted one while driving past so they must've been effective. After a fleeting glimpse of Mike Yarwood he'd screeched to a halt and backed up, before realising that it actually said 'Mike Yarwooden'. Intrigued, he came to the show anyway. And when that first one was over he came to several more with his wife, Kim, so we got to know each other. It transpired the couple ran a big pub themselves, the Royal Oak in Chorley.

The Laughingas in Leyland was going strong at this point, but I was getting tired of having to find fresh acts every week. Still, it was good for me to work out new songs, impressions and stories there, so I carried on regardless. Steve came to a few nights and had a good time and a laugh. We talked for a while and I let it be known I was

Stand-up Chameleon

fed up with of the process of running things at the Fox Lane Cricket Club. Shortly after which, while on an errand in Chorley, I called in at the Royal Oak – which as it happened was an old haunt of mine – and discovered that the interior had been redesigned. It now had a cellar bar that, in an attempt to be trendy, the brewery had called 'Clouseau's, with portraits of Peter Sellers on its walls. Walking down those steps I immediately knew this space would be an ideal new home for the Laughingas. After a bit of discussion, Steve and I struck the ideal arrangement. He would book the acts and I would just turn up on the night and do my usual stuff in this perfect room.

Opening night duly arrived and the venue, which held about 120, was full. Off to a great success it then ran and ran, not only with me but guest comics trying out their own material every other Monday. My own repertoire was expanding all the time and I was able to hone it at Laughingas mark two before performing it at the gigs I was getting from the Wigan agency.

By now, Chris Tarrant's *Stayback* had been and gone, with no spin-offs for my career. In fact, I'd almost forgotten I'd done it when a phone call came from the agency. 'Phil!' said Simon, the new boy in the office. 'Something you might be interested in… it's a strange one.'

At that stage I'd got used to fielding all sorts of offers and requests so, with a shade of indifference, said: 'Go on then, lets hear it.'

'Central TV in Birmingham are making a satirical TV show,' he said, 'and they wondered whether you'd be available to do the warm-up. It's hardly worth doing, fee-wise, as they are only offering £100.'

For the previous six months or so, I'd been ill with a terrible chest infection but had carried on working regardless, having a family and home to support. This wretched virus had resulted in several trips to the doctors and even tests at Preston Hospital. Nevertheless, while coughing and wheezing, I said: 'I still feel terrible, but even though I'm dying I'd better take it regardless because its TV and you never know what might come out of it. What did you say it was again?'

'Oh, just some sort of satirical show,' Simon replied. 'That's all they would disclose.'

And so, I turned up that day at Central Studios to be greeted by

The Tale Continues...

Peter Harris, a director I'd met on *Stayback* best known – until then – for his work on *The Muppet Show*, and producer John Lloyd, whose track record included *Not the Nine O'Clock News* and *Blackadder* among many other great programmes. It was explained to me that I was there to warm up a 300-strong audience; get them in the mood to watch a big screen on which a pilot episode would be shown. All the characters were to be tested out in this first ever showing, gauging audience reaction to each. Peter had suggested me for the job, recalling my ability to make people laugh with visual stuff, John said, and they would use the reactions to my performance as a laughter track for this new show, given it would be 'clean', having no voice mixed in with the guffaws. Also, I might generate a few chuckles and the odd titter. With a splutter from my chronic cough, I thanked both Peter and John and went to prepare my props.

Pic by Steve Taylor (now Steven P. Taylor), poet extraordinaire. Go check him out!

'Let me give you something for that dreadful cough,' said the Central TV nurse, who'd been put on my case. 'One of my specials,' she added, mixing the concoction together. 'It will pull you through your performance,' she promised, brimming over with professional confidence. 'Down the hatch!'

What tasted like brandy Night Nurse® – and God knows what else – slid down my throat and landed in my stomach with a bang. I did the show. It was a good one too. Everybody was ecstatic with my contribution and the characters on screen scored a big hit – some more than others. That was fine. The point of the screening was to find out which worked best. John came over when the audience had

Stand-up Chameleon

gone and congratulated me, remarking that he was impressed to the extent he would like me to join the team and do some voices myself. 'I'll be in touch and give you plenty of work,' he said before turning to walk away.

'Oh, one thing,' I said with a splutter and a wheeze as the special concoction began to wear off. 'What's the programme's name?'

'Oh, I'm sorry,' he replied, turning back. 'Did I not say? It's going to be called *Spitting Image*.'

Sure enough, he was true to his word. I did eventually contribute to the show. Once to do the voices of Mick Jagger and David Frost, and a second time to perform songs written for a Boy George send-up and ridicule Holly Johnson of Frankie Goes to Hollywood. The IMDb website also has me down as doing Norman Tebbit, Roy Hattersley, Adolf Hitler, David Steel and Scottish peace campaigner MP Gordon Wilson, although I'm pretty sure I didn't! I did meet others on the 'voices' team like Harry Enfield, Chris Barrie, Louise Gold and Steve Nallon. What I liked least about the experience was hanging about waiting for my 'turn' to be recorded. I also felt I didn't fit in too well, so wasn't overly upset when the job fizzled out in 1984.

It was around about this time too that Les Ward introduced me to some friends of his – a skiffle band called Please Y'Self, who played the Boggery Club and went on to do Glastonbury – a real nice bunch of people. In conversation, I explained that I used to have a comedy club and was now fortunate enough to have a mate running it, adding that I 'worked out' there on Monday nights. They told me they had recently appeared at a comedy venue in London called 'The Tunnel Club' and gave me the telephone number of the bloke who ran it. His name was Malcolm Hardee.

Shortly afterwards, I told Steve Taylor it might be a good idea if I were to take a trip south and see how they did it there, maybe get some comics and bands to come up north to the Laughingas, which did go on to happen – Jo Brand, Jeremy Hardy, Arnold Brown, Felix

The Tale Continues...

Dexter, Phil Cornwell and Jenny Eclair among them. 'I'll come with you,' said Steve, eager to get more experience in the comedy scene. So off we went to Greenwich, where I did a no-fee open mic spot. My humour seemed to go down a storm there, that first night.

Several trips to the Tunnel Club followed over the next year or so. Malcolm, the owner and compère, was some character – boy, was he ever! He is perhaps best remembered for a surreal act he did with two mates called The Greatest Show on Legs, where they danced in the nude, balloons covering the naughty bits, in a routine first seen on Chris Tarrant's *O.T.T.* in 1982. He had an Eric Morecambe-esque look about him, big black-rimmed glasses and what have you, but he was way more anarchic, outrageous and hairy, funny in his own way. He'd walk on stage going 'Oy! Oy!, that was his catchphrase, always acting really outlandish because I don't think he was that talented a performer, really. He relied heavily on things like getting his chopper out. I never saw him do that but it's gone down in comedy folklore. He wouldn't last two minutes nowadays.

Later, he had another comedy club floating on the Thames called the Wibbley Wobbley, a converted Rhine pleasure cruiser. I went to it once, never played there though. He'd compère that and then get in his little boat and row across the river – standing up – to another boat, where he lived. And this was after about sixteen pints. People warned him, 'Malcolm, you're going to die doing that...' and he'd say 'oh, fuck it...' – that was another of his catchphrases, 'fuck it.'

Sure enough, in January 2005 he tried the same trick, fell in, and drowned, aged 55. When they dragged him up out of Greenland Dock, he still had a bottle of beer in his hand.

I went to his funeral at St Alfege's Church in Greenwich and every man and his dog was there ... Vic Reeves, Harry Hill, Johnny Vegas, Phill Jupitus, David Baddiel, Jerry Sadowitz, Keith Allen ... all the alternative set ... Jools Holland played a hymn ... the funniest send-off I've ever seen. Someone put a lifejacket on the coffin instead of a wreath. Arthur Smith compèred it... absolutely hilarious.

The last time I saw Malcolm alive, though, was at the Edinburgh Festival in 1998. I went to another venue after my show, The Gilded

Stand-up Chameleon

Balloon, and Malcolm was just weaving around and banging into everybody, completely out of it. He saw me, went 'alright', mumbling away, and then just staggered on before disappearing into the crowd.

It all seemed a long way from those first paid gigs at the Tunnel when the big break every comedian longs for was, for me, just around the corner and came as a result of that *Spitting Image* warm-up.

In the audience, unknown to myself, had been a BBC producer who recognised me from *Stayback*. He sat in the dark Central TV studio watching my half-hour set thinking: 'Ah, so *this* is what that guy does when he's allowed more than a ten-second performance.'

I know that's what he thought because he later told me so, but I can't remember exactly what material I did on the night. It probably included my 'Gurning Song' – a pastiche of the Frank Ifield number, 'She Taught Me How To Yodel' along the lines of 'she taught me how to gurn', in which my entire face-pulling repertoire was preceded by a story of how I was invited to enter the Cumbrian Gurning Contest at Egremont in the Lake District. I might also have done my routine about the four-minute warning, and my underwater Hans and Lotte Hass sketch. No doubt I would have crammed in lots of impressions too. Anyway, this producer made himself known afterwards and said he'd be in touch. His name was Steve Weddle, soon a lifelong friend.

Re our chance meeting, Steve later told me he'd been on a train and met someone he knew. During a brief conversation they offered him tickets for a pilot at Central because they couldn't go themselves. Were it not for that fateful meeting, Steve would never have seen my set. Neither would he have then made contact with my Wigan agent to offer me a guest spot on *Pebble Mill at One* – the BBC lunchtime show he produced, broadcast live on weekdays from Birmingham. It was really popular, on air every day, and went on to run from 1972 to 1996. All the big stars guested and I certainly watched it regularly myself, so had no hesitation in saying 'Yes!' as soon as I got the offer.

Getting Spotted

The train pulled up to the platform. I stepped out, guitar and prop case in hand, and left via the station exit into the streets of London. Having walked a while, I stopped to get my bearings as to which direction to take to get to the comedy club I was booked for; a job taken months prior to *Cool It* going to air, although by then it had been broadcast.

'Phil!' a voice bellowed behind me. 'Please, quick, I must have your autograph!' It was a man in uniform. He'd followed me outside and, having caught up, spluttered: 'Here's a pen; put it there in my notebook,' out of breath. 'Hurry, I've got to get back on the train.' I could see he was desperate, so did as he asked after which he ran back at breakneck speed and rightly so. He was the now departing train's conductor.

This was one of the first times I got 'celebrity spotted' after *Cool It* and, because it was so new and unusual, I found it quite enjoyable. It made me smile. The novelty, however, soon wears off and before long you become wary. Worst case scenario is when you're alone having a quiet drink at a table in a hotel bar, like I was once in Scotland, and a tableful of people sitting opposite recognise you – you know they have – and begin a discussion about you. Of course there is one, completely drunk, who happens never to have heard of you, a fact you are aware of because their voice is so loud you've heard almost everything they say. This drunkard – a girl in my case – then staggers over full of false

Stand-up Chameleon

On stage at the Laughingas, watched over by Peter Sellers

courage and says: 'Is it true, you're a comedian?' 'It's true,' I reply, rather than two other short words I'd like to say. Now, with both hands on my table, up way too close for comfort, she says, 'You don't look funny to me. Say something funny,' she adds, trying to steady herself and stop from falling over. 'No, not here,' I say, taking a swig of beer. 'My friends say you are a comedian and you're funny.' 'Oh, thanks.' 'I've never heard of you, I don't believe them, do something funny, now!' Her mouth is now crooked, her face so distorted by booze it might be half-melted. What can you say in a situation like that? 'Good night, I'm off to bed?' Well, that's exactly what I did say, stepped around her and went.

During another 'quiet' drink in a hotel in Essex a slightly different situation arose. Four girls were sitting opposite me with a couple of blokes, who were buying their drinks. After a while these lads left and one girl said to her mates: 'See the bloke over there?' 'Yeah.' 'That guy told me he's a comedian off the telly.' 'Oh,' said one of the other three, 'in that case let's go sit with him, he's bound to have loads of money.' I was out of there before they'd risen to their feet.

Now, you may think calling this book *Stand-up Chameleon* means that I can blend into any background and therefore avoid all this, but no. I'm just like you. If I stand beside an old-fashioned letterbox in the street, I can't turn red and vanish. I did though, over the years, develop a knack for not being spotted. I'd have no problem with old pedestrians – if, say, a group of senior citizens tottered by I'd proceed as normal,

Getting Spotted

knowing they wouldn't be interested in my shows, nor have seen them, and therefore wouldn't know who I was. Groups of young people, on the other hand, would delay me, demanding I do a 'face', and be a real pain. In those cases, I'd whip out a handkerchief, pretend to wipe my nose and/or dive into a shop doorway, feigning interest in a pair of shoes, model aircraft or whatever in the window.

It is difficult to avoid being spotted by people who sit in cafés all day, observing pedestrians. I was walking down a street in Devon once when a woman ran out of one and stopped me. She explained she was an artist and asked if she could take a photo of me that she could later do a sketch from. Like a fool, I walked off all the way to her house and did a 'sitting' for her, leaving my address so she could forward it to me. It's now somewhere at the bottom of my memorabilia box.

Nowadays, I've had such a long break from TV that life is far easier in that I can walk anywhere and only get spotted on rare occasions. People sometimes feel there's a certain familiarity about me, and might say something like: 'You've got a look of that ... Phil Cool...', before adding 'No offence.'

Other sightings over the years have been in the most unlikely places. Holidaying in New Zealand in 2004, I got noticed by an Irishman during a river speedboat trip: 'I always remember a face, to be sure,' he said. 'I do, alright, especially one that had me in stitches, be Jabus. I can't believe it's you.' I've also been spotted by an Australian passport official at Perth airport. I knew he'd seen me, even though I was way back at the end of a fifty-yard queue. He was smiling in the distance, good at his job obviously. A relative must have sent him a *Cool It* video. I was clocked by an American once – in my local village pub in Lancashire! At first he kept quiet, pondering like. It was only when I left the pub to go home on this late and quiet night and was just about to turn the corner, fifty yards away up the street, that he came out and shouted this long rambling question: 'Hey! Buddy! Are you the guy who was on a TV show of the Montréal *Just for Laughs* Comedy Festival, who did an impression of president Reagan turning into a creature from outer space?' 'Yeah, goodnight!' I shouted back, before disappearing around the corner. He must've thought: 'God, some of these limeys are really anti-social.'

Once, I was out driving when my car broke down in a dodgy part of Preston. I left it by the side of the road and went into a pub. It was rough. I made a call from a payphone to a mechanic friend, bought a

Stand-up Chameleon

pint, and sat down at a corner table to await rescue. The staff and a few customers were showing signs of recognition, whispering, looking over and then away again fast. A short while after which one member of staff started collecting glasses and, on passing me, stopped. On behalf of the others, who'd egged him on, he discreetly enquired 'Are you Phil Cool?' Replying quietly, so only he could hear, I said: 'If I was Phil Cool, do you think I'd be drinking in a dump like this?' 'No, I suppose not,' he replied, before wandering off.

My growing paranoia re being spotted grew to such an extent that, to make it more bearable, Steve Hutt and I turned it into a game with ten points available for spotting a spotter. 'Spotter at ten o'clock,' one of us would say after spotting someone spotting me, in the manner of pilots looking for bandits during Battle of Britain dogfights. 'Ten points to me.' 'Yeah?' he'd say. 'Well, I've spotted two spotters, one at twelve o'clock and another at three, so that's twenty points to me.'

In the end you just have to accept that you've brought all this upon yourself. It is, after all, like the money, a by-product of the profession you are in, so you ought to stop whingeing about it.

The cheekiest encounter I ever had of being spotted during the fame years was when my wife Bev and I were in Manchester Airport, about to go on holiday at the check-in queue. A bloke came over from a long way off, shuffled right up close, and was soon face-to-face with me, our noses inches apart. He said nothing at all, just stayed like that for several seconds in silence, before turning and walking off. Halfway back to his family and friends we heard him shout: 'Yeah, it's him.'

Another strange and almost surreal moment came right at the peak of my fame, in 1991, on a hot and sunny afternoon in the USA.

'Ooh look, there's Goofy,' said a British mother to her children at Disney World in Florida. 'Let's have our photo taken with him.'

'And look, Mickey and Minnie,' said her husband. 'We'll have one taken with them too.'

'No, wait,' the woman then interrupted. 'There's Phil Cool. Let's have one taken with him first.'

My wife and two girls thought the idea of someone taking me for a Disney character hilarious. Not me. I was embarrassed. It probably showed on my face as I posed for their little Polaroid souvenir.

Alas, that was all such a long time ago. Nowadays?

I feel quite chuffed if I do get spotted.

The Tale Continues...

I was driven down to do *Pebble Mill at One* by Simon from the agency in Wigan. Entering the building we were greeted by a clearly excited young woman called Wendy Leavesley, who escorted us to a dressing room. We were taken aback by her loveliness and Simon, being a good-looking confident young buck, flirted with her as we walked through the area where the show was to be shot.

If you remember *Pebble Mill* you'll know that all the action took place not in the huge studio they had there, but the reception area. You may also recall how the cameras were positioned in such a way that, for most of the time, the presenters and guests were engaged in conversation with the building's glass frontage behind them, so any pedestrian walking by or traffic in the road was on screen. Steve Weddle, the producer, was among this hive of activity and Wendy took us to him. Steve told us that Wendy had been with him at the *Spitting Image* pilot, which was perhaps why she seemed so excited now. Having seen what I was capable of there she knew what effect I would soon have upon her colleagues on the programme.

Hot Chocolate, the soul and funk band fronted by Errol Brown, were the main guests that day. Steve took me to one side, lowered

Stand-up Chameleon

his voice and looked all around us as though he was about to share a secret. 'I've cut Hot Chocolate's screen time so as to give you more to complete the material you suggested,' he told me. 'Otherwise, I'm convinced you wouldn't get through it.'

The moment finally arrived and I was positioned on my chosen spot, waiting to go. In front of me was the *Pebble Mill* audience – a cross-section of the Brummie general public – cued to applaud as I was revealed by the camera. My EKO guitar was tuned and ready by my side. Up went the applause and I was off like a shot. I launched into the 'Gurning Song' introduction, which required a fair bit of miming to emulate the other contestants in Egremont. I managed a reference to Sellafield too, incorporating issues the place raised. This took maybe five minutes, which would normally have been seven, but I was motoring a bit to fit it all in a brief window of opportunity. On completion of the story I grabbed the guitar and sang:

> I went along to Cumbria, where all the gurners be,
> To try a learning gurning with my gurnalearnalee.
> *(Huge facial gurn)*
> I climbed up a mountain on a fine and windy day
> And met a fair young gurning girl
> in a gurning gurn chalet.
> She taught me to gurn, gurnalearnalee ... gurnalearnalee.

Extreme gurns, middle gurns, subtle gurns... they were all in there. The song finished, topped off with a spoken punchline. The little audience of seventy erupted into applause, having laughed through the entire piece. Then I quickly passed the guitar to a floor assistant and walked over to a couch opposite where I was interviewed by presenter Bob Langley. I can't remember what our conversation was about but it led to a tale about the four-minute warning, after which I ended with a few unusual impressions. Patrick McGoohan was one. I had him going on about not being a number but a free man and escaping from the village, which must have been because the 1960s show that made him famous, *The Prisoner*, had just been re-run on

The Tale Continues...

TV and that made it more up to date. Then I did a few Hollywood actors as cowboys and finished with Henry Fonda as a cop making an arrest. Les Ward of the Boggery folk club was there to give me a bit of support and afterwards enthused as much as anyone. Les was no stranger to Pebble Mill and knew several people who worked there while Malc Stent, his client, hosted a radio show there. Les, Steve, Wendy and the rest, still high on the show's success, all had a good laugh, a bite to eat and a drink in hospitality. Then for me it was back up the M6, driven by Simon.

※

Arthur Scargill, the Miners' Union leader, was prominent at this time, always on the news as the coal strike dominated the headlines. He was therefore well worth doing an impression of, I thought, and besides none of the other impressionists were doing him, which was strange. Perhaps they couldn't take him off or, more likely, didn't want to offend the 'left'. I never thought too deeply about such things so just went for him. What I did – and I've only ever done it once – was tape one of his rants from TV, then listen to it over and over until I eventually got the 'metre' of his speaking and mannerisms. I needed just one line to start with – one that got an instant laugh.

What came to mind was: 'I'll say this to all you people who say you can see right through me: let me make myself perfectly clear.'

I tried it at the Laughingas and it worked – my Scargill was ready to go. Meanwhile I'd been on the phone to Steve Weddle and Les Ward. Steve told me the *Pebble Mill at One* show got such a reaction he was going to ask his bosses at the 'Mill' if they would consider me for a pilot show. Steve had even thought of a name – *Cool It* – and if we got it made, and it was a hit with the powers-that-be, then I just might end up with a series of my own. He was going to set the wheels in motion, but emphasised that these things can take forever.

Les and I spoke about such things too, and it was growing ever more likely he'd become my manager once my contract ran out with the Wigan agency, only months away now. I told Les I was working

Stand-up Chameleon

on Scargill and he said that was a good move because with the coal strike intensifying it would be great for TV. *Spitting Image* might call me back to 'do' him for them. And then life carried on as normal as Steve beavered away at his quest to get Phil Cool on the box. Lots of phone calls, lots of meetings, lots of everything, keeping me up to date with everything going on until – bingo! Steve got a yes from his bosses. Where to do the show then became the issue. Ought we to find a theatre in Birmingham and shoot it there? Many discussions took place but eventually the day came once again at Pebble Mill.

I stood there in the big studio, ready to go with a jumble of material formed over several years. The previous night, I'd stayed at Les's house so was able to make an early start and feel fresher than if I'd travelled one hundred miles from home. In all honesty, though, I didn't feel fresh at all, having not slept due to anticipation of what lay ahead. The studio floor was left untouched – black. I used a mic in a stand, my EKO wired up and ready. Les had rustled up as many guests as he could, mainly from the Boggery, so as to ensure plenty of lively people in the 250-seater. The seats were tiered, so everyone would have a good view of the face hopefully about to blow them away. Just as I walked on to rapturous cued applause and was about to speak, I spied a 'late-comer' sneaking in on the end of a back row. Once underway, the hour sailed by. The show got a good reception and was soon, as they say, 'in the can', but according to the late-comer, who turned out to be Jasper, it should have been 'in the bin'.

He didn't voice this there and then, but I sensed he wasn't too impressed when we spoke briefly. It was only days later, at his house, that he gave me the third-degree. His main point was that times change and what once could be considered acceptable wasn't now.

'Phil,' said Jasper. 'You can't say: "Have you seen the lead singer in Hot Chocolate? His head's a Treat!"' (Treats then being a brand of chocolate-coated confectionery.) 'If he wasn't a black guy the joke wouldn't work, so you can be nailed for being racist. You can't go on about "snogging with a girl on the back row of the cinema who's got a big brown hairy birthmark on her neck", and refer to her as "Polo, the bint with the mole." It's derogatory towards women. You'll get

The Tale Continues...

slated for it. It's sexism!' He went on: 'And besides, there was a lot of waffle. You've got to be slick and precise with your diction on TV otherwise it looks and sounds awful on screen. It's too laboured, just get to the meat. You can either take on board what I say or carry on the way you are, it makes no difference to me. It's not my career, it's yours.' After which, I went away disgruntled and perplexed but did, over the following days back home, digest what the 'Carrott' said and came to the conclusion he knew better than I. He had been around longer, after all and knew what he was talking about. So, I decided it would be wise to examine my material and delivery more closely. I remain convinced that was the right decision.

Meanwhile, unbeknownst to me, Les Ward and business partner John Starkey were still deliberating over whether to manage me. I'd travelled down from Lancashire to John's house in Meriden with my wife for a meeting about this very thing, only to find John absent and Les alone with John's Old English Sheepdogs, totally out of control and diving over the three of us when as we tried to talk. Here was Les left to explain to us that they never intended to manage me at all when I'd been led to believe they had. The disappointment was awful and embarrassing, my contract with the Wigan outfit over, and I was very confused as to the problem. Compounding the surreality, Les had to keep breaking off from his explanation to scream at the marauding mutts. Julie and I left the house totally deflated. I did feel sorry for Les, having been left by John to deal with this on his own.

Strangely, not long afterwards I received a letter from John after doing another night at the Boggery in Solihull, saying something along the lines of 'I thought you were fantastic the other night, let's talk.' I don't know what reversed his view, it could have been a few things. It might well have been Jasper saying: 'You're crazy if you don't manage Phil.' Or maybe it was because I'd told Les that Max Boyce's manager, Stuart Littlewood, had been to a gig of mine and was considering managing me, which was true. Or perhaps John's letter was genuine and, after seeing me perform again at the Boggery, he had re-thought his decision. More likely, the 'change of heart'

Stand-up Chameleon

came after positive news had filtered through from London about *Cool It*. Still, whatever it was didn't matter because in the end John and Les said: 'Welcome aboard.' A five-year contract was signed. And that pilot? Well, it never did get transmitted, but what it did do was provide proof that I had potential and when Mr Weddle and his Pebble Mill bosses sent it to London to be judged by the big boys and girls there, it got the thumbs up. Their decision came through as: 'Yes, we think he has promise, so would agree to sign him for a series, but only three 25-minute shows.' There was a state of euphoria in Birmingham at Pebble Mill and plans were drawn up by Steve and Les to produce them. Back home, my wife couldn't believe it. None of us could. After all these years I was at last going big time.

Choosing material, of course, was the big issue and the more I had the better. Miners' strike still in full throttle, my Scargill was coming together slowly, a line here, a line there. Now though things were different. I had a TV show on the horizon and needed to think in those terms. You can do things on television that aren't possible on stage, so the wheels of my mind turned in a new direction.

I was also imbued with confidence, so much so I tempted fate by telling a few people I was going to be as big a household name as Daz soap powder, which turned out to be ironic. Shortly afterwards, while walking through the supermarket, there on the shelf with the washing paraphernalia was a product, in a box, called 'Cool It'. This made my wife laugh because I suspect that she (along with others I told) thought that all this television business was leading nowhere and I was a fantasist. Steve Taylor, though, seemed to believe it was going to happen. Sitting in the audience as I worked out my *Young Ones* sketch at the Laughingas, he must have felt it was like watching a boxer training for the big fight.

Phil O'Sophicool

I'm one of those many artists who have been not famous, then famous, and then not famous again. Being not famous again has never bothered me too much, although I'm sure that to some 'stars' the very thought of it fills them with sickening dread.

While starting out in the late 1970s, I worked for a whole week at the Gallop Inn in Harrogate with a formerly VERY big star. He had done the Royal Command Performance so many times in the presence of the Queen Mother and HM Queen Elizabeth II he'd been dubbed the 'Queen's Singer'. Now here he was, performing at this seedy cabaret lounge in North Yorkshire.

As a kid, I'd watched him on our little telly at home in Chorley and we had his number one records too, both in the UK and USA. In about 1978, when I worked with him, his style was now dated, his like having subsequently been replaced by rock 'n' roll, The Beatles, Bob Dylan and the new wave that followed. The small room in Harrogate was full, mainly of middle-aged women, all devoted fans. As I did my half-hour before he came on, frustrated at not being able to do any 'Gallop-Inn-knob rot' jokes as it would've caused offence among these blue rinse gals, I hardly got a look in, let alone a laugh.

When my spot was over, he came onstage and I watched from the side as he bellowed out his 'hits' with a still great voice, as though from

Stand-up Chameleon

a bygone age. The ladies swooned and cheered. Not so youthful now, he was more of a stage-worn dishevelled character, complete with a bit of a dodder and bulbous boozer's nose. It was a bit sad to see this former entertainment great with several number one hits to his name working such a downmarket joint. 'How things change.' I thought. 'One day, that will be me.' Departing the place on the last night, I never saw or heard him sing again.

All of which gave me a certain perspective on the business I was in, especially when, a decade or so later, I noticed his name among trivia and adverts in the bottom corner of a newspaper: 'David Whitfield dies in Australia.' I read the dozen or so words of brief description on the man and thought: 'That's the cruel old game for you; she shows no mercy, so fickle, so unforgiving.' Tenor David Whitfield of Hull, the first British artist to have a number one single in the UK and America, and once the Queen's singer, now laying cold on a morgue slab in Australia, aged just 54. Once everyone's darling, now almost forgotten, save for a few grainy images somewhere in the bottomless pit that is YouTube.

You know you are on your way out when you're watching TV and your name pops up on *Family Fortunes*.

For the uninitiated, that's a show in which two families compete against each other. It goes something like this: researchers survey the public beforehand, asking them to name things – 'an item you would pack to go on holiday' and the like. The reply may well be 'swimming costume' perhaps, or 'suntan lotion', 'book', 'passport'... you get the idea.

One family goes first and the host – which was Les Dennis at the time – asks each of them in turn to do likewise.

If their reply is the one a majority of people gave when surveyed it scores top points and pops up on the scoreboard accompanied by

---

'One will have you know that one has done the Royal Variety Performance...'

Phil O'Sophicool

the sort of sound you hear before a captain's announcement on an aeroplane.

If the reply is one that tallies with the second highest in the survey slightly fewer points are scored and so on, in a descending scale. If a family member replies with a guess that no-one on the survey matched they score no points, accompanied by a red X on the scoreboard and an unpleasant robotic ERRR-ERRR noise.

So anyway, I'm watching this pile of shite – don't ask me why – and part way through it, host Les says to a family member, 'Okay, Paul. Give me someone from the world of showbusiness whose first name is Phil.'

To which Paul replies, quick as a flash, 'Phil Cool'.

'Phil Cool?' Les replies. 'Okay, let's see if he is up there on the scoreboard. We asked a hundred people to name someone from the world of showbusiness whose first name is Phil ... and our survey said?'

'ERRR-ERRR!'

I once heard an interesting analogy of how most artist's careers are viewed by those who have control over showbusiness. Using myself as an example, it has five stages:

> **Stage One:** Who is Phil Cool?
>
> **Stage Two:** Get me Phil Cool!
>
> **Stage Three:** Get me a Phil Cool-type!
>
> **Stage Four:** Get me a young Phil Cool!
>
> **Fifth and Final stage:** Who is Phil Cool?

The Tale Continues...

I decided to go to London again to road test a few things, like my *Young Ones* skit and the Arthur Scargill piece I'd been working on, still unfinished and more suited to TV. Still, I could try it out and get the reaction of southerners. Steve Taylor offered to drive.

We parked up at Malcolm Hardee's club at the southern end of the Blackwall Tunnel and, walking in with my guitar and suitcase, were greeted with an 'Oy! Oy!' as per. 'Have a good trip?' Malcolm asked. We talked for a while, he gave me the running order and then we went for a drink. It would have been just the one for me as I don't booze before a show. It's always been that way, even in the early days. Until one night in Cassinelli's restaurant in Standish, having waited hours to go on stage, I stupidly ignored my own rule and could tell I wasn't doing the impressions as well as usual. It sent a shudder through me and taught me a lesson: that the impressions were more important than a skinful of ale.

Anyway, in Greenwich I prepared my usual props, ready for my spot. I can't recall who the other acts were that night, but I'd shared the bill at earlier Tunnel shows with Julian Clary and his dog, Fanny. Another time, I had a chat with a then relatively unknown Harry Enfield, who had been in the audience. This though felt different,

The Tale Continues...

the atmosphere less friendly, I thought. A rowdy bunch was standing at the back creating too much noise.

Scargill had recently given a well-publicised speech to members of the NUM and was captured by photographers giving what could have been some kind of solidarity salute, although in all probability it could also have been an innocence arm movement. Photographs can lie sometimes. Even so, those photos of Arthur accompanied a host of detrimental newspaper headlines insinuating he was anything from a thug to a Nazi and I was about to send him up myself. I had two new additions to my props ready – a lump of coal and a little packet of soot – both at the bottom of a plastic shopping bag. There was no proper ending to the routine, I knew it was incomplete. It had an ending of sorts, but only in my mind. My thinking was that I'd run it through, thereby learn it, and have it honed in preparation for my TV show. The proper ending would then be added by TV's technical wizardry. I'll try to explain it. If you imagine the complete televised sketch it would run like this:

(*As Scargill*): 'I'll say this, to all you people who say you can see through me – let me make myself perfectly clear. We are fighting for coal, lads.' (*I'd now put my hand in the plastic bag, dip my finger in the packet of black soot, pick up the cob of coal and hold it up*). 'This stuff, precious coal.' (*I would put my hand back in the bag, drop the coal, take my hand out again, my finger still with soot on it, scratch under my nose and sniff at the same time, depositing soot there as though I'd accidentally left a dirty little square patch of black coal dust over my top lip*).

'I've been involved with coal all my life, comrades, ever since I was a lad back in Barnsley. (*Simultaneously thrusting his arm out to point toward his 'hometown', at which point hundreds of camera flashes would capture him donning a little black moustache, arm in the air as though making the 'Sieg Heil' salute. The image would then freeze and spin around, as they do in old black-and-white films. And when it stops, we see the front page of a tabloid newspaper.*)

Stand-up Chameleon

But alas, the whole point was to show how facts can be twisted by the press. It could only be self-explanatory when performed on television, not on stage. It could be *prepared* on stage for television, however, which is why I did it that night.

I didn't see how it could be misconstrued as taking the piss out of Scargill, or that I was suggesting he was Hitler. Okay, I didn't think it through properly. In my naivety after being welcomed onstage by Malcolm, I walked up, did the *Young Ones* and other stuff, and then at the very end of my half hour set went into Scargill. It did well at first, but then as I got to the 'moustache' gag and my arm flying up like Dr Strangelove, all hell broke loose.

'You're out of order, pal,' bellowed an angry person at the back. Several more voices joined in as that whole end of the room erupted in curses and screams. All this above an undercurrent of babbling as the seated audience commented amongst themselves about what they'd just witnessed. I could almost feel the rope around my neck. Malcolm went over to those at the back, one or two members of the band The Flying Pickets among them, and reported back that what we had here was a whole coach load of depressed miners, all on strike, half-pissed and pretty angry at me for apparently having a go at Saint Arthur. So, I sent Malcolm back to this baying mob with murder on its mind with a few comments. One: I had just done a charity gig to raise money for miners' children's Christmas presents in Wigan. Which was true. Two: Both my grandfathers were miners. Three: I wasn't having 'a go' at Scargill; the piece actually had a twist at the end directed at press bias, but given how I'd been interrupted I never got to it. Of course this was only half true; the twist was only in my mind and in an imagined TV sketch.

Eventually, I went over to the miners myself and reiterated what Malcolm had said, apologised for not being clearer, and we made peace. Afterwards I allowed them to lecture me a bit about the evils of capitalism and Thatcher. They concluded by saying they were all really enjoying the show until I spoiled myself by insulting Arthur.

I just nodded and thought: 'Aw, diddums. What a shame.'

Hecklers, Drunks and Other Interruptions

Tales of hecklers on the showbusiness grapevine that I've heard down the years may be funnier than my own experiences, but not necessarily as strange. Let's see what you think.

One favourite featured a very famous British comedian who'd been enduring an onslaught of loud, semi-intelligible babble – always in the wrong places (like the pause before the punchline or just as everyone else stopped laughing). The audience knew his patience was wearing thin, that he could stand it no longer, and was about to respond with a lethal 'put down'. And sure enough he pointed at the nuisance in the front row. 'Hey, you!' he said. 'Have you just had a lobotomy?' The audience went wild at this sledgehammer of a line, except for the few people either side of the heckler. And as laughs gave way to silence, the guy, nodding and rocking in his seat, shot back a loud and agonising 'Yeah ... I haaave ... aaaggghhh.' Naturally the comic apologised profusely.

Another featured a comedian in some god-forsaken working men's club. Two minutes in and with no hint of a chuckle, he decided to 'have a go' at some guy who'd risen to his feet and was heading for the door. 'Hey pal,' he called from the stage, just as the guy was about to leave. 'Where do you think you're going?' At which, this guy turned around and said, casually but loudly enough for all to hear, in a broad Geordie accent: 'I'm just nippin' out, like, to check if the comedian's arrived!'

Stand-up Chameleon

There are many more where they came from, however the most memorable personally are those that happened to me over the years, some of them downright classics. The most recent being when I was doing a golf evening fundraiser in Billericay, Essex. Those three words – 'golf evening fundraiser' – still make my skin crawl.

I was assured beforehand that I'd be on stage at 9.30pm, do a half-hour set and be away and on my way home. Why do I still believe these people? God knows! At five minutes to eleven – and having stewed in the 'dressing room'(broom cupboard-sized office) since 6.30 – I was finally about to go on. I'd needed to be there so early to do a sound check before the audience arrived and from then until now they'd been squeezed for every penny in an auction for everything from a photo of some D-list celebrity to a health spa weekend by the DJ/compère/auctioneer. For hours on end he'd bellowed loudly at these golfers who'd clearly had enough. Then, just before I thought he was going to introduce me, this 'jack-off all trades' (not a spelling mistake) sent the audience to the bar for a comfort break and was soon pleading with them to come back into the room. 'Please, gentlemen,' he said (there was only one woman there), 'come take your seats, the act is waiting to entertain you,' which he repeated over and over again. Eventually the audience begrudgingly returned, weary at the whole long-drawn-out affair. They sat down, folded their arms and adopted a stern look of agitated contempt. Most would have been happier to talk between themselves, call it a night and go home, but no. 'Lady and gentlemen,' bellowed this clown through a microphone turned up to eleven, 'here he is, star of stage and TV, the one and only ... Phil Cool.'

I walked on and said 'hello' through a small radio mic on my lapel, sounding like I was whispering through a tea strainer compared to his hand-held job. The crowd fanned themselves with their programmes, apathetic to every line. A few people laughed, one over here, one over there, the more sober ones among them perhaps. Until, realising they were alone in their appreciation of my efforts, feeling embarrassed and quickly zipping their lips. I had now passed that certain point of caring and even stopped to explain the material I'd done in a sarcastic tone. Not because I thought they would understand, but because I wanted them to know that I knew they hadn't a clue. This stuff was either going over their heads, straight between their legs or both. I no longer gave a toss. I lasted about eighteen minutes before deciding to bail out. Not wanting to show I was fazed by this – though clearly I was – I held my

Hecklers, Drunks...

composure, but wasn't thinking straight, so muddled I foolishly came out with an exit gag I'd used many times before, but only in theatres and at gigs where I'd gone down well.

'Well folks thank you very much but I have to go now. If you thought I was brilliant my name's Phil Cool. If you didn't it's ... Rory Bremner!'

The room was silent. Not a titter arose, nor even half a handclap. I turned to walk off and just as I got to the edge of the stage a voice piped up from the back. 'Goodnight, Rory!' Ouch.

Hecklers come in many forms. Drunks are worst because they're not in a state to understand your response and are therefore totally incapable of being embarrassed into submission. Consequently, they go on and on and on until they are removed from the room by force. Everything you throw at them the audience loves, but not them. They are out of it and always shout things that are impossible to make out. Something like '*blubleaglayeguk*', for example, to which you'll reply 'go easy on the booze, pal, or you'll end up alcoholic before you're twelve.' Your audience will be in hysterics, the drunk respond with something like '*glashoudlight...kayya*.'

'See! This is what happens when cousins marry.'

'*Ganancukilop ye bastroud...*'

'You've been dining out at Thresher's, haven't you?'

The audience will still laugh for a while, but then get a bit weary of it. After one last gargantuan effort, the guy might just manage to string two words together: 'Fuck off!'

'Shame on you', I'd retort, 'for stealing Chubby Brown's catchphrase.'

The best way to deal with drunks is to ignore them and then they'll either stagger out to the toilets and not come back, or get bored and eventually shut up. One, at a corporate gig I did for some firm or other in the Great Hall at Warwick Castle, was different in that I could tell what he was saying. He only had two words mind: 'Washing machine'. That's all he said, constantly, throughout my set. Why? I don't know. He kept revolving his head and nearly falling off his chair. Perhaps he meant he felt like he was in a washing machine because the room was going round and round, as it would if you were inside one looking out. 'Washing machine. Washing machine. Washing machine,' he went on. I mean, what can you say to such an idiot? I decided just to let him get on with it. After a while he went into full-cycle, seized up in his chair and stared open-mouthed into space until I'd done. I later discovered he was the company's managing director.

Stand-up Chameleon

Aggressive drunks. If they make a move towards you while you are performing, you could try and defuse the situation, like I did once by saying in the style of Woody Allen: 'Please. I don't want any trouble. I would hate to be accused of being beaten up by a drunk.' Or, if you're that way inclined, you could call their bluff and say: 'I always carry a special spray to use on hecklers. It's called a 12-Bore'. That worked for me on several occasions.

Once, I was heckled by a dog. Well, not quite; more like upstaged. I was performing in a back room/cabaret lounge of a big pub in York called 'The Spotted Cow'. The dog didn't make a noise. It just appeared at an open door upon walking in from the yard. The sun was low and this hound's body cast a long, dramatic shadow across the floor. It strolled into the room, ever so casual like, and stood looking at me on stage. It was a beagle, I think, and had a comical cartoon-like quality. As it looked quizzically at me, the audience now focussed on it, looking at me. I forget what I said exactly. Something about beagles, laboratories and cigarette smoke probably, but there was much laughter whatever it was. Not for me, but the dog. This strange confrontation brought them to hysterics. The dog looked so serious and stared at me for a good minute. My script went out the window; hopeless to continue. The dog, after totally stealing the show, turned, still unimpressed by what it had witnessed, and casually walked back to wherever it had come from. And then returned, once more, later in my set. As this clever little mutt appeared for a second time I said something like 'I've got a bone to pick with you' and adopted my John Wayne persona. 'Don't tell me you've come back for yer paw.' If we had been a double act that night, I could only have been the straight man.

What comedians sometimes find more unnerving than having a heckler taking pot shots at them is having a guest in the audience who is either a fellow artiste, friend or family member. As the comic delivers the material they are at the same time imagining their guests' criticism, which is off-putting to say the least. Fear of offending is at the back of your mind too. I was once a guest at the Tramshed in Woolwich, South East London. The resident comedians, friends of mine, fronted a great comedy and cabaret night called FUNDATION. They'd invited me twice before but, on this occasion in 1985, I turned up. They did a song and routine about northerners and dressed for the part, complete with flat caps and braces. After the show they told me how hard it had been to get through, because they were halfway into the song before

Hecklers, Drunks...

it struck them that I, as a northerner, might have been offended after travelling down. They said they almost aborted the whole thing for fear of me walking out when they got to the line 'I'm just a big fat northern bastard'. Actually, I thought that was the funniest bit and kept telling them so. They didn't believe me and apologised for ages. Strange how such a small thing can be blown out of all proportion by the comedian's paranoia of someone 'out there' listening and watching in the dark.

Also in London, I was booked for a one night stand at the Dominion Theatre once. At the sound check that afternoon when the auditorium was empty, I was doing my 'one...two's into the microphone when a lonesome figure appeared in the front row of the stalls. I couldn't make out who it was because we were also doing a lighting check and I had bright stagelights on my face, so this individual was just a vague shape. When I'd finished, about to return to the dressing room to prepare my props, the shape called out. It was a guy, maybe in his sixties, with a Jewish accent. 'Come here,' he said. 'Talk to me a while.' Beckoned to jump down from the stage into the front row, I didn't know whether he was a fan, reporter, stalker or what, but I did so anyway and walked over. He said: 'Sit for a while. I've come to see you after watching your television show.' I wondered how he had got past security, or if perhaps he worked here. I wasn't alarmed; he seemed harmless enough. I let him go on. 'I think you are a genius and suspect you're so good at what you do because you have known sorrow in your life,' he said. 'Only a person who has been through great sorrow and pain could ever give a performance like you and I feel I am privileged to meet you. I am so looking forward to your show tonight. I will be in the Circle.'

By this time, I'd taken up his gesture of invitation to sit next to him and was beginning to feel a little uneasy as his voice began to break and his eyes well with tears. 'I have known great sorrow too my friend and understand yours,' he went on, grasping my shoulders and pulling me towards him. 'I was a young boy when I was sent to the death camp by the Nazis. I lay there with the dead as they rotted beside me in that vile place. My parents were... were...' he now broke up completely and was sobbing uncontrollably as he pulled me towards him.

One half of me wondered whether he was for real, and if he was, what he wanted with me. The other half was wondering if this was what I really needed to get into the mood to perform a comedy show.

'I am an actor, but not full-time,' he said, composing himself. 'I have, over the years, played small parts. Once I worked with the actor Peter

Stand-up Chameleon

Lorre.' He then spoke of working with Michael Caine, but didn't seem to have any affection for him. 'If you ever want an actor to do a sketch with you on any of your shows, I'd be grateful if you were to choose me,' he added. I was too shocked by this mysterious person to give the obvious response in 'Caine' mode – which would've been 'I am not bloody workin' with someone who doesn't have a kind word for me' – and anyway hadn't the balls for it. He then gave me – and insisted I take and keep – a yarmulke, one of those brimless cloth skull caps that Jewish men wear, saying it was his nephew's and would bring me good fortune. I took it, gave him a puzzled thank you, and said: 'Forgive me, it's time for me to go to the dressing room to get ready.'

'I'll be watching you on stage tonight,' he said, his voice still unsteady from the earlier outpouring of grief. Upon which, we parted company.

The Dominion was full that night, around 2,000 people in the place. The show went well, even though I kept visualising the little Jewish guy, out there in the darkness. I couldn't help but wonder if he was laughing, whether he really appreciated my humour or had just been after TV work. It also occurred to me that if he wasn't for real he was a bloody good actor, having put on a performance that shook me.

Eventually, I got to a part in the show where I did a Burt Lancaster impression – he'd done a TV mini-series in the 1970s called *Moses the Lawgiver*. I had a routine I called 'Carry On Moses the Lawgiver', which 'co-starred' Kenneth Williams as Aaron, Moses's brother. I'd done the routine every night on tour at venues around the country and by now was on automatic pilot, forgetting momentarily about the holocaust victim up in the Circle. So in I went, both feet, in my Burt voice:

> '...*and the good Lord God in heaven took his children out of the Land of Egypt and out of the house of bondage and out into the Wilderness for forty days and forty nights, give or take a couple of days either way, maybe a full week who knows?* (cue laughter) *And then my brother Aaron came to me filled with anger and so I said unto him 'Keep your hair on, Aaron!' Then he said unto me* (cue Kenneth Williams voice) *'Oooh, Moses! The children of Israel have asked me to tell you to stop messin' about and start makin' 'em laugh all over.'*

I was only a few words in when the little guy's image flashed into my mind. It would appear – to him – that I was having a deliberate 'go' at him and all he held precious. In actuality, it went something like...

Hecklers, Drunks...

(Burt Lancaster) *'And the good Lord God in heaven took his children out of the la... ah, the... a... ahem, well...* (and then in my own voice) *It's good ... ya... your a great audience tonight ... thanks for coming to the show...'* with the audience looking on in puzzled silence before I launched straight into another subject. As things turned out, it went on to be a great night, except for the silent heckler who had unnerved me from the shadows of the Dominion's auditorium.

The next morning I sat up in bed (no, not with the little Jewish guy beside me, alone) and for some reason decided to turn on the hotel room TV, which I rarely do, where the Breakfast television presenter was interviewing someone whose voice sounded familiar. My eyes still weren't properly focussed, I had literally just opened them on waking, so didn't pick it up at first, but as the interview went on there he was, the phantom Jew from the night before. Naturally, I was very attentive to what he said and could hardly believe what was transpiring.

His name was – no, I'll not say it – and he was a Nazi hunter, there in the TV studio to report on how he was currently closing in on one of the few remaining Nazi war criminals still at large.

Wow! Some distraction, eh?

I was certainly glad I'd aborted the Moses routine. Had I not done so, I might have ended up with Mossad paying me a visit.

The Tale Continues...

'If you like the shiny one, Phil, that's fine by me,' said Steve Weddle, as I stood in front of a mirror at Top Man, in Birmingham, trying on another jacket for size. 'Lets go with that.' This one, the last, was single-breasted, silver with long slim lapels, and fastened with a single button. The black trousers, black suede shoes and white T-shirt I was also to wear were already chosen and in the bag.

We were eager to get back to Pebble Mill, where *Cool It* was about to be shot. We'd a lot to get through. Steve paid for the clothes out of the show's budget and that was that, wardrobe sorted. Simple. Simple was also an accurate description of everything about that first series. The stage they built for me to work from was just a plain white platform about a foot high with three steps at the back to give it a bit of shape. On our return, we called into the huge studio to have a quick look and I walked about on it. It creaked slightly beneath my feet in the silence of that empty giant cube. I tried to imagine an audience there who I would be performing to in just a few days' time, something I've always done and still do before a show. 'Making friends with the room,' I call it. And having made friends, it was now time for a script meeting. I wasn't much looking

The Tale Continues...

forward to this because it meant that I would have to 'perform' the shows 'dry', i.e. in front of the few people involved with the look and substance of the shows. After a bite to eat in the BBC canteen, Steve and I entered a small room to find director David Weir, my now manager Les Ward, a typist to record the show's material, a couple of researchers called Claire and David, and an air of excitement for this first step of a groundbreaking Pebble Mill project.

Some of the material performed in the pilots was not going into the series because it wasn't up to scratch, however I'd written reams of new stuff since and it was far superior, which made up for that.

A spoof *Question Time* routine (still running after all these years) featured a cast of characters including Robin Day, Arthur Scargill, Roy Hattersley, David Bellamy, Sir Keith Joseph and more, but the bulk of the series would consist of tried and tested evergreen pieces like my E.T. The Extra-Terrestrial impression, Quasimodo singing the 'Bellringer Blues', my underwater Hans and Lotte Hass routine and an Eamonn Andrews *This Is Your Life* sketch, plus many more impressions, songs and crazy bits worked out and tested over many hours of stand-up. We had an hour and a half's worth of TV-quality material and needed an hour and a quarter for our three 25-minute shows. It was going to be some task honing the material down to its most economical form to give it the greatest impact on screen. Was I up to it? Well, I was, but never had a full understanding of the way television programmes are supposed to work, so a real blessing was that Steve had persuaded the BBC to appoint someone with a greater knowledge of these matters to join the team as an advisor. This person would eventually be credited as associate producer and there, with the others in that little rehearsal room, he sat. No sooner had Steve and I said our hellos than this person said: 'Right, let's get on with it,' as he looked at a rough script printed on coloured A4 sheets, probably transcribed from a tape recording of a live stand-up show. A first draft full of waffle and mistakes in other words. 'Eamonn Andrews,' he said, 'let's hear it,' before leaning back in his chair. I shuddered as I reached for the *This Is Your Life* book and stuck it under my arm while adopting the stature and facial expressions of

Stand-up Chameleon

the big-chinned burly boxer-turned-TV presenter and celebrity stalker, who could be seen as a precursor to Terry Wogan. Well, they were both Irish. I'd never performed a script without an audience before, except to myself while making stuff up. And here were seven or eight stern-looking people glaring at me. Anyway, I went for it:

> (As Eamonn) *Welcome to* This Is Your Life ... *some greasy little bleeder is in for one hell of a shock tonight. As you can see, I'm standing here in the shadows of this dingy backstreet massage parlour waiting for someone who thinks he's coming tonight for a quick massage. Ex pimp ... one-time grave robber ... a man who, believe it or not, just for the sheer challenge, started his own leper colony in Southport ... and he's about to walk through that door any minute. Now don't give the game away, I'd hate the little turd to give us the slip...*

All had been silent until a burst of genuine amusement came from our associate producer who, appreciating my having to run through it 'dry' with no audience and so likely find that uncomfortable and embarrassing, had broken the ice for me and the rest of the room by laughing out loud. By the time I got past Eamonn, I started sailing through the rest of the shows with confidence and by now the others were laughing too. Such was the intuition of the associate producer to help me out, he saved the day. I'd like to thank him for that – a bit late now – so thanks, Jasper.

During one script meeting, Jasper said how much he loved my underwater swimming routine with Hans and Lotte, the husband and wife oceanography team, but said the ending was no good. We needed to find a new one if it was to be in the show. So afterwards we both left the other people and went in a different room to thrash a new one out. After an hour or so of me reciting the script over and over again, a satisfactory finale still hadn't presented itself. Jasper made a few suggestions I wasn't keen on and I made a few he wasn't pleased with, even saying we should leave the original one in. I'd been doing it for years, but Jasper was having none of it: 'The new

The Tale Continues...

'Cool It', filmed at Pebble Mill, was a career changer

ending is somewhere in there Phil, but I'm damned if I can find it. Let's keep chipping away and it'll come, you'll see,' he said, pacing the floor and perhaps secretly wishing some comedy miracle would happen and we could both get off home. It was getting late.

The end to the routine had me (still miming the weightlessness of Hans Hass, in his underwater realm) happening upon what appeared to him as a body with its feet entombed in concrete. This body had a bracelet on its wrist and as Hans examined it, he read the engraving to his wife. 'Lotte, look who this poor bugger is,' he said, the bracelet now in his hand after breaking from the crustacean

Stand-up Chameleon

covered corpse. 'It's ... it's ... Paul Anka!' Anchor, geddit? Yes, I know it's a pun; a corny one too. All those years I really knew it wasn't good enough and now here I was, forced into finding a better pay-off.

This particular show we were working on began with Eamonn and finished with Hans and Lotte with loads of impressions, songs and stories inbetween. I ran through it all, fast-forward, in my mind, hoping something else would leap out that might finish the show after Hans and Lotte. It didn't. After a long day, brain fatigue set in. Jasper said: 'It's time to stop. Perhaps we'll think of an ending when were fresh.' 'Yeah,' I replied, wearily. 'It's driving me mad but let's just have another few minutes while I run through it one more time.'

So, I set off again, out loud, while miming Hans's movements in slow-mo so as to emulate being underwater. Jasper was ready to die from the tedium of repetition as I ploughed through the words again in that strange Austrian accent... 'Lotte and I discovered a rare coral reef where muff divers come from all over the world to dive for the muff, a rare tropical sponge...' and so on. 'Lotte and I discovered the entrance to a dark eerie ghost-like cave.' 'Lotte goes in first because I am frightened.' 'Lotte and I are spewed out onto this flat lifeless sandy bottom, only to find some poor bugger with his feet entombed in solid concrete, probably dumped off a motor launch for reneging on a deal, who knows?' 'See how this poor bugger hauntingly dances to and fro in the strong tropical current (*mime corpse swaying as Jasper looks surreptitiously at watch*) ...unrecognisable, covered from head to toe in a cocoon of crustaceans. I wonder who the poor bugger is? Wait, Lotte! He has a bracelet jingle-jangling around his rotting wrist. I will attempt to read it. (*Here I mime trying to catch hold of it as it moves with the swaying body*). Ach! It has come off! (*Hans now holds the imaginary bracelet*). And now, as I rub away the sediment of time with my scabby thumb, a name starts to appear ... Holy Mackerel, Lotte! (*Shocked as he shows her the name*). In the name of cod, look who this poor bugger is...' and again we were at the point when I'd say Paul Anka and turn towards the body.

This time, though, in a moment of inspiration, I came out with 'Blub! Blub! Blub! Glub! Blub!' in an Irish accent. 'You thought you

The Tale Continues...

had come here to photograph fish but, tonight, Hans and Lotte Hass, *This Is Your Life!*'

The delight on Jasper's face was priceless. We had found ourselves an ending. Now, we could start and finish with Eamonn Andrews. The other two shows would end with *Question Time* and my *Young Ones* routine in which I did impressions of Rik, Vyvyan, Neil, Mike and, of course, Jerzei Balowski, Alexei Sayle's landlord character.

Whenever we had any material changed or rewritten slightly, Les Ward helpfully arranged 'try out' nights at Midlands venues. And once the material for all three shows was finalised, we then needed a camera script so director David could capture my performance with all the right shots, i.e. long shot for a full body mime or action, close-up facial when I slipped into a Quasimodo, or mid-shot when required. This meant going through the material on the studio stage for several days prior to each recording. We had a dress rehearsal too, so if the clothes presented any problems they could be altered.

One revolutionary thing for me was having the option to use a small 'clip-on' instead of my usual line microphone on a stand. I remember the very moment it was offered during the first rehearsal. 'Do you want your usual mic, Phil, like you used in the pilot show, or to try one of these?' a technician asked, as I was about to start. 'Oh, I'm sure I'll be more comfortable with the mic stand,' I said. 'It's what I'm used to, but as this is only a rehearsal I'll try the little one, see what happens.' What happened was I discovered this immense freedom to perform. It enabled me to move around on the stage free to gesticulate with both hands, without hindrance, a godsend for all the mimed bits we were about to shoot. It opened up a whole new world of performing. I could now, if I wished, roll on the floor and bang both fists on the stage unencumbered by the need to stay 'on top of' a microphone in a stand, or be forever taking it out to move around. I've used a small clip-on radio mic for stand-up ever since.

After *Cool It* was broadcast, other television comedians were soon following suit. Most of them use one now.

Tales of Nutty Bits – not Naughty Bits

*'I sometimes play to all-women audiences...
whether I satisfy them or not, I still try to perform well.
I mean, who cares if they fake a standing ovation?'*

You may have heard it said that the number one quality a woman wants in a man is a sense of humour. Really? I don't think so.

It's strange how when you're famous for comedy women will laugh at this 'sense of humour' and may even give you starry-eyed glances as their laughter subsides. And if you're not famous for comedy, the same women will hear alarm bells ring when you make a move to be funny and probably run a mile.

As a man, it also depends on how handsome you are. If you're dead handsome and not that funny, they'll laugh a lot. If you're dead funny and ugly, they might laugh a bit before telling you to go away. If you're extremely handsome and not funny at all, they might laugh just enough to pacify you, before asking you in for coffee. Extremely handsome and extremely funny? They will wet themselves and short-cut the coffee. If you are extremely handsome, extremely funny and famous, you'll dwell in the realms of the Gods.

What, then, if you're not handsome and not funny and not famous?

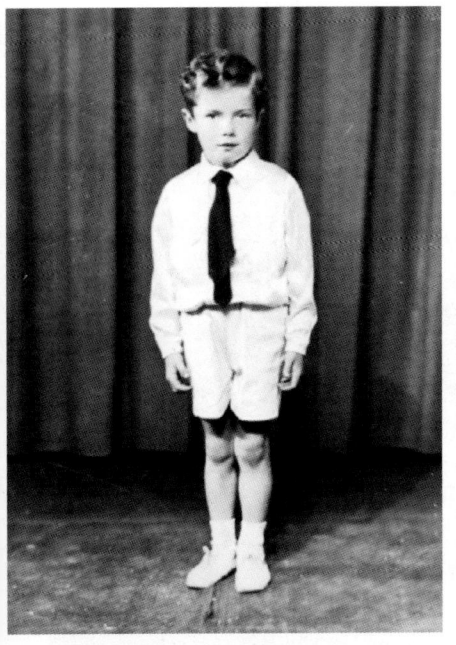

Curtain up, *above* – seven years cool...

Wearing my first long pants, at my big sister's wedding, *above*.

St Augustine's teachers, *left*. Can you spot Phlegmy – and guess which one is Fester?

The only existing photo of my class at St Augustine's, *right*. I hope I'm easy to spot among this motley crew...

Michael Kavanagh (Psychedelic Sid), Mick Randle, yours truly and Bill Hunt, *above,* at the bar.

Right: Owen Woods, 'Mr Tambourine Man'.

Below: The Carrott and me at my comedy club, Laughingas on Fox Lane, Leyland, after his show.

Dennis Almond and me in a photo booth on Chorley Bus Station, *above.*

Making my entrance at The Tunnel club, as introduced by its owner, Malcolm Hardee, *right*.

Above: Is it Bob Dylan, of Duluth, Minnesota? No, it's Phil Cool, of Chorley, Lancashire.

Left: A soundcheck at the Laughingas in the early days, in front of some of my homemade artwork.

Left: Happy days during the making of the first series of *Cool It* – with David Lancaster, Les Ward, me and Steve Weddle.

Right: Steve Hutt took this when Dame Joan Collins came backstage to say 'hello' during a twelve-night run at the Royalty Theatre, Kingsway, London. I am doing my Kirk Douglas impression...

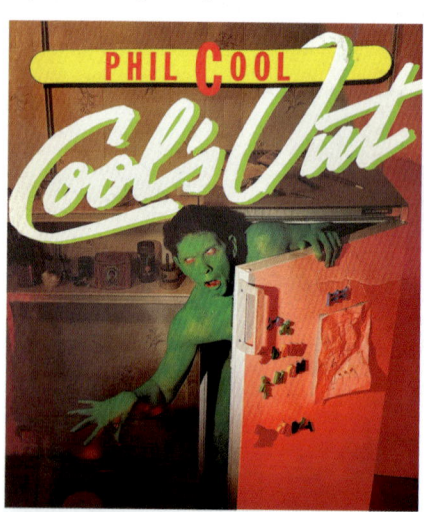

Left: This isn't my first go at doing a book! *Cool's Out* was published by David & Charles, with a cover by Grub Street Design, in 1987...

A minstrel prepares to die on stage, *left*. Doing *The Secret Policeman's Ball* with good sport Richard Branson, *right*.

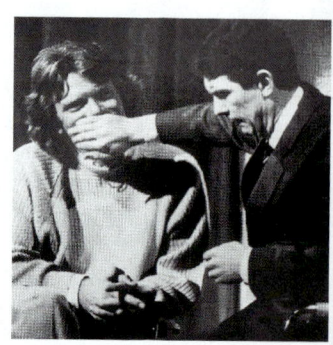

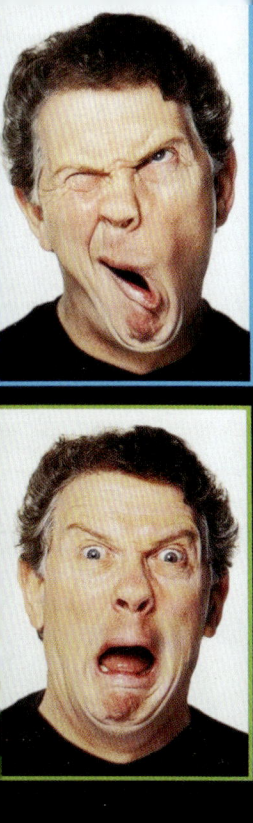

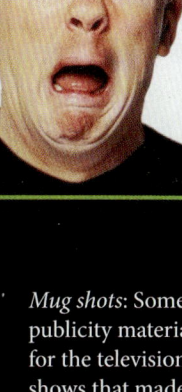

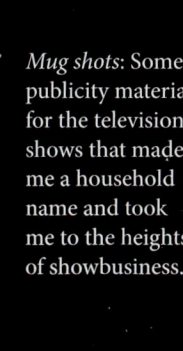

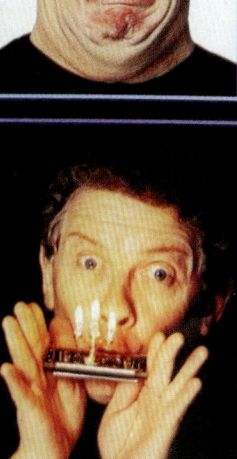

Mug shots: Some publicity material for the television shows that made me a household name and took me to the heights of showbusiness.

Above: Bev and I get married in the sunshine with family and friends enjoying the occasion.
Below: Me, Joe and best man Bob Johnson. *Below right*: Mike Harding takes the stage Pics: John Birtle

Left: Sid and me at my 50th... and my daughters Jenny and Rachel, *right*, at the same celebration.

Above: Enjoying a pint with Steve Hutt at my 50th. Not sure who this is with, *right*. Gromit?

Left: On stage with the great Bill Wyman at Sticky Fingers.

Above: Three stills from *The Motorist*, the little film I made.

Above: In the snow with Joe.

Left: Music was my first love and it'll be my last.

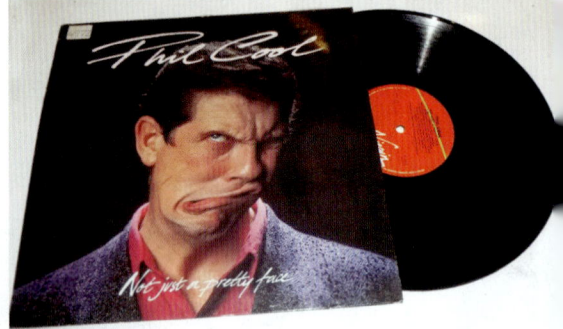

Above: The album I made for Virgin back in 1986.

Above: Keith Donnelly having a bowl of soup between tunes in the South Atlantic.

Right: Here's a 13½lb salmon I caught on a Willie Gunn fly on the Spey.

Nutty Bits

My advice is to work at your comedy, become famous and make the most of a bad job.

You might say: 'Won't this be the same if you swapped the whole thing around and took the view of the other sex?' Well, I just hope you don't ask because I've no answer to that as I'm not the other sex. You might ask also: 'What about Rasputin? He was an ugly potato, but had women all over him.' Alas, history hasn't documented any of his funny chat-up lines, but maybe he found the Lynx formulae years earlier or it was his position of power – another aphrodisiac. All theory of course, although having been not famous, then famous and then not famous again, in the sense of being once again able to walk down any street without being harangued, I do at least have a bit of an insight.

Young women would visit me backstage and in theatre dressing rooms after the first *Cool It* series aired, some of them students doing some kind of thesis on me, whatever that means, often entering the dressing room in a 'zombie-like' state, mesmerized by this clown with a Lancashire accent. That old svengali 'fame' had hypnotised these poor females through the screen. Nothing untoward went on. I was happily married, with two daughters, and loath to jeopardise a settled family life. Living a double life is my idea of hell, so potential sexual encounters were resigned to the realms of fantasy. This is not a wise admission to place in a book because many may not read on if they know there are no juicy bits coming, but I'm sorry I don't do juicy bits.

Since the magic wand of TV waved for me, close encounters were often there on a plate, but I heard a cartoon voice in my head – the one I remember from *Popeye* when a talking human skull, on the shore of a poisoned water hole, told him 'you'll be sorry' as he was about to take a drink. So, no. There are no juicy bits.

Nutty bits? Well, I had as my TV persona a profound effect on one young girl. I only discovered this as she told me her story ten years later as a grown woman. I had just arrived at a theatre in Lowestoft, carrying my guitar and suitcase through the auditorium, and she was placing flyers for forthcoming attractions on the seats. She was dressed in an usherette's uniform and as I walked through she looked over to me and said: 'Oh! It's you.' I couldn't deny this. I was standing there. She then said, placing another flyer as I listened attentively in the silent auditorium: 'It is you, isn't it? The one who does that reptilian creature from *V*?' 'Yeah, that's me,' I replied, with an innocent smile. I had noticed she wasn't smiling as she laid down another flyer and came back with,

Stand-up Chameleon

'I was in our kitchen a long time ago, washing the dishes, when my father shouted from the front room:"Come quick and look at this fella on TV." I quickly walked into the room still drying the cup I held with the pot towel and there you were. One minute you were Terry Wogan and the next you were turning green and peeling what seemed like a mask off your face. You ended up transforming into this terrible green monster and I flipped. It made me go into shock.'

As her tale unfolded, I began to feel uneasy. My innocent smile by now had turned upside down, into a guilty sulk. Placing the last of the glossy flyers she said, 'I'm alright now,' before concluding: 'I was in therapy for six years.'

After gulping silently, I said: 'I'm sorry, but I don't know what to say. I don't do that routine anymore, so ... ahem ... I hope you'll be watching the show tonight.' I never saw her again, but I do hope she's alright.

By the standard of today's youth, losing your virginity at the grand old age of eighteen would no doubt be a cause for shame, but in my day it was just about acceptable so I admitted it back then, as well as now. I was eighteen, she was thirty-two. Her name was Edna and she was a bus conductor. I clipped a clippie. If she's still around she'll be 90 now. Bloody hell! Even so, between the ages of 18 to 27, which is when I met my first wife, my carnal knowledge was non-existent and making it up as I went along amounted to disaster after disaster, girls putting up with me for one or two dates if I was lucky. If a film were ever to be made about my love life it would be called 'What Women Don't Want'. This, I'm sure, would not have been so had I been to a mixed sex school in my teens and had the company of a few girls at that crucial time, but no. Leaving an all boys school, girls were a different species. There were, however, odd times when things did seem to click naturally, but I don't do juicy bits, do I, so here is another nutty bit.

In 1973, the council house in which I lived with my mother was being redesigned and refurbished by the council. It was such a big job that we and the rest of the terraced residents had to move out until it was finished. Ma moved to my sister's house in Chorley town centre. It was a lovely home so she was pleased to be there. I moved in with my workmate, Dennis, about five miles away. His was an old terraced house but clean, warm and homely. He lived there with his wife and son. One day I asked if I could bring this girl back to stay overnight in the spare bedroom. They were sympathetic for me to get my end away and broadminded enough to say yes, but still slightly reluctant because

Nutty Bits

they weren't too keen on her; she had a reputation as a wrong' un. But anyway they eventually said fine, just this once. Dennis, his wife, this girl and me said our goodnights on the upstairs landing, then went to the room we'd been allocated. Dennis and his wife retired to the main bedroom after pointing out the bathroom, also off the landing, plus the airing cupboard for towels.

After about what seemed like an hour in bed together, this girl raised herself up on an elbow and said to me in a soft voice: 'I want a shit.' I didn't answer, but lay there thinking: 'She can't be saying what I think she said because if she did want a shit she'd just go and have one; she wouldn't need to tell me. She must have said something else and I missed it. Besides, a girl wouldn't come out with that anyway.' So I replied: 'You what?' 'I want a shit,' she said softly. 'Oh, she's said it again,' I thought. 'I'll ask her to speak up, so I'll catch what she's actually saying.' And so I said: 'Can you speak a bit louder?' 'I want a shit,' she said, too loudly this time. There was no mistake. She was definitely saying 'I want a shit.' And this time it was followed by an impatient 'Well!?' 'She can't be,' I thought. 'I'm not having it.' I was about to say: 'Well go and have one then,' but stopped myself. 'This is ridiculous,' I thought. 'No one would say that. No, the fault lies with me. I'm missing something here.' So I raised myself up on one elbow, so our faces were closer, and said: 'Now, please, would you say what you just said, only slowly and clearly.'

An air of impatience took over. 'I ... want ... a ... shit,' she answered, clear as day. By now, any trace of romance – or lust – had gone out the window. 'Bear with me, please. I'm not getting this, I pleaded. 'So please, just one last time, would you say again what you just said, only this time enlarge upon it and explain in detail and stages exactly what it is you actually require?' She sighed, looked at me in the landing light that filtered through the ajar door. 'I want a shit, so I can put my arms through the sleeves, pull it over my shoulders, button it up at the front, and tip-toe across the landing to the bathroom.'

Relief flooded over me. I was tempted to say: 'Oh, you mean a shirt!' but stopped myself just in time on realising she would then have had to say: 'Why? What did you think I said?' Upon which, of course, I would have had to admit: 'I thought you said you wanted a shit.' Then she would have said: 'Do you think for one minute I would say such a thing? What kind of girl do you think I am?' She was from Chorley, but with a trace of scouse in her accent, an early lesson in subtle differences in dialect that can be such an important element of comedy.

The Tale Continues...

'*Coo! Coo! Coo! Coo!*' said the ring-necked doves, down Les Ward's chimney. It was 5.00am on the morning of the first *Cool It* recording. I'd stayed at his house in Solihull to get a good night's kip before this very important day. Les had as always made me welcome, reassuring me all would be well, but the excitement and uncertainty only gave me what felt like a minute or two of shut-eye until, finally, the doves prompted me to get out of bed.

Tired I may have been, but I went to Pebble Mill determined to deliver a high energy performance that day. There would be time to rest once it was done. Whenever I've heard doves cooing since, however, it does takes me back to Les's spare bedroom.

When completed, series one of *Cool It* had, like all programmes, to be run past the 'powers-that-be' in London before transmission. And they had a problem with it. A gag in the *Question Time* routine was deemed too offensive. As I said before, TV people like to meddle and you've got to let them. The gag in question wasn't written by me, actually, but one of those jokes doing the rounds at the time of the Cecil Parkinson scandal, when the Conservative politician was found to have had an extra-marital affair with his personal secretary,

The Tale Continues...

Sara Keays, and fathered a daughter he never met or acknowledged. Well, I incorporated it into the show like this:

> **Robin Day:** (*pointing to someone in the audience*): Gentleman in the third row ... yes, you sir ... big drooping eyes ... sharp features ... your question please (*Then I'd do my Jasper Carrott impression and ask the panel my question...*)
> **Audience member/Jasper:** I'd like to ask the panel, right, what's the similarity between Cecil Parkinson and MFI?
> (*MFI being a furniture store*)
> Pause as no one responds.
> **Robin Day:** Well, no one on the panel seems to know, so, perhaps the gentleman who asked the question could enlighten us? Sir, what exactly *is* the similarity between Cecil Parkinson and MFI?
> **Audience member/Jasper:** One screw in the wrong place and the entire cabinet falls apart.

The joke was just right for the sketch. But, no. Word came back that it must be replaced with something less offensive. Less offensive to whom I'm not sure. Cecil Parkinson, I should think. So, with the help of Les Ward I wrote a replacement gag, Sir Keith Joseph doing some lines about top civil servants also in the news at the time.

Of course, the new bit seemed funny as we wrote it, but it hadn't stood the test of a live audience and when edited into the space left by the now removed MFI gag stuck out like a sore thumb, not funny. It had to go into the show, though, being all we had, shot in an empty studio one afternoon with no audience. The director and editor tried their best to put a convincing laugh track together but the ambience wasn't right, my timing too slow; it looked laboured and dreadful. To make matters worse I'd just had my hair cut, thinking the shows were done. Shooting the original, it was much longer. What viewers saw when it went to air was a guy with hair that magically shortened itself for 90 seconds and then magically grew long again. Still, Cecil Parkinson was saved any embarrassment. I mean, come on; as if he

Stand-up Chameleon

Robin Day interviews another politician

would have ever watched it in the first place. Thankfully, the big wigs had had their little 'meddle', were satisfied and didn't make any more intrusions over the next two series or to a *Cool It* Christmas special.

That first show aired in August 1985 and went out on a Friday at 10.00pm on BBC2. I was living in Leyland back then with my first wife, Julie, and our daughters, Jenny, then eight, and Rachel, six. We sat excited in anticipation in front of our telly. The gap between the previous programme ending and *Cool It* beginning seemed to take forever. There had been little or no pre-publicity but Jasper reckoned that was no bad thing; people would feel they'd discovered me by themselves and spread the word. As the final seconds ticked away, the butterflies in our stomachs did a little dance and the BBC2 logo came up. A woman's voice said something along the lines of '...and now let's spend a cool half-hour in the company of Phil' and that was that. The *Cool It* theme tune I'd written especially blasted out over titles featuring my animated figure twisting and gurning into various contortions, as devised and drawn by Marcus McGuinness. On the final note, cartoon Phil's head exploded and the programme

The Tale Continues...

began. We sat and watched it, hardly speaking to each other. I was amused by how my two girls couldn't understand how their dad was 'in' the television. When the show finished, they both went to look around the back of the set, puzzled as to where he had gone.

The first series didn't make me much money as my management had, rightly, accepted a fairly modest fee. We'd have done it for free, to be honest. After all, it was national exposure, a first step to 'greater things'. The phone was red hot, even before the next two shows were aired. All kinds of offers were made but I was very selective as to what I would and wouldn't do. My 'dream', if you like, was to do the big theatres like Jasper, Billy, Max and Mike. So, when the manager of Leeds Grand phoned Les and asked: 'Will Phil be interested in playing my theatre? If so, I would like to call the show *The Mad, Mad, Mad, Mad World of Phil Cool*', Les said to me, 'Shall we try it and see what the turn-out is like on the night? It'll be a good indication of how the series has been received by the public and a yardstick to gauge what size venues to book for your first tour.'

If you've read this book's preface you already know my answer. Stepping out before that great first ever crowd in Leeds, I heard them explode with delight for their new bendy comic hero.

All comedians must feel the same when, after years of rejection, humiliation and hardship, they finally 'arrive'. The applause goes on and on. So much so that you have to beckon them to stop and before you utter your first sentence they are at it again. The hysteria is such that you only have to scratch your nose, or give them a certain look, and they are falling in the aisles in fits and convulsions. And when your best material is finally delivered, the applause and laughter is almost deafening, yet also wildly invigorating. You feel that, there and then, there is no greater sound on earth – and so it was.

Later that night, in the hallowed space of the Grand's auditorium, the lights must have gone out with a long sigh of contentment. And, when its outside doors slammed shut, a peaceful hush must have descended save for a faint rumble of traffic from the city outside. The dust would again have settled, lying still for a while.

A little part of me is still there, I feel, resting among it.

It's a Funny Business, Comedy. Sometimes.

I have sometimes theorised that comedy/humour can be likened to a silver seam running through consciousness – but only while it remains there can it be said to truly exist. Unlike geological seams in the rocks of Earth – which can be mined, extracted and turned into a commodity of greater value – comedy disappears before it reaches the surface.

Long ago, I once watched an hour-long TV programme in which the late writer, satirist, composer, director, social theorist and all-round intellectual clever dick Jonathan Miller tried to analyse comedy. By the time it was over neither he nor his viewers were any the wiser.

He just couldn't nail it down. So elusive a concept is humour that no matter who tries to unravel its mysteries, he or she is destined to fail. I have my own thoughts, equally unresolved. It might somehow be connected to the way in which human nature is 'flawed', and connected also to the empathy we have for one another. We look at the failure of others and think 'thank God that's not me,' don't we? I know of two excellent comedians who did prison gigs for TV, one was transmitted, the other not. Both failed miserably. Having had the idea they must've thought: 'Wow, yeah, it'll be like the Johnny Cash album *At San Quentin*.' Wrong! Music and comedy are different mediums. It was probably only by dying the death that the two realised your more hardened criminals, except at the most basic and profane level, don't have a sense of

It's a Funny Business...

humour because they *can't* empathise with their fellow man. Which, of course, is why they are in jail in the first place.

Even for someone like myself, who has made a living for around half a century writing and performing it, comedy still has me scratching my head. For instance, one story I tell is received differently depending on whether it's told on stage or slipped into casual conversation. It works great in the latter instance. I once told it while having breakfast in the company of folk comic/singer Vin Garbutt and singer-songwriter and ex-Fairport Convention guitarist Richard Thompson, in a guest-house with their wives and road manager. We had performed at Trowbridge Festival the previous day and Richard's manager started talking about his mobile phone app. It was an ingenious bit of apparatus that, when held out towards a singing bird, could both identify its song and name the culprit. I said I knew a bit about birds myself and told them how I learned it all by collecting those little cards that came free with Brooke Bond tea. You could stick them in an album if you wished, or keep them loose. Information about the bird was printed on the back.

One I read about was a spotted flycatcher, a small brown secretive thing that gave its position and identity away by its song, described by the card as a single high-pitched note repeated at regular intervals of a second or so that sounded like a wheelbarrow with a rusty wheel. Out and about on walks through local fields in the 1950s, I had been able to verify this many times. On hearing such a call in a bush or hedgerow, I would stalk and actually see the bird up close, as described by Brooke Bond. Richard, Vin and company must have been wondering where all of this was leading. 'Once,' I continued, 'I was walking with my mates down by the canal in the height of summer, so the grass was tall. As we moved along the towpath we had to sweep it aside with our arms. There were houses with gardens and allotments adjacent and as we approached them I heard this bird do its thing. 'There,' I said. 'Did you hear it?' 'What?' 'That high-pitched squeak? There it is again.' I'd held my finger in the air. 'It's a spotted flycatcher.' 'How can you tell?' 'It's easy,' I replied. 'Its call is a single high-pitched note that sounds just like someone pushing a wheelbarrow with a rusty wheel.' No sooner had I said this than the tall grass parted and a bloke appeared – pushing a wheelbarrow with a rusty wheel.

My little audience around the breakfast table must have loved the tale because they bellowed out loud. Whether they believed it or not, I don't know, but it did actually happen. And yet when I tell this spotted

Stand-up Chameleon

flycatcher yarn on stage, which I have done several times, it has never worked. Why? Perhaps the spontaneity of just slipping it into casual conversation does the trick, whereas if it's part of a stage show and obviously premeditated it's less believable and therefore less amusing. I really don't know. If it's neither of those then I'm still baffled.

If a comedy piece flops first time around and you've a gut feeling it should be funny, keep the faith and stick with it. Just a slight change in delivery can make it work. I did a Jo Brand impersonation once that, when I first tried it, made a few people groan disapprovingly. It's part of a longer routine, but one bit in the middle was formulated in such a way that it didn't do the job well enough. Jo explains she has been to see her doctor about 'girly problems':

> **Jo:** So I walked in his surgery and said I've come about my girly problems. He never answered, just kept staring through the window with his back to me. 'Excuse me,' I said. 'Can you give me some advice about cellulite? 'Yes,' he said. 'They're the worst mobile phones you can get.'
> *(No problem with that gag. It always worked.)*
> **Jo:** Then he snapped on a surgical glove, like doctors do. 'Right, Ms Brand,' he said. 'Girly problems. Take your clothes off, please, I'm going to examine you.' When I first stripped off for this man years ago, he just laughed. This time he collapsed in hysterics...
> *(Still fine... it was the next bit that brought the adverse reaction.)*
> **Jo:** So, he examined me down below like doctors do, then he said: 'Right, Ms Brand. You can put your clothes back on. You've got albatross.' 'Albatross?' I said. 'Go on, educate me, what's that?' He said: 'It's like thrush, but ten times worse.'

I used this in several gigs, each time getting dirty laughs from a few in the crowd while some groaned and others stayed silent. A scriptwriter friend tried to analyse the gag with me once and concluded it would always be offensive because of the images the word 'albatross' brought to mind. One night, however, I changed it slightly. I can't remember if I thought of the change beforehand or it came spontaneously in performance, but the same bit now went:

> **Doctor:** Nothing to worry about, Ms Brand. You can put your clothes back on now. I'm going to give you a prescription for

some special cream. Use lots and lots and it will prevent you from developing albatross.
Jo: Go on, educate me. What's albatross?
Doctor: It's what you end up with when thrush is left untreated.

Everyone in the audience laughed... no groans, no dirty laughs, just the kind all comics hope for, big wholehearted ones. The script goes on a lot longer, but it's that particular gag that interests me most. How going from the actual – 'You've got albatross' – to the hypothetical – 'prevent you from developing albatross' – works miles better. It magically transforms the also hypothetical punchline to something you *might* end up with rather than something you've actually got.

It also shows that if you persevere with a script that isn't quite right, it can come good in the end. It's true, some I've persevered with have never worked properly. Yet I have only given up on them after weeks, months and even years of trying them every which way.

My attempts at an Eddie Izzard impression and script, for example, never quite hit the spot, although again I kept at it for ages. The script, totally fabricated, was inspired by us working on the same bill together at the London Palladium for the charity Children on the Edge. Before I eventually dumped it out of prolonged frustration, it ended up going like this (and please remember this was well before Eddie also became Suzy at a time when gender and identity issues weren't quite so toxic):

I met Eddie Izzard backstage at the London Palladium once. He came around the corner in women's clothes. I must have looked startled because he said: 'What's up? You never bumped into a cross-dresser before?' 'No,' I said, 'but while drunk I did once collide with an angry wardrobe.' I like his style, though, the way he moves on stage (*do Izzard walk*). I also like how he does this thing with his mouth (*go into an Izzardesque mouth and head movement before launching into a full-on impression...*)
Eddie: (*strutting*) If you wonder why I like to wear women's clothes its because it makes me feel good and, besides, it helps me get in touch with my feminine side. Which, incidentally, is lesbianic, which means I'm not gay ... well, could be, but not ... I am (*nod*) ... not (*shake head*) ... no, I'm not, just kidding ... I am ... not ... am ... you can't check, can you? No, I'm not gay ... but you know something? When I'm in front of a full-length mirror in

Stand-up Chameleon

> me fishnets ... high heels ... split leather skirt and bra under me see-through blouse ... and in full make-up and orange wig ... just for a split-second I feel as though I could be a woman trapped in the body of a pregnant beluga whale.'

Prior to 'beluga whale', I tried 'old English sheepdog', 'mutant walrus', 'giant duck-billed platypus' and a ream of others, but could I get the bastard thing to work? Could I hell as like. The script went on:

> **Eddie:** I like me woman's clothes warm and straight off the woman, which, when you come to think about it, means I've got to choose some pretty strange-shaped girlfriends...'

If the audience were particularly good, they'd go with it. If they weren't, I found it uncomfortable to do. In the end, all those years of struggling with it amounted to a waste of time and effort.

The trail of material I've left behind that didn't quite come together would fill several books – if I could remember it all. Some of the other stuff that didn't quite make it, though, still amuses me. Like Dreadlock Holmes, an idea I had once of a Rastafarian sleuth set in 1950s London, dressed in tweed, with a trusty sidekick. 'Elementary, me dear Leroy, let's reggae on down to Baker Street, fill me pipe wi ganja, play some cool sounds on me violin and solve the case...' Many years after writing this down, someone else has had the same idea – a detective called Dreadlock Holmes, based in Middleham-by-Sea, now appears in a book of short stories by the writer John Agard.

I've been inspired by the Old Testament too. How about a police drama (TV execs love 'em) set in biblical times, whose screenplay might go like this: 'Freezeth! And turneth around slowly. Now raiseth thine hands, Joshua, and leaneth against the walls of Jericho. Now, spreadeth thine legs, for I am about to searcheth thee for all manner of things displeasing to the Lord thy God.' That was an extract from *Jacob's Crime Crackers*, another waste of energy. These days, most people don't know their Bible so it's lost on them, just like my 'Sermon on the Mount' sketch with John Wayne playing Jesus. Although I did manage to get it on an episode of *Cool Head*, on ITV, way back in 1991.

Some material has never got beyond my own thoughts. I've always wondered what reaction I'd have got had I stuffed a big cylindrical piece of sponge down the front of my pants and walked out on stage to open the show singing Sinatra's 'All of me... why not take all of me...' Fortunately, we'll never know.

In 1988, I appeared on *A Night of Comic Relief*, directed by Geoff Posner and written mainly by Richard Curtis. I was asked if I wouldn't mind coming to London to take play the part of Charles I. I agreed. It turned out, though, that I had no script and was just going to be seen in one scene, as the monarch, and then another with my head tucked under my arm. To make it work, I had to visit a model maker in London the week prior to the shoot so a fibreglass replica of my head could be made. This I did. It took a full day. I sat on a chair whilst the chap and his helper covered my nut in a liquid rubber-like solution, so I had to breath through a tube. I had to remain still and imagine my facial expression was neutral beneath all this goo, holding the position until instructed that it was all set and ready to be removed as the mould.

This thing cost a grand or so, and when I saw the completed model on arriving for the shoot, it made me realise just what an ugly git I am. 'It' had a stump of a neck, which seen from the bottom was blood red, as though 'it' had just been severed. There was also a whiteish bit that could have been taken for a vertebrae and spinal column. Horrible, but I loved 'it'. I was on a 'no fee' for this and, as a gesture of thanks, Geoff said I could keep 'it' as a souvenir '...as 'it' is no good to anybody except maybe yourself.' I was delighted and brought 'it' home in a box, where I took 'it' out and stared at 'it', wondering how I could use 'it'. I'd stand in front of the mirror and hold 'it' beside my head to compare the two and judge how realistic 'it' was, looking back at me, complete with 'its' own wig. I figured that from a distance a person might be fooled by 'it' and after playing around with 'it' for a while put 'it' back in 'its' box in the spare bedroom wardrobe. Though 'it' stayed there a year or so, I'd still occasionally think about how I might use 'it' to make an audience believe I could be in two places at once, or, that the false head was real and my actual head was false. Any ideas, though, when I thought them through, seemed far too complicated and contrived.

But then one day an idea came out of the blue that I was sure would work due to its very simplicity, so I set about making it happen.

What I did was buy two identical flat caps (not cat flaps), a broom handle and a six-foot long piece of thick black cotton cloth. This cloth, also about six foot wide, and two six-foot lengths of metal carpet grips, I'd bolt together in a T-shaped frame. The cloth was then fixed to one end of the horizontal bit of the frame so that when I lifted the vertical

Stand-up Chameleon

piece of the metal 'T' it would hang down from the horizontal piece of the frame. And this cloth was weighted at the bottom, so it hung taught and straight.

What the audience saw when I eventually tried it on stage was me walking out with this contraption while wearing one of the flat caps. The other, identical, was stuck on top of the false head, which had the broom handle jammed up a hole I bored into its severed neck. All this hidden behind the cloth. On reaching centre stage, I'd then raise the T-frame bearing the black cloth to three inches under my chin. I'd then give a last look at the audience, turning my head from side to side in a robotic movement with the same neutral expression the model head had, do a quick smile, and go back to the neutral look. A second later, I'd lift the T-structure – keeping the model head on the broom handle concealed – to a height of fifteen feet or so while, behind the cloth, raising model head until it appeared fully, complete with flat cap and neutral expression, above the top edge. The audience could still see my legs, but now my head was fifteen foot higher. I'd then twist the broom handle so the head would 'look' from side to side. Not exactly in David Copperfield's league, sure, but so silly it didn't half make em' laugh. After milking it for a few seconds I'd then bring it down slowly behind the cloth, lower the frame with the cloth still keeping the whole apparatus out of sight, and walk off.

In fact, I kept this silly trick in my set for a whole tour, by the end of which I was getting so bored I did a variation. Now, after milking laughs with the head, I'd drop the frame with the cloth accidentally on purpose. I'd then get even more laughs, revealed as holding this replica head on a stick. It was fun while it lasted, but I don't do it anymore. Why? I've aged and the head hasn't. Like the portrait of Dorian Gray. I've still got the thing, though, in a box in the spare bedroom. I think my wife, Bev, has forgotten about it. If she outlives me, she might be in for a nasty shock one day, while clearing out the wardrobe.

※

Of all the bird-brained routines I ever dreamed up the one that comes to mind as most ludicrous was a thing I did with the assistance of my good mate, the Geordie tale-telling guitarist Keith Donnelly.

I had bought a pair of those brogues you see in old gangster movies, the black and white ones with patterns made by little holes in the top. I'd chosen them to wear for a Roaring Twenties birthday party and, when it was over, figured I'd never wear them again. About to put them away in a cupboard forever, though, another idea came.

First, I had special brackets made out of flat sheet metal angled at 90° and fixed to the heels. These shoes could now stand vertical, with their toes pointing up. When placed on the floor, as shoes would normally be, the brackets were slightly higher than the heels and had little holes where a long fishing line could be tied. At the front, the toe area had little ring hooks screwed into the soles, where other, shorter, fishing lines could be tied. The idea was that when the shoes were in the wings, toes pointing out towards the centre of the stage, they could be pulled either way by these lines. All this set up beforehand, the ends of the short lines marked with a piece of coloured tape so they'd easily be found later on the floor. They were now ready to spring into action. At some point in the show, Keith would secretly hand me the short fishing line and I'd pull them on from the wings so they could 'walk' on stage. Very unrealistically, I must add, because of course the shoes couldn't lift while stepping, just slide in a shuffling fashion. Keith would then take cues from me as to when to pull the long lines, while I went through a Humphrey Bogart-type script in the style of the Sam Spade detective movies. It went like this:

Bogie: A knock came on my door that night (*knocking noise by Keith*), so I walked over and opened it real slow (*I would mime opening it on the edge of the stage, just behind the curtain, make a verbal creaking sound, then look down at the shoes and back up to eye level*). It's you, huh? You might as well come in. (*I would walk backwards here, having taken the short lines from Keith, and pull them in such a way that the shoes followed me to the middle of the stage as though an invisible person was in them, which got a huge laugh as they shuffled rather than walked.*) Why don't you step out of those shoes and dance? (*Here I'd drop the lines and mime holding an invisible woman in a waltz position, about to dance, then set off around the stage for a while with her. Putting my lower hand in a few of her invisible taboo regions, I'd get back to the short lines on the shoes, stop, and continue talking*). It sure was a swell idea wearing those kind of shoes. Nobody would guess you're a dame. Let me help you back on with them. (*Here, I'd kneel, hold*

Stand-up Chameleon

the shoes for her a second, then pick up the lines again, stand up and say) but you didn't come here to dance, did you, sweetheart? You came here to kill me! *(I'd then put both fishing lines in my left hand and throw a punch with my right, at the face of this invisible woman. Pulling up the lines with my left, the shoes would then stand up, the toes pointing at the ceiling, as though this invisible woman had gone down with the force of the blow. If Keith could get the timing right, he clapped his hands to coincide with the punch and fell over in the wings, on boards, to create the sound of the invisible body hitting the floor.)* Get up! *(I'd say, pulling the short lines with each hand, making the shoes now tip back from their upright position, flat again, Keith taking hold of the long fishing lines tied to the back of the shoes, ready to pull them.)* Okay you dirty double-crossing dame, get out of my office *(I'd say, jabbing a finger at an invisible chest)* and don't call on me again. *(Shoes now move backwards, as I speak and jab).*

I must say, it was all more Benny Hill than Penn and Teller and of all the times we tried it in front of an audience we must have got it right only once or twice. The fishing lines would get snagged and we would get one shoe collapsing on its side and stopping while the other wandered off on its own. Yet the more Keith and I goofed up, the more the audience loved it. We ended up in stitches ourselves many a night. In the long run, though, it became a pain in the arse, so I scrapped it. I've still got the shoes though and, no, they are not stored next to the head. Having read this, you may wonder why I bother to mention the 'head' and the 'shoes' thing in a book. Well, anyone starting off on a comedy career who reads it and is doing stand-up – and who adds an oddball idea like these into their performance might just lift it to another level and set them apart from the rest.

You may remember a TV series entitled *Masterclass* shown during the 1990s. It engaged experts in given fields to instruct amateurs in how to improve their art. One episode was hosted by Mark Knopfler, the wonderful guitarist from Dire Straits, who advised some wannabe guitarists. I was flattered to be asked to host a comedy masterclass and readily accepted. It was an interesting experience, but although the programme was aired I never actually saw it, nor did I watch the complimentary copy I was sent. I felt that it was a bit of a cheat. The programme featured three young comedians who had put together

It's a Funny Business...

an act. I was to give them tips on performance, delivery and so on and then say who was most likely to make a career of it after seeing them work an audience of eighty at a tiny venue in Newcastle. Looking back it had the feel of a reality show. The trio were chosen because they hadn't – or so they stated to the producer – appeared on television before. I knew one had. I'd seen him more than once – he specialised in impressions of *Coronation Street* characters – but I kept my mouth shut and kept his secret. The other two did characters they'd invented. They'd walk on stage as their character and go through the script they had written for the part. It was pretty unexciting stuff really, but the impressionist guy was very funny and I howled at his Kevin Webster impression. So, naturally, he was picked as the one most likely to make it – unsurprising really, as in many eyes he already had by getting on TV. Looking back on all that nonsense I have to ask myself whether the notion of a master giving help and imparting comical wisdom to a class is not somehow totally bogus. Can comedy be taught? I doubt it.

Comedy really can't be analysed in the same way as playing a musical instrument. It might be described as the most subjective of all the arts. You may listen to a singer-songwriter and not like what you hear, yet as time goes by grow accustomed to it and eventually become a fan. Van Gogh's paintings were ridiculed by his contemporaries, but a hundred and fifty or so years later people rave about him. Comedy doesn't work like that. It is judged instantly and often of its time.

Also the more comedy is picked at and dissected the more elusive it is. It's questionable whether there is such a thing as a comic genius; a person can never be one hundred per cent sure that what they think is funny will actually *be* funny when put before an audience. With me, from the very start it was a case of busking it, a trial and error process.

While he was in power, I had a Tony Blair impression. Because I had neither a decent script for him or was able to get the voice quite right, however, I chose to do a silent version and just mimic his movements and dummy-like facial expressions. It served me well, went down great with audiences everywhere, until I thought I'd get my finger out, write a decent script and work on his faux-plebeian 'mockney' voice. So off I went on my new little quest, to nail Blair in this way at a gig.

I noticed how one thing impressionists failed to spot is how he had – and still has – trouble with his L's when they come in the middle of certain words. World becomes worwed. Sometimes he omits the T at the end so 'got' becomes an abrupt 'go-'.

Stand-up Chameleon

Which resulted in the following:

> **Blair:** Wewl, what wiw my legacy be? Y-know, wiwl future historians look back and say: 'Yes, that was Tony Blair, the man who saved the Labour Party from Socialism, then went on to save the Catholic Church from Christianity. He persuaded Pope Benedict XVI to allow Alastair Campbell to take a fresh look at the Commandments.' Yes! And because of this, future historians wiw say, 'Tony Blair was finally canonised by His Holiness to the status of sainthood. He became known as Anthony, patron saint of honesty and founding father of new Catholicism.' Historians of tomorrow wiw say, 'That was Tony Blair, the man who couldn't pronounce the letter L and yet saved it — the worwd that is — from the dark forces of Conservatism.' And yet, dear beloved brethren, I say unto you with trembling lip, 'the poor you sha-w y-know always have with you, but no-me, I'm afraid. I'm off to the United States to advise those less intelligent than myself.'

Tony then walks away and, as he does so, waves to the audience, his waving hand soon stopping its waving motion and his thumb rubbing his fingers instead, to signify all the money he's going to be making.

I tried this out several times, sure the script was a winner, yet the only laugh I got out of the whole piece was the money rubbing fingers bit at the end. Needless to say I went back to the silent Blair.

You never know if something's going to score with an audience or not. The only thing you can be sure of is if you write ten pieces, one will be great, one will be good and one will be acceptable. So you've got three. The other seven you can forget.

Write another ten and then you'll have six, and so on. Keep on writing and you'll find the great ones that really crack people up. Then keep building over the years until you have a large repertoire you can add to with whatever springs to mind.

Or subtract from, with stuff that's dated or you are now bored by.

The Tale Continues...

A sell-out tour followed that first *Cool It* series, which was amazing given that the first show only got 1.9 million viewers, a small amount by 1985 standards. As Jasper predicted, though, word soon spread and we reached well over two million by the third and last one.

Letters of congratulation came from all avenues of showbusiness. Michael Grade, back then Controller of BBC1, wrote a quick word of praise to Les Ward's Starward business partner, John Starkey, who was also Jasper's manager: 'Dear John, Phil Cool is brilliant, let's talk, yours etc...' A letter from legendary comedy writer Barry Cryer said simply: 'Dear Phil, I'd like to write for you, how much do you charge?' Plenty of other similar responses came in, including several offers for commercials, which I refused. I had no clear reason for doing so, couldn't at the time give a sound and solid argument as to why I wished to reject them. I just instinctively felt it wasn't for me.

At the time, I mined lots of material from TV ads and the idea that you'd see someone, usually a celebrity, lying through their teeth about some product or other. Doing the same would have left me in an awkward position. I didn't totally rule it out but pleaded with Les that we should let them go and reconsider if anything more suitable

Stand-up Chameleon

turned up. Naturally, Les wanted me to say yes as the money would have been great, quick and easy, but to his credit he respected my wishes and graciously passed. Besides, theatres were full; my career was going from strength to strength. His business partner, John, was there as a consultant with advice if needed and also handled contract negotiations. As expected, the BBC soon wanted a second series.

One problem with doing the shows from Birmingham was that the 'Big Boys' in London seemed to see the place as some kind of a joke, in fact any town north of Watford was 'out in the sticks'. These days things seem to have changed somewhat, although recalling the fuss some of their employees kicked up when asked to go to Salford after that decision was made in 2006, you wonder. I'm sure some still think the north is all cobbled streets and chips with everything.

Anyway, communication and requests from us had to go through Steve Weddle, who then passed them to Pebble Mill. From there, they'd then have to go through a number of people in London before reaching the real decision-makers at the top. After which, the whole process went into reverse until an answer came back. It seemed to take forever. Even so, things got done and eventually John Starkey was negotiating a fee for *Cool It* series two. He got a nice tidy sum too. Yet, for reasons I'm still not quite sure of, this next run wasn't for the usual six shows, but five. Did they not trust me with six? Five was fine by me, anyway. The name of the game now was to get the material together. A bit of good stuff that hadn't made it into the previous series helped with that, while touring forced more ideas from my lump of grey matter, so it began to come together nicely.

These five shows were to air in 1986. Jasper was still involved and sharpened up the scripts with me. While at his house one day, I told him I had written a poem called 'Feeding Caviar to Pigs' and would like to put it in. The idea was to tell the audience that Richard Burton once said he hated audiences (true) and I would do an impression of him by reciting this poem in mock-Shakespearean rant, as if he were on stage in some godforsaken working men's club.

'OK,' said Carrott. 'Let's hear it.' I cleared my throat and started. 'I am feeding caviar to pigs...' I spat, in my best gravelly Welsh tones,

The Tale Continues...

'...This vintage wine that should be savoured, going down in swigs.' Maintaining that Burtonesque raspiness, I took the poem to the end.

Before Jasper responded there was an awkward silence. I broke it with an abrupt: 'Needs a bit of work doesn't it?'

'Yeah, Phil. You can't put that in as it stands. It needs something adding, to contrast with the seriousness. Let's hear it again.'

So off I went once more until, betraying my lack of confidence in the thing as overlong and having too few – or no – laughs, saying: 'Sorry, I should never have suggested it in the first place. On second thoughts, let's not bother. It's just a silly poem.'

'Oh, no,' Jasper said with a smile. 'We'll make it funny, you'll see'. Reaching for a book on Shakespeare from his bookshelf, he told me: 'Go on. I'm waiting.' So, channelling my inner-Burton once more, I began again in that strange rhythm of speech:

I am feeding caviar to pigs ... this vintage wine that should be savoured, going down in swigs ... for this yet another of those nauseating gigs ... where I am feeding caviar to pigs.

My first joke not a titter not a flicker of a smile ... my next line so inventive, you missed it by a mile ... I am feeding caviar to pigs and its stifling my style ... but never mind, you all can play your bingo in a while.

I am feeding caviar to pigs ... a Rembrandt in a junk shop unrecognised by every Tom, Dick and Harry ... breathing in the smoke from all the cigs ... here, feeding caviar to pigs.

'Stop there,' said the Carrott. 'That's far enough with the serious stuff. We need to interject some real Shakespearean extracts.' Breaking off from thumbing through the great bard's works and gazing up to the ceiling, the machinery of his mind went into action. 'We need to get better known phrases in, like 'a horse a horse; my kingdom for a horse.' Pausing for a second, he added: 'Try it like Norman Wisdom.'

So I went into Norman mode: 'A horse [pronounced *owerse*], a

Stand-up Chameleon

owerse, my kingdom for a *owerse*, just as Norman would have. Jasper laughed: 'Now we are getting somewhere but it still needs setting up. How's about something like: "Granted, there were times when I would pander to the demands of light relief," said in your Burton voice of course...'

I then took over, extending his line: 'But Shakespeare wrote for king and peasant, vagabond and thief...'

'Now,' said Jasper, "do the horse bit, but come in as Norman half way through.'

'A horse! A horse!' I said, as Burton, then quickly morphing into Norman Wisdom physically and in voice, added: 'My kingdom for a *owerse* Mr Grimsdale ... ha ha ha ... you should see your faces.'

At which, Jasper cracked up and we knew we had a strong bit in the making. Within an hour, it was done. When I did it at the next script meeting everyone concluded it was strong enough to finish a show with. 'Caviar to Pigs' was quite a long and sophisticated piece, sophisticated in that it ridiculed impressionists, which meant I was essentially rubbishing my own craft. It was also a long piece in that it eventually included Rik Mayall, John Cleese and Jimmy Cricket, all being outrageously silly within this mock Shakespearean stuff delivered so seriously in Burton's mellifluous baritone.

In opinion, the best piece in the second *Cool It* series though was a routine about playing a nightclub in Stockport called 'Quaffers', a true tale enhanced here and there for maximum effect. The stage in that place actually did come out of the dancefloor to an ear-splitting rendition of the *Thunderbirds* theme tune. Anyway, the piece ended on a high as I did an impression of an Aquaphibian from *Stingray*, that other Gerry Anderson puppet show of the 1960s, before my face 'got stuck with cramp'. During the last few seconds of the show, I can be seen gradually disappearing on the now descending stage back from whence I came, face still contorted (mimed, of course).

That second series was great fun to make and each of its episodes finished with a very strong sketch, 'Caviar to Pigs', 'Quaffers', 'Rolf Harris' (painting the studio audience), 'Wogan' (revealing himself to be a creative from Alpha Centauri), and a stand-up routine where

The Tale Continues...

It was a proud moment when I collected this certificate at the London Hilton

I did impressions of Griff Rhys Jones and Mel Smith in the style of *Alas Smith and Jones*. My Griff is reading out Oscar nominees at an award ceremony when he has a heart attack, dies and goes to heaven, only to discover God and Paul Daniels (who he has just slagged off) are one and the same person. Griff's spirit was shown apparently rising out of his lifeless body as it lay on stage. I don't think special effects had been used before much, if at all, on television during a piece of stand-up, but that was just one of the things that set the *Cool It* shows apart. The first time we used effects was in series one, when I asked if it was possible to make me disappear as I leapt into the air at the end of the *Young Ones* spoof, as used to happen in the sitcom. It was – and the *Cool It* team did. They also incorporated some lovely lighting changes and occasional gobos, images cast by a spotlight. For instance, the stained glass window that suddenly appeared when I did the Rolf routine on the Sistine Chapel ceiling was a gobo. The whole Pebble Mill team right down to the researchers, floor workers and, well everyone really, 'gelled'. Perhaps that was because we were all part of something new, fresh and exciting for Pebble Mill.

I don't know who it was that nominated Phil Cool and *Cool It* for

Stand-up Chameleon

the 1987 Royal Television Society 'Original Television Achievement' award but, whoever it was, thank you.

The RTS presented me with it – as witnessed by our great *Cool It* team – at the London Hilton, on Park Lane. Nowadays, it hangs on my wall at home. 'To Phil Cool for 'Cool It', an original Television achievement,' it reads. Newspaper reviews too were excellent, which led to more offers for TV commercials, corporate gigs and such, but I was only interested in doing stand-up in theatres, so let them go. Meanwhile, Les would line up big tours in 1,000-2,000 seater venues and I'd sometimes do several nights in the same place. All sold out, though not overnight. Mobile phones and the internet were only in their infancy and there were no social networks as such, so the word spread at a limited pace. This, combined with me keeping a relatively low profile by turning down such programmes as the *Wogan* chat show and adverts for everything from beer to banks, kept the brakes on the fame thing. Had mobiles, Facebook, Instagram and what have you been at the stage they are nowadays, the Phil Cool phenomenon would have gone stratospheric, I'm sure. Still, I was more than happy with what I had. Here I was, an electrician from Chorley, doing what I'd worked and hoped for from the start. It couldn't get any better.

Around this time, Les, John and Jasper were together working on a programme they called *Stand Up America* and went to the US to shoot it. Jasper was its host and each one featured half an hour of mixed stand-up from names then on their way up like Jerry Seinfeld, Gilbert Gottfried, Emo Philips, Rita Rudner and Kevin Pollak. Jasper spoke to them in the dressing room before their short set and after. It was a very good programme and Les and John made lots of useful contacts. One day, John asked if I'd like to try my luck over there, if so he would set up a few theatres for me to work in. I didn't enthuse about the idea. I suppose that somewhere deep down I knew that to crack the States I'd really have to live there a while and tap into the American psyche, which would have required a lot of determination, work, time, a strong desire for global recognition and the rest. So I took the easy option. 'I'll pass,' I said, 'stay here in the UK and carry on as usual.' Yes, folks. That's just about how ambitious I am.

A Winter's Tale

Heading for Yeovil, the outside lane of the M5 was beneath a foot of snow, so south-bound vehicles like mine had to crawl in the slow and middle lanes, where it was compacted by wheels. I had a little more confidence than most, as the front-wheel drive of my new Austin Maxi gave me a lot more stability in such testing conditions.

I was due to play an armed forces base in Somerset, one of several I'd been booked for in the South West in 1981. It was always the case that no matter how well you played, the level of appreciation you'd receive at these places depended on whether you performed for the junior ranks, corporals or officers. Most times you only found out who your audience was going to be on arrival, checking in at the gate, so driving down you'd be pondering your fate. If it was officers, you stood a good chance of doing well. And even if you didn't, you would still be treated courteously with a minimum of embarrassment. Similar with the corporals. Get the junior ranks – squaddies – though and anything could happen. I remember doing a Christmas gig at the Yeovilton Naval Air base, HMS Heron. As the clubroom filled with junior ranks before the show, I sat making observations. It was the only gig I've ever been booked to play when people were so drunk they had to be carried in. Needless to say, I just went through the motions to ensure I'd be paid. A payment which would, more often than not, come via several agents.

Stand-up Chameleon

I had many an adventure in my beloved Austin Maxi

But back to the M5, where I was heading south. I hadn't travelled far. The night before I'd been working at the Army Apprentices College on the Severn Estuary and survived a young audience's indifference. Id blagged a bed for the night in the billet blocks. Some guy, not a squaddie but with a stripe or two, corporal maybe, had taken pity on this poor rambling minstrel and lent him his room. As I lay in the single bed, just before killing the lightbulb and going to sleep, I looked at a rectangle of paper my host had cut out from a glossy magazine and hung on the wall. A close-up of a woman's genitalia – in colour. Grateful for his room, I nevertheless couldn't help but wonder if he'd hung it there because it was a self-portrait.

Chepstow to Yeovil meant passing several junctions south before swinging south-east on an A road. Approaching my exit, the weather worsened. By now there was thick frozen slush on top of the snow that had previously been falling straight down and was now being whipped into swirls by gusty chaotic winds.

The Maxi pulled up the slip road and I was finally off the M5 at last. Heading cautiously down the A road I felt lucky to have this new blue Maxi because the old green one had had a thing about snow. A year or so before, I'd been driving north on the M5 when, without warning, the wretched thing's windscreen shattered into mosaic fragments with a startling explosion as I was doing 70mph-plus and overtaking. *Boom!* In a fraction of a second, I was driving blind and gently applied the foot brake while smashing a bigger hole with my fists to get a better view. There wasn't much traffic, luckily, so I was able to keep the car under control and steer it safely across to the hard shoulder.

What to do next? After going through every swear word in the book I covered my hand with my scarf, made another fist and smashed the rest of the windscreen into fragments. A sign said the next junction was a mile away. 'I'll go for it,' I told myself, clearing glass off the seats.

Have you ever driven without a windscreen in winter? Thought not. It's the act of a mad person. I'd gone a few hundred yards and was starting to turn blue when my luck changed. It got worse. As if on cue: snow. I could feel the cold crystals forcing themselves through my clenched lips and then seeping into the gaps between my teeth. Cold, cold snowflakes impairing my vision as they slammed at great speed into the slits my eyes had soon become. 'I can't go on. I'll have to stop,' I heard myself say, somewhere in the igloo that was my head. Pulling over again, I once more tried to work out a plan. My prop case on the backseat became part of it. In there, were many peculiar things. As the snow got heavier and began to form a layer across the top of the dashboard, I set off again in Elvis sunglasses, a Rolf Harris beard and a Humphrey Bogart trilby on my head, all of it held in place by a silk scarf thing I used for a John Wayne neckerchief, tied under my chin. I also had an Ian Paisley-type overcoat on, but no gloves, and was using one hand to steer while the other wiped the lenses of my sunglasses. Eventually, the old dark green Maxi – now white inside and out – limped off at the junction. Reaching the highway at the end of the slip road, I chose to turn left not knowing whether I'd find a garage sooner that way or not. One mile. Two miles. Three miles. No garage. Then way off in the distance I spotted something; was it a mirage born out of peering through ice? No it really was a garage. As I pulled onto the forecourt it became evident that this was one of those old-fashioned

Stand-up Chameleon

private affairs that do repair work and such, so my soul received a little glow of hope. A huge door was open, obviously a mechanic's workshop. I rolled the Maxi towards it and parked up. On hearing the creak of a door hinge, a pair of mechanics looked up from working on an engine to see what looked like a bow-legged snowman clambering out. Two hours later, I was driving home. These guys, nay, gentlemen, had postponed their work while one drove off to pick a new windscreen up and hurried back to complete the job, while the other kept me supplied with hot tea during the wait. I was deeply grateful, even if I did keep discovering a new shard of glass digging into my arse every few minutes. Needless to say, the snow had by now stopped.

Fast forward to this Yeovil trip and the snow came at me and my new blue Maxi in the hypnotic way it does at 40mph or more. The light was fading and I hoped to reach Yeovil before darkness fell. The snowstorm got worse as I cut through it, it violent swirls tearing twigs and branches from leafless trees lining the roadside, forcing me to slow down and dodge them. Way ahead was a sight to behold – and not a nice one. One bloody great hill lay before me, on it I could see six or so cars all making attempts at conquering this little Everest. As I got closer it became evident they were doomed to fail. Some slid down sideways, others were stationary. I patted the dashboard of the Maxi and said: 'We've got to go for it, lad,' presuming it was male. 'Just get yer head down and go.' Increasing speed I made a dash for it to perhaps dangerous levels. 'We' reached the foot of this perilous slope, the key word in my mind now being 'momentum'. The Maxi climbed the hill as other cars slid down strewn at strange angles, all, I presume, travelling or intent on travelling in my direction. By now it was every driver for him or herself. With my foot hard down on the accelerator, the front wheel drive dug into that hill, flat out in third gear. I couldn't take the straight route up, but had to zigzag through these other vehicles as they came at me from all ways. Eventually, the Maxi reached the crest and as it levelled out again – jubilation! I roared a cry of relief out loud for me and the Maxi, patted the dashboard, slipped it into fourth and went easier on the accelerator. The road from then on was straight and on the flat. I'd travelled a couple of miles in fourth rather than the fifth Maxis were famous for, so as to keep more control in this still treacherous weather, when headlights appeared in the rearview mirror. It must be a vehicle that had also conquered the hill and, what's more, it was gaining on me, so I was intrigued as to what this vehicle was as

A Winter's Tale

I tootled along at a safe speed, headlights now picking out the hypnotic snowflakes. I slowed down even more, so the car behind would catch up and it did. As it was about to overtake me I yielded to the left slightly and as it passed laughed out loud. It was another Maxi.

Coming into Yeovil it was almost dark and the snow had stopped. After making enquiries I found the person responsible for booking me, a pleasant chap who was astounded I'd actually turned up. He explained that the event had been cancelled and if I would follow him he'd show me why. 'I'm going to have to pay you, anyway,' he said as we walked along the wintry pavements of the forces base. 'At least you'll be rewarded for your determination, which is well appreciated.' Then, as we turned a corner, he pointed and said: 'But look at that, where you were going to do your stuff tonight. Good job it happened this afternoon and not when the place was full, eh?'

There it was, the long wooden building that served as their 'family club' obliterated. During the storm, a huge tree had gone over and literally cut the place in half. 'Come with me now, Phil, and I'll get you your fee. It's cash,' he said as we walked together. I asked him if he knew of anywhere I could stay for the night (always short of money in those days I didn't want to blow my small fee on hotels and such; being the breadwinner I needed to take home as much as I could. 'There's one or two pubs and a few local guesthouses nearby,' he said, handing me an envelope marked 'artist'. 'But there's not one I can think of that might put you up here on the camp. Good luck.' We shook hands and then he turned and walked away, as I did. A second or two later though I heard his voice behind me. 'Hang on,' he said. 'I'm being unkind here. How about I ask my wife and daughter if they wouldn't mind you coming to our house for tea and staying the night in the spare room?'

'That would be great, I'd appreciate it,' I said, feeling relieved that I didn't now have to go hunting for digs, a chore I always hated.

'Welcome to our humble home,' said his wife. 'I believe you're going to dine with us and stay over?'

'Yeah, it's very kind of you to invite me,' I replied, tapping the snow off my shoes on the front doorstep.

'Come in and make yourself comfortable,' she smiled, helping me in with my guitar and suitcase. It was a home supplied, I think, by the MOD on what looked like a council estate, among rows of small semi-detached pebble-dashed houses. As I entered I was introduced to their young daughter, who put the kettle on for us all, and I settled in. The

Stand-up Chameleon

guy explained that he was a mechanic who worked on helicopters, as his wife beavered away in the kitchen making sure there was going to be enough food to go around at teatime with an extra mouth to feed. A coal fire glowed, making it all so warm and friendly in stark contrast to the dark, cold and cruel night that had descended on this corner of England. They were interested in what I did and said they were sorry that circumstances had prevented the show going ahead. We chatted some more and, before I knew it, a huge plate of meat, veg and gravy was handed to me as I sat on the sofa. 'I hope you don't mind eating off your lap?' I was asked, as I took the warm plate and cutlery.

'No, not at all,' I said, eager to get stuck in.

'We usually have TV dinners rather than all sitting around the table,' said the daughter as she walked in with her dinner plate and sat across from me on a comfy-looking chair. All four of us sat eating and talking as the TV screen lay silent and grey, catching only our reflections. The electric light was left off too, allowing the fire to cast its orange spell about the room, creating shadows of the furniture over the walls that pulsated as the glowing embers flickered in the grate.

After dessert and a mug of tea, we all cleared our plates away, the TV stayed silent and the conversation led to me explaining that I was working on a new song about what we had just discussed. 'Oh, go on, Phil. Let's hear it then,' said my lady host. 'I'd love to hear you do it, especially as Prince Charles.' So I opened up my battered guitar case, took out the EKO I had then, and launched into a short song about Charles and Diana. Three hours later, I put the guitar back, having gone through my entire repertoire of songs, impressions and stories, and all to an audience of three. The fire had almost died, my host family were all laughed out and happy, and the day came to a close. We all said goodnight and retired, with me given permission to have a lie-in.

Drawing the curtains the next day at the crack of noon, I was pleased to see rain falling slightly and the snow looking sad and dirty, so knew the road out of Yeovil would be a doddle this time.

The guy and his wife had long gone (to work maybe) and, after I came downstairs, their daughter made a quick brew for me and wished me well. I left the house, suitcase and guitar in hand, with a treasured memory. Driving away from this humble home in Buckle Avenue, I felt as though I had captured a glimpse of the kind side of human nature and was better for it myself.

The Tale Continues...

In 1987, I took a break from *Cool It*. As almost all my material had now been shown on national television, I'd need more – and it would have to be written and tested out on the road.

What Les did was book me into smaller theatres to experiment with new ideas. If they went down like a lead balloon, two hundred people would see me struggle with them rather than two thousand. So, off we went Les, Keith, Gilly and myself, to often remote places like the little Welsh towns – at which, incidentally, I was always given a great welcome – where I'd try out impressions, songs and stories.

Underpinning it all was an agreement between John Starkie and the BBC for a third *Cool It* series, this time featuring six half-hour shows. Six! Wow! I was honoured. Not only that, but a fifty-minute special was also being discussed. When the time came to make them, Steve Weddle, Les and I agreed we'd need to change the format slightly to give viewers something fresh, other than just stand-up.

I relished the thought and began writing all manner of crazy routines to be performed with other actors, not just myself. And these sketches would be direct extensions of my stand-up material, in other words carry on the theme it had taken. An outstanding one

Stand-up Chameleon

was about Paul Daniels, a little magician with a big name at the time, that required involvement from the audience and an actor. A tall woman was required, so when she stood next to my Paul he'd look *really* small, which was fun to do. Probably not for the real Paul, though, if he ever saw it.

We shot it half in the studio and half at the top of Ilkley Moor, in Yorkshire, a location that doubled up for what 'Paul' assured us was Mount Sinai, where Moses received the Ten Commandments. It was all part of a long-winded contrived trick executed with the help 'an audience member' – i.e. an actor, Sara Sinden. Around six foot two, she was perfect, 'Paul' inviting her on-stage to help with his 'trick'. After 'selecting' her (most of the audience must've known she was a plant, adding to the fun), they walked hand in hand towards a table. Sara, aka 'Doris', sat on a chair of normal height behind it, while I, as Paul, sat next to her on a very low chair, which got a huge laugh as she now towered over him. He then asked for a personal item that she produced from her handbag, a ruby-encrusted cigarette lighter given to her, she said, by her late father on his deathbed. Paul, with the help of Doris, then put this lighter in a cloth, folded it up and said: 'Mind your fingers', before producing a glittering hammer from beneath the table. After which, he set about smashing the lighter to bits and said, in that distinctive accent of his: 'What you have just witnessed, ladies and gentlemen, is a recording; but stay tuned as we go live to a mystery location.' Upon which, we now zoomed into a screen behind him and 'cut to Mount Sinai', where I, 'Paul', was being given a lift to the summit on Doris's back. After a few of his trademark condescending remarks, the lighter turned up in a bucket of donkey shit.

Throughout the routine, Paul continued to tell her, 'Say yes, Paul', in a sexist tone or better yet, 'Say I'd love to take a bath with you after the show, Paul.' The sketch must have been about twelve minutes long, so took up half the programme, and concluded with Paul maniacally commanding Doris to: 'Worship me, Doris. Worship me,' as his head expanded (low-tech special effects), growing bigger and bigger until, cackling and yelling with as much male chauvinism as he could muster from such a tiny frame, a bolt of lightning blew him

The Tale Continues...

to bits, leaving only his wig, smouldering on the ground. Finally, a God-like voice boomed: 'NOW THAT'S WHAT I CALL MAGIC'.

Another piece written to make that third *Cool It* series different was my 'Bugs Mercury' impression, shot in an empty studio that we did up like a rock concert stage, with fancy lights.

The character – as you've probably guessed – was a cross between Warner Brothers' cartoon 'wabbit' Bugs Bunny – 'What's up, Doc?' – and Queen frontman Freddie Mercury. For it, I did my best rabbit face, complete with Mercury-esque moustache, while strutting and singing 'I want to break free' in Bugs's voice, clad in a black leotard and studded belt. Halfway through, I turned around and was caught at a strange angle by another camera, to reveal my backside and a fluffy round bunny's tail that I wiggled for all to see.

For some strange reason, this was one of the hardest things to perform for me ever. We kept going for another take to get it perfect and by the time we'd done fifteen I was knackered. Maintaining the Bugs face and Freddie movements was really difficult. Maybe that had something to do with using dry ice to get the right look on camera. I had a feeling all the oxygen had been sucked out of the air. It was worth it, though. When the studio audience saw it on monitor screens during my stand-up routine, they cracked up in all the right places.

A guest on one of the shows was Geoff Capes, the Olympic shot-putter and professional Highland Games competitor who twice went on to be named World's Strongest Man. Geoff helped me on a spoof I'd written of the Paul Simon hit 'You Can Call me Al', taken from the latter's 1986 album *Graceland*. I'd penned this pastiche with the same sort of nonsensical lyrics the single had. Geoff was a great sport and learned it off by heart so he could mime it for the show. He played the same part Chevy Chase did in the video, while I was Paul, complete with pink room and door in the back wall that I would walk in and out of while Geoff 'sang' the lyrics and tooted a flute much as Chevy had. In the first half of the sketch I sat twiddling my thumbs. In the second, I'd go through the door and re-emerge as someone else, Ronald Reagan first up. Then it was Rolf Harris and finally J.R. Ewing, the oil baron played by Larry Hagman in *Dallas*.

Stand-up Chameleon

The song started with:

> *Well, I guess this song came down to me*
> *as I was drivin' along in my Africar.*
> *With only the feel of a steering wheel*
> *instead of the steel of the strings of my guitar*

A tune similar to *You Can Call Me Al* then closed with:

> *We're all goin' down to Southfork,*
> *Southfork, down in Dallas, Texas*
> *to see what makes Miss Ellie sad*
> *to see what makes ol' JR bad*

Geoff picks me up here, while I'm playing guitar wearing JR's stetson, boots and suit, and carries me off and through the door.

We also used camera tricks in the series, split-screen effects that enabled me to do some pretty surreal stuff. I'd play two people, one each side of the screen. By refining their exact positions on camera we could make them appear to interact and even touch. In one such sketch I played Charles Bronson and Clint Eastwood as a comedy duo performing in a Mexican saloon. Charlie and Clint, as they were billed, came in looking like they'd been on the trail a long time, real dusty and mean. The doors swung open and shut with a creak as they left the street and stood looking at their Mexican audience (who the viewer doesn't see but hears the babble of in the background).

Charlie: 'Looks like we got ourselves a real nice audience, Clint.'
Clint: 'Yeah, real nice.'

At which point one heckler shouts: 'Go home, Americanos! Your act, it stinks.' Clint responds by folding back his poncho, drawing his Colt 45 six-gun and blasting the critic dead (always a fantasy of mine). Charlie then says: 'Clint has a way with hecklers, now laugh!'

'Yeah, go on, punters. Laugh. Laugh real hard,' adds Clint. At first, the crowd nervously does as ordered, before their laughter builds to a great volume. Upon which, Charlie and Clint introduce the next

The Tale Continues...

act, which he calls 'The Two Rons'. Here, we cut to a flag, the Stars and Stripes, where two versions of the US President deliver a script between them, one Ronald Reagan finishing the other's sentences.

I used to enjoy impersonating the flamboyant jazz and blues singer, art critic and writer, among much else, George Melly. We did a sketch where I played Michael Parkinson interviewing him. My Melly was very good but my Parky needed work; we went ahead with it anyway. As George walked to his seat they both 'met' and seemed to shake hands. I'd written a song for Melly to sing called 'Jazz goes on and on and on' that I enjoyed every minute of performing. I later heard that George himself saw the sketch when it went out and loved it. He also admired the suit the wardrobe department made for me to wear as him, so much so that he bought it to wear at gigs, after a few alterations. It was yellow with multi-coloured bars across it and, to my own amusement, I saw him wearing it on telly years later.

※

Steve Weddle brought in several writers to help in this third series, a thing that I found hard to bear. A lot of artists feel at ease delivering material written for them, but I've always had a problem with it. For some reason I don't feel sincere delivering stuff supposedly tailored to my style, but it's in there somewhere among the self-penned gags, routines and sketches.

Watching those six shows today, the material that came from my own experiences is obvious in how I appear comfortable delivering it. Jasper wasn't involved this time – he may have thought me capable of dealing with it without him. We kept in touch, though, and he often enquired as to how everything was going.

Cool It series three went out on BBC2 in September and October 1988. Something that did please me was how Steve persuaded the BBC to include the making of 'trailers' in the budget. So this we did; two very elaborate ones in a big studio that were great fun to do.

In the first, I had a foggy street built in the style of 'Olde London', cobbles, gas lamps etc. I was to loom out of this mist in the guise of

Stand-up Chameleon

You know you've cracked it when you feature in the Beano

John (in real life, Joseph) Merrick, the 'Elephant Man' of Victorian times, with a cloth bag over my head. I'd then walk up to the camera and say, slurping my words in the way John Hurt had in the David Lynch film: 'Good evening. If you would like to see me with the bag off, watch *Cool It* on Thursday nights, at nine o'clock.' Then I'd walk back into the fog and disappear.

The other trailer was a Mick Jagger impression set in the future. Here, 'Mick' was old and infirm, sitting in a wheelchair. When we made it he was still married to the American model and actress Jerry Hall, so it starts with him shouting 'Jerry!' over a slow and roaming camera shot in what could be his home which captures old photos on the wall and mantelpiece. There is other memorabilia too as Mick's voice rings out again – 'Jerry!' – before the camera reveals a half-eaten Mars bar in a glass case. 'Jerry!' he again yells, now very agitated, until the camera finally rests on him, revealed as an old and grey grumpy old rocker in a wheelchair, with a blanket tucked over

The Tale Continues...

his knees. The BBC makeup department pulled out all the stops with me on this. 'Jerry!' Until suddenly, from the side of the screen, a 'Jerry' (i.e. chamber pot) appears, a woman's hand holding it out for him. 'Thanks,' he says, before addressing the viewers: 'Ere! Better watch *Cool It* on Thursdays, nine o'clock. Phil Cool is gonna do an impression of me. Now, if you'll excuse me... I've gotta use this.'

We were all pleased with both and thought they'd be affective in growing ratings. If they were shown at peak times for a fortnight before the series went out, who knows, they might bring in an extra million or two viewers. Not so, I'm afraid. Shortly before the third series was due to be transmitted, Steve was asked by someone in London, who we thought to be head of the BBC trailer department, if we wanted *Cool It* to be included in an autumn season promotion. This was a big trailer that included clips of forthcoming attractions. If so, would he send in a choice clip of *Cool It* and it would be part of that. Steve explained how we'd been budgeted to make two trailers of our own and so had spent a lot of time and effort in making them. We were looking forward to them being shown.

'Oh, that's not happening now,' came the reply. 'Every show has got to be trailed in one big trailer.' After Steve and I discussed this, we decided to decline the offer (wrongly, in hindsight) in the belief that it would be wiser not to reveal any material from the series, so an element of surprise could be maintained for the viewer. We added that nor were we happy at our trailers being scrapped. So, let me be clear now as to how muddled I saw the situation then.

As we've seen, the second series of *Cool It* had won the BBC a Royal Television Society Original Television Achievement award. Yet now, as a mark of appreciation, the third series wasn't even going to be trailed. This is when it struck me that my career could well be at the mercy of some jerk in their trailers department. Looking back, though, we really should have humbled ourselves and accepted their offer; sent them a clip of 'Bugs Mercury' maybe, short and punchy. After all, you really can't tell these people what to do. They have their own agenda and tell *you* what to do. You live and learn. It never got trailed but *Cool It* again went out to the nation and was well received.

Stand-up Chameleon

At the time, however, while my series was on the air, the BBC *did* broadcast an individual trailer for *Alexei Sayle's Stuff*, a series soon to take over my slot when our shows came to an end. Not only that, it was shown something like three times a night for two or three weeks! What was the difference? Alexei's series was made in London, while mine was made in Birmingham.

One *Cool It* series three show pulled in an audience of just under ten million, although I can't now recall whether that was when it got repeated on the back of *Fawlty Towers* and inherited John Cleese fans. Still, it's a hell of a lot of viewers. At some point during the first airing of the series I was invited to a celebratory meal by the deputy head of Pebble Mill in Brum, my management welcome to come too. Wow! Were we going to hit the town first and end up in the finest restaurant in town? Or were we in for an even greater surprise?

Well, when Les Ward, John Starkey and I arrived, the deputy head awaited us alone in his office upstairs, greeting us with smiles and handshakes. 'Sit and make yourselves comfortable' he said, gesturing towards chairs around a table. 'Your show is about to start,' he said, glimpsing at his watch. 'How did you enjoy making the series, Phil?'

'Oh, it was very interesting. Exciting, too, using actors in routines and sketches rather than just stand-up. It was also great fun writing and performing elaborate music pieces and working on location was particularly enjoyable,' I said, wondering where all this was leading.

'Oh... well... okay, then,' he said, going over to a huge TV set and switching it on. 'Let's watch tonight's show.'

We sat, all four of us, in silence for the minute or so as the final images of the previous programme flashed before us. 'And now,' said the announcer, 'it's time to *Cool It* with Phil.' After which, we all sat through the next half-hour in silence. No one looked at anyone else.

Of course, Les and I had been so close to the material, working with it and watching it for the last month or so, that it was hard work to sit through it again in the sterile atmosphere of an office in Pebble Mill. I thought, 'I'll be glad when this is over so we can get away for the meal and drink.' Eventually, after what seemed like an hour and a half, my half-hour show was done. It was a good one too, although

The Tale Continues...

not the strongest of the six. 'Well, that was a good show,' our host said with what seemed to be a forced smile. We replied similarly back across the table. The atmosphere, though, was discomforting. It hung there, making for awkward conversation. It couldn't possibly get worse, could it? Well, yes, it could and did. 'Ah, the meal,' said our host as the door opened and two women in 'dinner lady overalls' came in, pushing a trolley. On it, celebratory Beef Stroganoff straight from the canteen next door, dished it out from a big pot. We carried our plates back to the table and couldn't eat it quick enough and go.

Next day, John Starkey said: 'I was extremely embarrassed for you, Phil,' though it hadn't really bothered me too much at the time. Now, well it all seems so amusing.

It did, though, make me wonder: 'Are the BBC trying to tell me something in their long, roundabout sort of way? Like – go!'

There was still the fifty-minute *Cool It* Christmas special agreed to, though, that went out in December 1990. Particularly interesting to perform, it had some very unusual stuff in it. Little cheeky-faced Scottish weatherman Ian McCaskill was a guest in one routine when I did Terry Wogan interviewing him. Every time Ian's turn to speak came, Wogan put his hand over Ian's mouth to shut him up and soak up more of the limelight. Which left poor withdrawn Ian sitting in silence as he was inundated with ever more blarney. A show stuffed with impressions, stories and mimes ended with a bang – our now King and then Prince Charles fantasising about fronting Dire Straits, while morphing into Mark Knopfler. Using early computer wizardry, our director David Weir somehow managed to superimpose a stadium audience in the foreground as Charles/Mark belted out 'Money for Nothing' with the band at the back of him.

In total, those three *Cool It* series and one special episode had amounted to seven and threequarter hours' worth of material. The pressure of constant writing and finding new ideas had worn me out mentally and I needed a break.

Steve Weddle asked what I wanted to do next? 'Nothing,' I said. 'I want to leave it for a while. I've had enough for now and want a bit of space.' He understood.

A Rant

Showbusiness is a different animal than it was when I started out. It seems now as though the whole nation worships the God of Fame.

Just look at all the tacky showbiz gossip magazines lining the shelves in newsagents and supermarkets; one reason everyone thinks they can step right into the part without putting in the time and evolving slowly and organically. Everybody wants a quick fix, epitomised by the bogus 'talent' shows that take up so much television output.

In my youth, if you told your dad you wanted to be in showbusiness he'd look at you as if you were deranged, deluded or both. Not now. Everything has been reversed. Today, a kid might say: 'Don't be angry at me, dad, but I want go to medical school and become a surgeon.'

'Medical school?' snaps dad. 'Surgeon? Over my dead body! You'll be an Elton John tribute act and like it. Elton will still be going musically for generations, even when he's dead and gone. Listen to "Rocket Man" and "Crocodile Rock", get the big specs on, lad, and fancy costume. Once you've established yourself and know all the words to 'Goodbye Yellow Brick Road' and are making a bundle, *then* you can think about medical school. After that, if you do become a surgeon and it all goes pear-shaped, you'll have a proper job to fall back on, won't you?'

There's a tribute act for every band and artist out there nowadays, always somebody, somewhere, parasiting every entertainer there has

A Rant

ever been – and it's getting worse. They all have slightly-altered names so as not to get into legal trouble. The Illegal Eagles. The Counterfeit Stones. The Bootleg Beatles. And the names get worse as time goes on. Fake That. Nearly Dan (not Steely Dan). You could have a prize for the daftest one. Jeff Leppard? Fred Zeppelin? Or how about By Jovie?

There must be hundreds of Roy Orbisons out there, walking into lampposts because they can't see through their thick dark glasses. Elvis Presleys are most abundant. I seem to recall the comedian and actor Hugh Dennis doing some research on the phenomenon. He found that before 'The King' died in 1977, he had 157 impersonators worldwide. Well, at the last count there were 295,000. Hugh reckoned that if the numbers continue to rise at the same rate of growth, by 2050 a third of the Earth's population will be Elvis impersonators. There are so many, of every race and creed, that each one tries to find some angle or means to differentiate themselves. Thus we have big fat Elvises. Mini-Elvises. Skydiving Daredevil Elvises, who drop in at your barbecue despite the threat of high-voltage powerlines ... 'I'm bzzzzzzzzzzzzzz all shook up' ... and landing medium rare on the lawn.

Where will it all end? There doesn't seem to be the slightest decline; the tribute disease goes from strength to strength. Alvin Stardust turned up at one theatre, did his usual show and following a great night given rapturous applause the manager said: 'That was fantastic! Is there anyone else you can do?' He'd been billed as an Alvin Stardust tribute.

Some old people can't get their heads around the concept, totally baffled by it. I read about one old guy telling his daughter he'd seen, in the local paper, that Robbie Williams was on at a pub round the corner. 'No,' his daughter said. 'That's not *the* Robbie Williams, it's someone doing his songs.' 'No its not" insisted the old boy. 'It's Robbie Williams. It says so in the paper. Look.' His daughter gave up trying to explain. Later, her dad reminded her. 'Shall we go to see Robbie Williams?' he said. 'It's great value for money.' 'What makes you say that?' she asked, patiently. To which her dad replied: 'He's on with the Bee Gees!'

It's not just musical acts, either. Comedians, too, succumb to this warped activity. Tommy Cooper gets the tribute treatment, you may have seen the tour dates in the Sunday papers. It's a bloke with a fez on for goodness sake. Peter Kay has been targeted by some bloke who looks slightly like him from a distance, having the (piss-taking) good grace to put him in his music videos. As I write, I notice John Cleese has brought a stage version of *Fawlty Towers* to the West End, possibly

Stand-up Chameleon

in response to the rip-off merchants who've been copying it for their own ends at corporate do's and such over the years. To my horror, I was told by a reliable source that someone in Australia has even been doing a tribute act to me. Come on! I'm not dead yet. This person does routines I wrote for *Cool It* shows called 'A Tribute to Phil Cool'. And the final insult? The bastard's getting bigger audiences than I am.

Those who have entered *Britain's Got Talent* (or as I prefer to call it 'Mock the Afflicted') must have thought: 'Won't it be great if I win? I'll get to play the *Royal Variety Performance*. Well, for the winners it likely was. Call me a cynical old bastard, but when I did it I found it anything but great. It's for charity, no fee, but that didn't matter as you got to meet Prince Charles – as was. That was an experience, I must say.

My go came at the Lyceum Theatre in 1998, the show's seventy-seventh year. Also on the bill were The Spice Girls; Boyzone; Lily Savage and Maureen Lipman (with the *Annie* and *Oklahoma!* casts respectively); Martine McCutcheon; Jane McDonald; B*witched; and Barry Manilow; the whole thing hosted by Ronan Keating and Ulrika Jonsson. Another comic to appear was the aforementioned and back then barely known Peter Kay, just named runner-up in that year's Perrier Awards. Shortly after his 50th birthday, our now King was there too, up in the Muppet box with his then girlfriend and our now Queen, Camilla. Back-lit and so silhouetted, I could make out this huge pair of ears from the stage and thought: 'If he ever falls out, he'll just glide across the auditorium.'

At the end, we performers followed choreographed instructions to form ourselves into lines and remember our positions. I was front right, centre-stage. When the curtain finally fell, we at the front were to turn around, backs to it, and wait for the Royal Couple, who would travel down a back stairway and emerge on stage. This they did, before walking slowly along the line engaged in brief conversations, no doubt thanking everyone for services to charity. Charles seemed to take ages before getting to me. As he got closer, I could hear him jest with the others and caught snippets of what he was saying. Camilla was even closer, no more than a yard. Unlike now, at this point she was having a hard time with the press and suffering a lot of cruel jibes about her appearance (not from me – I considered such jibes cheap). Now here I was, seeing her close-up and, behold, making a discovery. If I screwed up my eyes a bit, so my upper eyelashes started to brush against my lower ones, I found ... it didn't make the slightest bit of difference.

Eventually, His (then) Royal Highness, Prince Charles, reached me.

A Rant

He stood and paused for a second, princely like, and in the knowledge that I do impressions did that lip-wetting movement of his with his tongue while fidgeting and fiddling with the ring on one of his little fingers. 'Oh, Mr Cool I suppose you must spend a great deal of time looking in the mirror?' And then, with hardly a pause, I blurted back my impression of him: 'Oh, I'm sorry. I thought that's what I was doing now,' only at a level he wouldn't quite hear. He might well have done, though, because, he gave me a two-second blank look and moved on.

Am I a royalist? No. Not particularly, although as I write I am part-way through a book that claims royalty is better than democracy. I like to stay open to new ideas, having an enquiring mind. Democracy, it says, is just a caretaker for a short period of time. I'm not so sure. We are fine with King Charles, but if we'd had King John might not have been. If there's something about royalty on telly my wife, Bev, loves it. I just pick up the guitar and go in another room. Not because I'm being disrespectful, but because I have no interest in it really.

In the end, appearing on the *Royal Variety Performance* did nothing whatsoever for my career. The material I did was pretty unusual too. Bill Clinton, at the time US president, revealed himself as an alien in 'The Clint-ons', a *Star Trek* spoof with Captain Kirk, Mr Spock and Co. Yet when I was introduced by Ulrika's disembodied voice from a mic in the wings, she just said: 'Phil Cool'. Not 'Welcome... Phil Cool,' or 'Ladies and gentlemen... enjoy the many faces of Phil Cool', or similar. No, just a dull monotone 'Phil Cool'. When I see the Royal Variety show now it all seems to belong to another era. The world has since changed. Britain certainly has and I suppose comedy changes with it.

Did I choose comedy? Not really. Now I'm retired from it, I find it strange how my career took that entertainment path rather than a music one. It chose me, I think. It didn't come easily, but instinctively. It gave me an amazing ride, with no regrets. My fifteen minutes of fame lasted a good twenty years. Now?

I'm content with a life that isn't quite so hectic.

The Tale Continues...

As 1989 became 1990, I continued to turn down commercials. Pizza Hut ... Plax, the pre-brush plaque remover mouthwash ... a beer, the brand of which I can't recall ... someone from the Netherlands even made an enquiry after Dutch TV screened the *Cool It* special.

She wanted me to do a commercial for the Bank of Holland (there was only one bank in Holland, I was told, making the need for a commercial even more of a mystery). I could name my price, though. She sent a script with the offer and a letter stating that only I could pull it off, due to my unique talent and style etc. Les reported back my thanks, but that I'd said 'no'. She was having none of it, didn't believe him. In the end he got me to speak to her direct, to convince her I really didn't want the job. She pleaded with me over the phone, telling me I was welcome to bring my wife and kids. 'We'll treat them and yourself to the best hotel and a trip around Amsterdam city,' she said. I thought: 'Yes and we could all go window shopping together.' 'Please, please, please...' she went on, in her seductive accent. 'Sorry, I'm not doing it,' I insisted and, after a long stunned silence and brusque 'goodbye', that was the end of that. Poor Les. His awkward artiste had let another fortune slip away, yet he never grumbled.

The Tale Continues...

In 1989, I'd done my biggest ever tour – over ninety shows right across the UK and Ireland – and by the time I'd finished, had had it up to my neck with comedy. I was sick of coming up with ever more impressions and felt as though I was forever jumping through hoops and would welcome a long rest and fresh look at things.

At the end of the year, Les was contacted by Central TV: would he and I be interested in hearing their proposal? 'Well, no harm in listening,' I told Les, after he passed on the message. A meeting was arranged at John Starkey's house, a sizeable pad with a nice feel to it. Enchanted garden... modern red-brick exterior... warm friendly interior... plush lounge... big sofas... deep pile carpets... spacious modern kitchen. 'Phil,' Les said, as he introduced me to our visitor. 'This is Judith, Judith, meet Phil.' The Judith in question was Judith Holder, a well-respected and highly-placed person there with a lot of clout. Over the next hour and a few pots of tea every promise in the book was lavished upon me. Oh, if I would only be part of the Central TV line-up. I would, she said, be given virtually anything I wanted artistically. I'd be nurtured, given the golden treatment, taken to new realms of the business and looked after, considered a long-term artiste who would be guided by all the best people in television. Les and I said we'd be in touch after thinking things through, the meeting over. Judith left and Les and I didn't speak for a while, just stared at each other, pondering decisions that needed to be made.

I said earlier that I didn't know how television worked. Well, I didn't at the time of that meeting and, I admit, still don't to this day. For me, the ideal scenario would have been to keep my old *Cool It* team and have the making of the shows transferred to the BBC in London, but that was wishful thinking – fantasy, no less. In reality, there was never any response from London to that effect. Could that ever be? Did the powers-that-be at the BBC there think it wasn't appropriate to take something like *Cool It* from their colleagues in the Midlands and bring it to the capital? Or did they not even give it a thought? Had they got more important things on their minds than some relatively insignificant show from the Birmingham sticks? Is the whole thing like one big chess game? If I'm poached from the

Stand-up Chameleon

BBC by Central TV, could I then be poached back by the BBC to London? The truth will never be known and that period in my mind is now rendered to ifs and buts. Weighing up the equation: on one side I had the great team at Pebble Mill with all that we had built together and, on the other, promises from a woman I'd only just met.

Those promises, though, were pretty impressive. Namely that I would be given the sort of attention of which I was worthy and be provided with whatever it took to further my career, long-term. Was it to be 'Out of the frying pan and into the fire' or 'Nothing ventured nothing gained'? Les and I discussed this over what remained of the day, then separated. I went back north to agonise over the decision, as it was mine alone, Les wasn't persuasive one way or the other.

There was a twinkle in his eye and peculiar expression on his face the next time we met, as he awaited my thoughts. I expressed to Les that the sense of loyalty I felt towards Steve Weddle and the team at Pebble Mill was over-shadowed – in my mind, at least – by the constant indifference and apathy shown by the BBC in London. Getting anything out of them was an arduous procedure. This made the Central TV offer more attractive; if their promises were kept, then we could have greater control over my career direction.

'Let's go for it, Les,' I said, with a tremor of uncertainty. But there, I had said it. 'Good! I think you've made the right decision,' he replied, looking pleased as I recall. Mind you, that might have been his response had I said: 'Let's stick with Pebble Mill'. I'll never know.

Decision-making is always a pain in the arse. His artiste though had at least made one and Les would take the reins from there. Needless to say there would be dismay at Pebble Mill, but life moves on and, sadly, the place itself was only to function for another few years. The studio was closed in 2004 with the building converted for a new purpose. Today, BBC TV in the midlands has its headquarters at The Mailbox shopping complex in Birmingham city centre.

Pebble Mill, meanwhile, lives on only in the memories of we who were lucky enough to have worked there.

Fringe Benefits – Making it in Scotland

Scottish theatres are full of the ghosts of all the English comedians who died in them. Had I appeared at any, in a variety stage show say, I'm sure my own would be among them. Fortunately, I only ever did them after having had success with my national TV shows, so stood a better chance of survival. I can't say I've had a bad night in Scotland.

I performed at the King's Theatre, Edinburgh, several times and the city's three thousand-seater Opera House only once. My show there wasn't actually part of the Edinburgh Festival, but for some reason the booking was taken on what I think was that year's first night. I had a very good show and with my manager, Les, went to a few venues on our day off to see acts that were part of the Fringe. We saw the Italian playwright and satirist Dario Fo, the dearest act in town at six quid a ticket, who did the entire thing speaking two sentences in Italian and stepping back. His interpreter then stepped forward to repeat what Dario had just said in English. It too was a huge venue and packed. He was on for an hour and got one laugh, or rather his interpreter did.

We also saw Mullarkey and Myers – ie Neil Mullarkey and Mike Myers, the latter a complete unknown with the Austin Powers and Shrek years still ahead of him. I said to Les: 'He looks the part, belongs up there. There is something so special about him.' After the show, I was lucky enough to speak to them both and told Myers he'd go far.

Stand-up Chameleon

The next time I saw him it was on the big screen in the film comedy *Wayne's World*, in which he became a big star alongside Dana Carvey in 1992, Mullarkey working on its script. Their little Edinburgh show got plenty of laughs, unlike Dario Fo's where the audience had proved more interesting. Bored, my attention drifted to the seats around me in which his audience was pretending to be amused when they clearly hadn't the foggiest idea of what was going on. People would slyly look around to see if others were getting the joke – and nobody was. Yet they clapped when they thought they should, the greatest example of 'The Emperor's New Clothes' I'd seen, laying bare the pretentiousness.

I've played the big theatres in Aberdeen and Glasgow; in Inverness, Dundee, Perth and smaller towns too. Sightseeing has always been the main afternoon pastime. Due to its dominance on the Stirling skyline, the Wallace Monument was easy to find, but could I find the Gromit one? I could not, having to wait until 2021 when a bronze one to the pair was unveiled in Preston. I did, however, spot a peculiar carving at the bottom of the mound on which the stone monument stands. Its sculptor must have been on super strength lager while chiselling the thing out of the block, his version of Sir William looking more like that of Mel Gibson and Hollywood – well, almost. A poor attempt anyway. So here we had magnificent rendition of the defender of Scotland on the crest of the mound, and at its foot a Braveheart with an actor's head and a body totally out of proportion. Mutant Mel also smells. The faint trace of ammonia in the air made me smile, as I envisaged a line of male Jewish tourists waiting their turn to relieve themselves on the thing – 'That'll teach you to rewrite history, you anti-Semitic bastard.' He's not there anymore, I'm told, the man himself now more famous for seeing his work torn to pieces by film critics who claim he distorts historical truths. Fair play, he's promised to make up for it with his next film project, *The Eight Wives of Henry the Sixth*.

Yes, I've done gigs all around Bonnie Scotland and loved it, the country and its people are so welcoming. It took a long time, though, before I was persuaded to do the Edinburgh Festival, what with the Dario Fo experience and convincing myself it was no place for me.

In an attempt to raise my profile, Steve Hutt contacted Richard Brecker, head of a PR company called 'Up Front TV', and he proposed that I do a two-week stint at the 1998 event, figuring it would rekindle interest in Phil Cool. The venue, the Pleasance, was an old Presbyterian church that had become available following a cancellation. It was mine

Fringe Benefits

for hire if I made a quick decision. I said 'Yes' and it was arranged. Steve, Richard and I also took a trip to Los Angeles to do some comedy clubs there later that year, but that's another story.

Scottish television, on learning I was doing the Festival for the first time, got in touch and enquired as to whether I'd be interested in doing reviews of my own on several acts who were performing there. This, they said, would be from the perspective of an Ed Fest 'virgin', making it a little different from the norm. Their idea was that I would pick out a few acts from the Festival guidebook that sounded interesting to me and then go out with a film crew to watch and/or interview them. I'd then report back to the studio, show the footage to the audience and comment. It would be a good exposure for me and thereby bring more people to my own show when it began at the Pleasance.

All of which sounded fine, but deep down I instinctively knew that I'd make the world's worst interviewer. To keep everyone happy, I ignored that and said yes. I must choose four acts – any more and the piece would go on too long – and the lucky quartet were:

1) Rob Newman of The Mary Whitehouse Experience and then Newman and Baddiel fame who (supported by Sean Lock) had in 1993 become the first comedians to play and sell out London's 12,000-seat Wembley Arena. Rob had been working solo ever since.

2) A Canadian comedian whose name now sadly escapes me. She was doing a one-woman show. Not stand-up, more of a monologue.

3) A bizarre comic/magician performer from either the USA or Canada, name of Rudy Coby. He was 'very Jim Carrey' in style, although I wasn't too sure whether Jim Carrey wasn't 'very Rudy Coby' because so much 'thespionage' goes on in the comedy business.

4) Ken Kesey, author of *One Flew Over the Cuckoo's Nest*, the novel later adapted into the groundbreaking Hollywood film of that name starring Jack Nicholson and directed by Miloš Forman in 1975.

I was told that Kesey had been chosen by the US government to conduct experiments into the effects of LSD on the human mind, back in the 1960s. His own mind, that is, and those of his Beat Generation pals. A tribe of them set off across America in a custom-built coach, flowers in their hair, living madly. The culmination of which was the *Cuckoo's Nest* film and some TV documentaries charting their progress. Kesey also did stage performances of a counter-culture hippie variety among other such antics. I knew little about all that, but whatever it all entailed was shortly going to have to talk to him about it.

Stand-up Chameleon

Rob Newman did not disappoint, although you get a whole history lesson before he gets to the real funny bits. Still, his show was very interesting and entertaining, his Tony Blair immaculate and the other few impressions he did equally impressive. The quick interview I did with him the day after his show was just superficial and amounted to no more than a touch of mutual admiration.

The woman with the monologue was quite clever, but the only thing in her show that really impressed me was a simulation of a helicopter hovering overhead while she spoke loudly over the noise. She achieved this by drumming on her rib cage with the palms of her hands, very fast, close to the mic. It's very effective. Try it now and you'll agree. Along with her name, I can't remember what I actually asked her, but it might as well have been 'what's your favourite colour' for all I cared. It's a hard thing to fake, interest, and that certainly showed when our 'chat' went out on television.

Even with Rudy Coby, my questions were so dull and uninspired he could only answer with 'yes' or 'no' while giving me a look that went right through me that said: 'Can I go now, please? I'd much rather be somewhere else.' I'd seen his show before we talked, a very high energy performance full of tricks performed in quick succession, lots of leaping around, bangs and flashes going off and backstage accomplices not quite keeping out of sight, perhaps due to the venue being unsuitable. I wasn't full of praise for him later, though did point out qualities such as 'kids would like it as he has the look of a comic character, almost'. I also described him as 'cartoon-like' due to his plastic quiff hairstyle. He moved in a jerky animated way too. Think of Jim Carrey in *The Mask*. Was it really him, pulling all our legs?

A room in the Royal Hotel at the end of Princes Street had been converted into a temporary studio where all things on fringe subjects were discussed and aired, including my Ed Fest virgin opinions on these four acts. There I sat, in front of an invited TV audience, reporting on Rob Newman, the helicopter woman, Rudy Coby, and now Ken Kesey. A day earlier, when Kesey and I spoke, I'd been waiting ages for him to show himself from the dressing room of St Mary's Hall, another old church converted into a venue. It still had pews and I've played it myself several times since. Kesey's show was due to start at 7.30pm and I'd been given a message to wait in the main space with the camera crews until he was ready to talk. We'd been there since half-five and often seen him and his friends peek around the dressing room door, look at

Fringe Benefits

us, shake their heads, whisper something to one another and then go back in. 'What is this paranoid behaviour?' I wondered, looking at my watch for the tenth time. 'The result of a lifetime of hallucinatory drug taking?' He left it to the last few minutes before the audience came in before he and his fellow performers ambled over. I hadn't done any research on him, except for 'basic facts' I'd read on an A4 sheet. I felt he expected me to be clued up on his background when the cameras started to roll. Well, I wasn't. After making a real plonker of myself with a question that betrayed my ignorance of his life story, he gave me the gravest of looks and corrected me. Then, after another attempt at jump-starting a conversation, I got him to speak, which developed into a roll that I just let him get on with, nodding and interjecting with the word 'great' when I clearly didn't mean it. The studio audience picked up on this and groaned when they saw the footage. I repeat, interest is hard to fake; it makes you realise what a genius the likes of Parky and Terry Wogan really were. After Kesey had gone on for a minute or two we mercifully ran out of time, the camera crew packed up and went, and I stayed to watch the show. Lucky me.

I left before the break, not waiting for the second half. Next day in the Royal Hotel 'studio', relaying my experience of the four fringe acts, I cringed as we watched the footage on a big screen. The programme's host rounded up by asking what I thought about Kesey and his show so I told her the truth: 'I walked out before he was halfway through.'

'Why would you do that?' she said. 'Ken Kesey is such a revered artist and literary icon.'

'Well,' I said, 'he rambled on, took about five minutes rearranging the mics on stage, never spoke, which to me was an indication of someone who is so far up his own arse it would have taken a search party to go in and get them out. After saying his fellow artists were finally ready to do something, he read a dull extract from one of his books. No one genuinely laughed. No one was enthralled. No one was impressed. It was an audience pretending to appreciate it, so as not to lose face. He might as well have been talking in Swahili for what I or anyone else could grasp of it.' She stared at me open-mouthed. 'Then Kesey and his people joined in some song that sounded like a bunch of amateurs in a pub. And while all this was going on, some weird guy in the audience, who was dressed bizarrely, not unlike those on stage, kept standing up, waving his arms around and shouting gibberish at no one in particular, probably high on acid himself.'

Stand-up Chameleon

The studio audience and host were clearly now uncomfortable. I went on: 'Kesey made me wish it was all over and so, being impatient, I walked out.'

'And the nuisance guy on acid? What happened to him?'

'He walked out too!' I said. At which, the audience cracked up. I don't know if they believed me or not, but it was true. He had.

With my own show at the three hundred-seater Pleasance, the first night was full and the other thirteen came close to it. Meanwhile, in a hundred-seater black box studio upstairs, a young guy billed as 'a pint sized Les Dawson' was playing – Peter Kay. I popped in one night and caught his show. At last, some real talent. Young Peter got great reviews, leading to his Perrier runners-up prize and Royal Variety appearance.

My reviews were mixed. One guy said: 'It was worth the entrance fee just to see Phil Cool transform from Jack Nicholson to Bugs Bunny.' Another – most likely young – critic gave me a write-up that was the verbal equivalent of throwing acid in my face. Still, if you dish it out you've got to be able to take it and, believe me, I can and I do.

During my time at the Festival that year I watched other shows, as you do, and can't say I was overly impressed by any, pledging I wouldn't work there again. As it turned out, however, I would end up doing two more. So much for pledges!

The second time I did it came four years later, in 2002. I was there for an old mate, really, a promoter called Kevin Williams who I met filming a commercial in 1984. We met up for the first time in years and he asked what I was doing lately. I told him of various failed ventures like a TV pilot, *Ghost in the Machine*, which featured several characters I invented. I also reminded him of the little three-minute film I'd made years ago called *The Motorist* and hinted that I was of a mind to revive my song-writing ambitions and actually do some on stage. It would be awkward to mix serious songs with comedy, though, as the audience would always expect something funny to happen in the middle of a serious song, and therefore never take my serious songs seriously. To overcome this, I said, I would have to assume an alias, disguise myself.

Kevin seized on this. 'Why don't you do just that?'

'In what way, exactly?' I said.

And being his innovative self, Kevin replied: 'Be your own support act?' Brilliant. Why hadn't I thought of that? So, having already dreamed up the name JD Meredith for this fictitious singer everything seemed to fall into place as though it was meant to be. When I told Kev I was

Fringe Benefits

halfway through recording an EP of six songs on CD, he said: 'Get it finished on time and we can sell it at Edinburgh.'

Kevin had acquired a small venue on the Royal Mile. where he'd set up a big screen and projector to show *The Motorist* and other short videos I'd made over the years to keep the audience entertained while the changeovers took place. I'd be backstage taking off the JD Meredith country and western clobber, beard, long hair etc, and underneath I wore a 'new look' Phil Cool outfit of black hose leggings and the sort of stripey black and white long-sleeved T-shirt with which French mime artists are synonymous. Also, a pair of clunky black slip-on shoes. This costume, I figured, would look peculiar but in a good way and make slipping other garments on and off over throughout the show easier. I paid a tailor from Clitheroe to knock more stuff up... big black smock thing for the Jo Brand piece ... fancy pink jacket for my Eddie Izzard sketch ... and a tartan waistcoat that had a long dangly flap at the back for a Billy Connolly routine. Chunky shoes did for Brand and Connolly and I'd sparkly pink ones for Izzard. Everything was ready and in place. The JD Meredith CDs were delivered on time and so off we went.

Over its fortnight run, one quirky thing happened to make me smile. Right at the beginning of the show one night, a guy in the audience ran out of the room thinking he was at the wrong show upon hearing the announcement: 'Ladies and gentlemen, would you welcome on stage all the way from the USA... JD Meredith! Somebody on the door sent him back in. Among the other acts Kevin booked for the two weeks were: Elvis the Girl, a tribute act, and Dana Gillespie, a great blues singer who told me she'd slept with at least eight of the people I impersonated, naming two. I couldn't resist and said, in my best Sean Connery: 'Oh, well. In that case how about a trip down memory lane?' There was also a young – and bizarre – comedian called 'Silky' and Sylvester McCoy did a one-man play, *Hello Dali*, so I was among some unusual folk. Kevin put Sylvester up in the same digs as me, out towards Leith. I'd tell the audience I was staying in the same flat as Sylvester, the only Scot to play Doctor Who, which he was at the time. 'It's a strange experience, going into that place,' I'd say. 'From the outside it's tiny, but when you go through the door...'

Kevin asked if I'd do a guest spot on afternoon chat-type shows to plug my own and I agreed. Will I ever learn? One of several I did was with Greg Proops, the American comic who had risen to UK fame on Channel 4's *Whose Line Is It Anyway?* improv show. He had a few guests

Stand-up Chameleon

on before me. One was Omid Djalili, the Iranian-British comic, who went down great with the studio audience. After which, it was the turn of an American woman who had written a book about being sexually abused by her father. This serious traumatic subject introduced a heavy atmosphere to the room and, once Proops finished interviewing her, she stayed seated while I – waiting in the wings – was introduced to applause. Proops, a brilliant comedian, had a sarcastic dig re my 'having mastered an American accent' during one early impression. 'Almost as well as you have, Greg,' I replied. But as it all went on it became difficult for me to get a word in edgeways, being the laid-back bloke I am. Proops, on the other hand, was extrovert, very confident and cocky. The American theme went on and in an attempt to overpower his incessant interruptions and dominating manner, I manoeuvred into my Forrest Gump. Complete with vacant Hillbilly expression, I set off:

> **Gump:** I brung mi gal, Mary Lou, home to meet mi momma. I said: 'Momma, this here's Mary Lou, we's a-gonna get married and, guess what, momma (*here I put my arm around an imaginary person, as though showing pride in this Mary Lou gal beside me*) 'she's a virgin.' Momma said: 'You can't marry Mary Lou, Forrest, especially if she's a virgin.' I says: 'Why not, momma?' She says: 'Well, if she ain't good enough for her own family, then she ain't good enough for you...'

This got a massive laugh from the audience and Proops, but still sitting there, clutching her book, was the poor American woman, wondering how insensitive we all were, no doubt. Oblivious to the hurt this may have caused, I sat back as Proops rounded up the show, stood up and left. The penny only dropped hours after: 'What have I done?' Later that day Greg Proops relayed a message to Kevin to say he thought Phil Cool was very brave. Bravery? I don't think so. Stupidity borne out of fear, more like.

Billy Connolly swears a lot, which is something I've never done on stage. However, when impersonating him over the years I've often been tempted to let the expletives fly, to make it more realistic. On meeting David Baddiel during the making of a short film in 1999, I told him I'd never used the 'F'word on stage. 'Try it,' he said, 'and see what happens.' For a while afterwards I pondered changing my approach to Billy and writing them in, in a non-gratuitous way, to ridicule swearing itself.

Fringe Benefits

✳

In early 2002, I started up another comedy night, once a fortnight at a local venue with guests, to ease me back into performing after a heart scare I'd had in 2000. It didn't work too well, but I got a couple of new Jo Brand and sweary Billy Connolly routines of it. By the time it folded a few months later they were well honed and ready for Edinburgh that August. I already had a Connolly wig from old, but put together a more recent purple/pink tash and Van Dyke beard that looked the part.

My new routine with him was a strange mix of Connolly and *Dad's Army*. My Billy told the tale of how he'd been to Edinburgh on a trike during a world tour of Scotland and witnessed young comedians overusing the 'F' word. He takes a wee boy who's just finished his act to one side and gives him a stern lecture on how it loses its venom and power to shock the more it is used. 'I don't know who you get it from,' he says. 'Imagine,' Billy tells this imaginary comic, 'if everyone used the 'F'-word ... The Pope ... The Queen ... it would become meaningless and ineffective. What kind of world,' he rants, 'would we be living in? We wouldn't have all those quaint and innocent TV shows we all enjoy so much.' The Big Yin goes on: 'Take *Dad's Army*...' before saluting and adopting the persona of Clive Dunn's elderly Lance-Corporal Jones:

> **Jones:** All present and correct for duty, Mr Mainwaring, sir...
> **Mainwaring:** All present and correct for duty? But your dick's hanging out, Jones.
> **Jones:** That's because I've been wanking, Mr Mainwaring.
> **Mainwaring:** But you've been on guard duty, Jones. Don't you realise wanking on guard duty is an offence punishable by firing squad?
> **Jones:** No, that's falling asleep on guard duty, Mr Mainwaring. It's wanking that keeps me awake.
> **Mainwaring:** Very well. Now listen, men...
> **Private Pike:** (*interrupting*) Mr Mainwaring, sir...
> **Mainwaring:** Shut the fuck up, Pike (*pauses*). Where was I? Oh, yes. The War Office informs me that German paratroopers have landed on British soil. Anyone coming into contact with one must respect the Geneva Convention.

Jones: If I see a German paratrooper park his parachute and come towards me backwards, Mr Mainwaring, I'll stick me fuckin' bayonet up his arse.
Mainwaring: But that would be in breach of the Geneva Convention, Jones.
Jones: I don't give a fuck about the Geneva Convention. The Germans have bombed Liverpool, incinerated Coventry, blitzed London and keep sending doodlebugs over the English Channel. They've obliterated France and now they're attacking Russia.
Private Frazer: Oooooh! We're awl fuckin' doomed.
Mainwaring: Wilson! What do you make of all this?
Sergeant Wilson: Does it really matter what I think? After all, I'm not in charge, am I? You are.
Mainwaring: You facetious twat, Wilson.
Pike: Mr Mainwaring, what does *suffecious* mean?
Mainwaring: Shut the fuck up, Pike. Now listen men, between now and the end of the war, I want you all to get the fuck out of my sight. Oh... and Jones?
Jones: Yes, Mr Mainwaring?
Mainwaring: Put your dick away.
Billy Connolly snaps back into his own voice here, telling the young comic who is supposed to be listening to all this...
Connolly: See what I'm getting at, son? Riiiight! So, the moral of the story is – if you're gonna use the 'F'-word just fuck a little, don't fuck a lotto.
(*Connolly was then appearing in a TV ad for the National Lottery*)

The fortnight ran smoothly, and I enjoyed my alias JD Meredith doing 'his' four straight songs, with little breaks provided by videos on the big screen as I changed backstage. It was all quite fun. One night, Rory Bremner popped in, bless him. He once gave me a half-compliment in a newspaper. 'Phil Cool is brilliant,' he was reported as saying, 'visually.' Later, I returned that half-compliment during an interview of my own: 'Rory Bremner is the greatest impressionist radio has ever produced.'

All the acts Kevin booked went out on the town together and had a few beers here and there, including Elvis the Girl. Although she was a very attractive young woman, I wasn't sure about the sideburns. I did though like the way she said 'thank you very much'.

When the festival had been and gone, I bought myself a projector

Fringe Benefits

and big screen on a stand, taking the same show with four character additions on the road to smallish theatres. The first was Psychedelic Sid, which was an impression of my old mate really, but with a more elaborate script. I had all the props, wig, bandana, beard, tash, gob-iron and holder, fake joint etc. I like to think I 'did' him with affection, as a tribute. Even though the crowd didn't know the actual Sid, they still found this archetypal hippie funny. The second character came from the murkiest corners of my imagination: Isaac Hunt, Explorer. For him, I'd have tweeds on and stick a cushion up my front, to make me portly. Before I walked onstage in his clobber and a grey moustache, his name would come up on the big screen. Then I'd walk centre-stage, point at it, and bellow in my best Brian Blessed: 'Take a good look at that! Now you all know exactly what I am ... an explorer!' and waffle on about adventures in far-off climes and how I was taken captive by six foot tall naked Amazonian women. Character three was a Frenchman called Wigan Pierre – the stripey top helped with this one too and I wore a black beret. He was supposed to be a Wiganer who'd moved to France, spoke pidgin French, but kept sliding back into his native accent. Alas, I couldn't get the damn thing to work, so eventually scrapped it.

Character number four was Piapoint Sykes, a humble inventor. He was desperate to patent his ideas and make a fortune to provide for his fiancée, Daphne. During the sketch he explained what had inspired the patents he had pending. 'One dark night when driving home during a storm and drowsing at the wheel, I would have crashed my Model T Ford and plunged over a cliff had I not swerved to avoid a cat, whose eyes had been illuminated by my headlights,' he said. 'So, the very next day, I cried 'Eureka!' and developed – I suspect you may guess what it was – yes, an ingenious device – The Cats Eyes Stimulus Pad! It's a mat one sits on while driving when tired which delivers a fierce electric shock at ten-second intervals to keep the motorist awake.'

This sketch was called 'The Cool Night Air' and performed like a segment of a stage play. The script also made clear it was set in 1912. Piapoint was dressed in evening suit with a white silk scarf and walked out at the top of the sketch onto the stage, sat on a chair and didn't speak for ages. The lighting was dappled, as if moonlit through foliage, and background music played over sound effects of the babbling voices of party guests. All of which created an illusion of him having walked out of a party in full swing into the garden. Just as the audience were beginning to wonder where it was leading, Piapoint suddenly becomes

Stand-up Chameleon

alarmed on noticing the crowd out there in the dark, so speaks. 'Oh! I'm sorry,' he says. 'I didn't notice you there. Don't mind me. I've just left the revellers for a while, to sample the cool night air.' He goes on to explain, with a sob, that back at the party Daphne is being wooed by a rich fellow, Horatio Pringle, who is intent on stealing her away on a trip to New York to expand his empire (he's in cardboard). After a tale of woe, the cats eyes story, other patents pending and gags about inventions like the widget (a device to ease chaffing on plump ladies buttocks: 'Every shop in the land will one day sell them!'), he forges on with 'Forgive me. I must get back to win back Daphne's heart, before she leaves with that scoundrel Pringle in the morning.' And then, just before he steps into the wings, he turns back to the audience and says: 'He'll travel there in luxury too, the lucky blighter ... on the Titanic'.

This elaborate stand-up show went on for a year or two until I got tired of all the changing and the time it took to pack everything away and went back to a simple show. Still, the Edinburgh Festival had been the very thing that had set all those ideas in motion and at least for that I can't knock it. I swore again, though, that I wouldn't do it again.

Jump seven more years, to 2009, and there I am once more, driving up to do it again. Such is the influence of my old mate Kevin Williams. 'It's a great venue this time,' he said, 'and my swansong at the festival.'

Kev told me this latest place had won an award in 2008 for best new Edinburgh Festival venue. What he didn't say is it was so far out on the edge of the city it could've had a Berwick-on-Tweed postcode. I did eight nights as part of Kevin's line-up, which included a one-man adaptation of Oscar Wilde's *The Picture of Dorian Gray*. Dana Gillespie was there again and we had a swing band on the bill called The Jive Aces. Even so, the whole thing turned out to be a bit of a damp squib and finally put the mockers on my ever doing it again. Honest!

So what do I think of the Edinburgh Festival?

All tossers and no cabers.

Before I left Ed Fest for the last time I did, however, have a mystery solved for me. Over the years I've always been baffled as to why the annual Royal Edinburgh Military Tattoo is called that. A local, Tam, put me right. 'Ah, the Tattoo, yeah. See, Phil, it's called a 'Tattoo' because it would cost more to have it removed than what it cost to put it on in the first place.'

The Tale Continues...

The Central TV building was, as its name suggests, right in the centre of Birmingham. I'd been there before for *Stayback* and *Spitting Image*. Having signed to Central, Les and I were now beginning the process of determining what shape a new series of Phil Cool shows should take, so turned up at Judith Holder's office for a discussion.

Which writers should we engage? Which director? And so on.

Judith asked how we envisaged it and from that first question to the very last moment of the six shows to be transmitted it became a nine-month nightmare. Sure, there were odd times when we had a laugh, but generally speaking the series was fraught with angst, clashes of opinions, uncertainty and lack of vision, not just on the part of the 'new team', but from myself also.

In hindsight, the whole project was too ambitious and the die was cast when Les and I stated in the first meeting that we didn't wish to abandon stand-up, but keep it in. Yet we would like to add elements like sketches, with a sitcom woven in for good measure. Simplicity, always a key factor in all good comedy shows, never got a look-in. Thus we'd made a rod for our own backs, or rather mine.

An ITV show has commercial breaks, so a 'half-hour' show is

Stand-up Chameleon

actually two halves of twelve and a quarter minutes. Now, to cram stand-up, sketches and a sitcom involving other actors into such a slot is very unrealistic, but that was what we chose to do. Adapting to my new position of having wishes granted, I requested Geoff Posner as director as he was – and remains – the best in TV comedy. Geoff couldn't do it, though. He was working with Josie Lawrence on her Channel 4 sketch series *Josie*, and recommended John Kilby, director of *Not the 9 O'Clock News,* who agreed to take it on instead.

It transpired that John, against all odds and frustrations, in the end pulled the series through and made it presentable. He and I got along together fine. For the moment, though, Judith recommended a writer called Ian Davidson.

Ian was a nice enough guy from the 'old school' style of writing who Judith expected to bring stability. I wasn't too sure and wanted more 'off the wall' writers involved as soon as possible. Meanwhile Les, Ian and myself met and between us settled on the concept of breaking off from the stand-up. Ian said: 'Remember that Woody Allen film, where we got a glimpse inside his body? Bulldozers shifting vast amounts of cannelloni in his stomach? How we glimpsed him acting as one of his own sperms about to bail out of an aeroplane as a metaphor for an ejaculation? Well, we could do something along those lines, but instead just take the viewer inside Phil's head, where sketches [i.e. thoughts] would unfold.' The little sitcom would be going on in there too. 'Then we'd somehow transport the viewer out of Phil's head and back to stand-up.'

Les and I thought he had excelled himself with this because up to then he'd just presented us with a bog standard sketch about the problems of lighting a barbecue. This idea sounded very 'brave' indeed. The technology for such an elaborate concept didn't really exist then, though. In our naïveté, we chose to give it a go anyway.

When next we spoke of other writers, the ones who came to mind were the guys who wrote *Red Dwarf,* Doug Naylor and Rob Grant, as they were really different and fresh. We had to count them out, though, as they were not so surprisingly working on another project.

Jasper had engaged two other writers for his shows, the guys

The Tale Continues...

behind *Max Headroom*, a computer-generated character played by actor Matt Frewer, who was quite ground breaking in that he'd been said, in 1985, to be the first of his kind, in days well before what we now know as AI. So I spoke to Jasper about these guys, Paul Owen and David Hanson, and he said he's been impressed with their work and they may be just right for us, putting Les and I in touch with them. They came on board and, eager to get started, wrote a little sitcom pilot that was shot at Central's new studios in Nottingham.

We tested out several actors for that, Steve O'Donnell being one, who as it happened stayed on board for the series. The action revolved around a room with a counter in it, like you'd see in a hotel reception, people coming and going as 'thoughts'. It would start with Steve saying to camera 'Welcome to Phil Cool's brain, go in and find out what he's thinking today.' This pilot, which lasted about twelve minutes, was criticised by a few of us for its writing and look. Les gave Jasper a sneaky peek, 'sneaky' because he wasn't supposed to be involved, and one good point he made was that Steve had been given all the good lines. Les and I then made this point at a meeting, as if it was our own observation. Lots of other faults and weaknesses were discussed over the next day and we all concluded that we'd scrap the pilot and think some more about the way forward. So the necessaries were put in place for writing sessions to begin at Central's offices in Portland Place, London. I stayed at the Holiday Inn, near Edgware Road, as the outline of the series took shape.

I forget how long I was there, but it seemed like an eternity. Day in, day out, unproductive. Every day, in that room, we would meet. John Kilby, being the director, wasn't involved in the writing process but had to be there too. After all, he had to shoot what was written and advise if it was shoot-able. This whole story about the first Phil Cool series for Central is so complicated that it hurts my brain just writing about it. So imagine how difficult it was to actually make.

Our *Max Headroom* writers, Paul and David, were now with Les, Ian and me and the sessions became increasingly unbearable. Days and weeks flew by with nothing on paper. Poor John hung around for hours on end in another room, going crazy. Others involved in

Stand-up Chameleon

A 'Cool Head' was indeed needed – even our publicity shots were complicated...

the shows, like the set and stage designer, were constantly enquiring over the phone about how we wanted the set and stage to look so they could get on with designing and building it. Occasionally Judith would call in, stay a while, ask how we were progressing and, as we never had anything to show her, grew increasingly anxious; agitated that time was running out. Sometimes John Kilby would sit in on a writing session and upon hearing what we proposed erupt in fury, rightly pointing out it was impractical beyond budget and wouldn't work anyway. Paul and David got disillusioned and seemed to spend more time talking to their agent about other matters via their early mobile phones in a corner. These writing sessions finally turned into a monstrous literary nightmare and imploded. Paul and David had argued all along that the concept of stand-up, sitcom and thoughts/sketches all going on in my head was trying to write the unwritable. By this time, Ian Davidson was, I'm sure, wishing he'd never got involved in this whole sorry mess. I was now far less ambitious for how it should be structured and so waved the white flag.

The Tale Continues...

A compromise was finally reached in that the whole series, now to be called *Cool Head*, would chiefly be stand-up on a stage in the studio before two hundred people, with an *Alice in Wonderland* kind of trip down into my mind. But even without the sitcom it was still a pretty tall order.

At last we agreed on how the interior of the 'mind' would look. Breaking away from stand-up, we'd cut to a segmented revolving head of the kind you might see in a medical programme, John's idea. He said it would be quick and slick. We'd be on that for a split second then cut again and the viewer would 'arrive' in a pink-white tube (six foot in diameter, with blood vessels in it) to discover a character roaming around as a 'thought'. If it was Prince Charles, say, he'd come out with something like 'Oh, I am highly honoured to have you here. Welcome to the west wing of Phil Cool's brain, do go on in.' The camera would then leave him and race down the tube through a revolving door and we'd cut to a shot on the other side. The viewer would then be inside the main 'cortex', which was a big space with pulsating veined walls fused with purple and red flashing lights. Here, the action or 'thoughts' would be revealed to the viewer.

Dillie Keane, of cabaret trio Fascinating Aïda fame, a very funny woman, also got on board with *Cool Head*. She played my 'feminine side', putting on an adorable Lancashire accent. To make this clear to the viewer, Dillie was dressed the same as I was, in an orange shirt and black trousers. When 'discovered' by the viewer we were always engaged in some activity or other; we had to be doing something, didn't we now? It might be riding exercise bikes or perhaps repairing some broken down bit of memory tape. We would argue about the content and nature of the stand-up currently being performed 'out there.' Was it too aggressive? Too rude? Dillie, being 'feminine me', would argue against violence or vulgarity, while my masculine side, represented by a Jack Palance-type bloke I played, took the opposing view, arguing for as much smut and violence as the audience 'out there' could take.

Is this concept complicated enough for you yet, reader? Reader? You still there? If not, don't worry, it gets infinitely more so.

Stand-up Chameleon

One episode was written in which my brain was dying from alcohol abuse so the Rational Union of Brain Cells came out on strike, each played by extras in globule-like costumes, carrying placards and chanting stuff like: 'No more booze!', 'Alcohol destroys brain cells!' 'We've had enough drink!' and 'Enough is enough!'

Celebrity chef and restaurateur Keith Floyd was the villain of the piece. Running riot through the pink tunnels of the brain with bottles of wine under his arms, he, or rather I, doing my impression of him, would suddenly stop to face the camera and say: 'Follow me. I'm about to make some delicious pea soup.' We'd then cut back to the stand-up in the studio where I'd be doing a bit on the subject of booze. Meanwhile, back in the brain, the president of the Rational Union of Brain Cells – in the form of our old friend Arthur Scargill – would deliver a speech to his protesting members, Keith Floyd by now demonstrating his culinary skills.

'Pea soup? It's easy take a pea,' Keith says, before picking one up and putting it in a large aluminium pot, before adding the special ingredient. 'And now, in goes the wine, to enhance the flavour of the pea.' He picks up one of several bottles under each arm and pours, laughing manically until, having tasted the dish, deciding there's too much of a pea flavour. At which, he sticks his hand in, pulls out the pea, tastes it again and says 'perfect.' Then he downs the lot, spilling most of it down his front. We cut again and the viewer is back in the studio, where I'm still doing stand-up related to alcohol. Clever, eh? Yeah. So clever nobody could understand it. Needless to say, *Cool Head* didn't receive the same acclaim as *Cool It*.

Making it, I was so frustrated, sick and tired of the whole damn thing I couldn't wait for it to end. Looking back now – and watching it occasionally – my verdict is that it was too ambitious, too complex. Had there been advanced computer graphics in 1990, we might have been able to make it easier to understand.

What I'd originally asked for, when production began, was a studio crane on silent rubber wheels whose arm extended from a heavy metal chassis. Normally, the whole thing moves through the studio as the arm extends or retracts, on the end of which is an

The Tale Continues...

ordinary camera. I wanted a small one, with a fisheye lens, so the operator could extend the crane's arm down to my head as I delivered the last line of stand-up. This little camera would then go right up to my ear, say six inches away, and zoom into my earhole, at which the screen would almost go black. There would then be a cut and the viewer would find themselves slowly moving down the pink tunnels of the inner ear and perhaps encounter an ear-mite along the way, chomping on a piece of wax: 'Don't mind me ... just go on in.' The viewer would then be taken further down these pink tunnels via a set built from Styrofoam and gauze and know they were inside the mind of Phil Cool.

Today such a thing would be easy for TV production to create, not then. We had to make do with the 'cut' from stand-up to the revolving head model and then cut again to the pink brain tubes.

Still, at least we tried to be different, even if *Cool Head* seemed at the time a real turkey. However, with the passage of time, a once perceived turkey can be seen as a phoenix risen from the ashes, a cult classic, no less. Who knows?

The only correspondence we received from the public about *Cool Head* was a complaint about a song. And in fact it was the only song I didn't write in the series. Paul and David were its creators.

It went 'Schizophrenia – don't let doctors come between ya; I know yer problem cause I've been ya...'

A mother wrote in saying her son suffered from the condition and it was disgusting to make fun of people inflicted with it. Central put out a complex justification for it, in an attempt at an apology.

Wales

I have, over the years, found many a warm welcome in the valleys. The best gig I did in Wales, though, was in some out-of-the-way little spot whose name I can no longer recall. Was it that place with the very long and unpronounceable name? The town that rock 'n' roller Chuck Berry once stayed at, which inspired him to write 'Johnny B. Goode'? 'Gogh-gogh-jonee-gogogogh jonee-begoch.'

The venue was part of a Carrott and Cool UK 1992 tour of small theatres that we saw as a work-in-progress adventure, given we were both trying to forge new material. It was a civic building with a high stage and about 300 seats, crammed to the rafters. This was a General Election year, Neil Kinnock battling John Major, and someone told us it was the Labour leader's constituency, so must have been somewhere in Gwent. The locals didn't like him one bit, although would vote for him to keep the Tories out. Due to this – and given that this particular Wednesday night was election eve – I knew we were in for a great show as I'd just perfected a routine about the pair. While the Carrott and I waited to walk on stage, there seemed an extra-special buzz in the air.

As the stage lights went up and Jasper and I wandered on, the place exploded in a huge burst of energy. The Carrott, too, had some good election material, which got them rolling about and set the scene for me and my crazy piece on the subject. It was one of my most enjoyable pieces to perform. I did a real mean Kinnock impression and my Major wasn't bad either. So, when I put them together as rivals – Superman versus Lex Luthor, with Roy Hattersley as his bumbling sidekick 'Bibbsey Spittlechops' – we had what you might call the perfect storm for the perfect gig. The audience was so receptive and responsive that my confidence soared to new heights. The performance was flawless, quite likely the ultimate stand-up moment of my entire career.

> **Kinnock:** (*Luthor*) Bibbsey, we need a plan. Superman is gonna drill through the sidewalk and crash through that ceiling any minute now, dropping right into our underground lair.
> **Bibbsey:** (*spitting as he speaks*) Lex, I have the perfect plan to put Superman in his place.
> **Kinnock:** (*wiping his face with a hanky*) Oh, we're gonna drown him, are we?
> **Bibbsey:** No Lex, listen. What we need is green kryptonite.
> **Kinnock:** Oh, yeah? And where are we gonna get some green kryptonite tonight, Bibbsey? Woolworths? A car boot sale?
> **Bibbsey:** Give me a second, boss. (*Hattersley turns away to sneeze, while at the same time pulling something from a pocket, sneezes again, then turns around with a green lightbulb hanging from one nostril, swinging like a big snot bubble*) See, Lex?
> **Kinnock:** (*mimes giving Bibbsey a slap*) Less of the jokes, Bibbsey. This is serious. Any second now, Superman is gonna drop in ... too late. Here he comes. (*I whirl around to emulate a spinning Superman, slip my John Major specs on and do his theme tune – da da da da da etc – in the voice of John Major*)
> **Major:** (*Superman*) Da da da etc... (*stops spinning and holds a Superman-esque pose, arms folded in naff macho kind of way, and faces the audience, daft Major face at the ready*) Got you, you dirty rat! I'm going to put you where you belong ... behind bars.
> **Kinnock:** Don't make me laugh, Superman, don't make me...
> **Bibbsey:** (*spitting*) Yes, don't make us laugh, Superman. Don't make us lau...! (*slap*)
> **Kinnock:** (*having slapped Bibbsey*) Stop aping me, Bibbsey. No, Superman, you'll never take me alive. Do you know why? Because you're not the right man for the job.
> **Major:** Well, I've got the job, I like it, and I'm going to keep it.

Stand-up Chameleon

Les, my manager, took this photo during a gag I did with Britain's tallest man, Chris Greener, on the set of 'Cool Head'. You can still watch it on DVD – or if you can find a working video player in the loft!

※

Major had actually used that very line only a short while before on TV and it was repeated over and over again on the news. So the volume of laughter it generated almost took the roof off that little theatre, laughter that might still be echoing through the valleys to this day.

You must appreciate, though, that words on pages like these can never truly convey the power of a good comedy piece. You really do need to have been there at the time to appreciate it in all its glory.

The Tale Continues...

Shortly before the making of *Cool Head* was completed, Central TV and other independent television companies just happened to go through a process of being 'streamlined' in order to be 'more efficient'. Accountants were called in to advise on money-saving strategies; in layman's terms giving people the sack and running a tighter financial ship. All of this fostered a dark mood of despair, people not knowing whether they were in for the chop or not.

Interest in our series, from all quarters, seemed to disappear. One of the first signs all was not well came with the studio audiences for my stand-up; half the seats were empty. It was close to Christmas too, in itself suggesting a poorly thought-out plan. Believe me, its not very inspiring staring at empty seats during a performance. So much for Central taking care of me as an artist.

Some people jumped before they were pushed. Our producer, Judith Holder, was one. Her boss, Tony Wolfe, who'd popped in the studio occasionally to remind me of how much I was appreciated at Central TV, went too. I've never seen him since. *Cool Head* got a ten o'clock slot on Sunday nights and disappeared without a trace, never to be repeated or mentioned again.

Stand-up Chameleon

My attitude was 'Let *Cool Head* rest in peace'. It had been ahead of its time, but was my TV career over? It did cross my mind. Several cruel comments came after it was aired. One that comes to mind was from a woman in Clitheroe, who stopped me in the street. She didn't have the discretion to take me to one side, just blocked my path and unloaded her seething unholy opinions at a volume that could have been heard in Preston. 'What the hell are you playing at? I was a fan of your BBC shows, not anymore. That one you've just done was rubbish, couldn't follow it. It doesn't make sense. It's not funny and they've spoiled you, dressing you up in wigs and make-up and costume. I'll not be watching anymore of it.'

I tried to interject – 'hang on, it's only a TV show...' – but couldn't get a word in as she set off again. So, before the few passers-by who were slowing up curious as to what this tirade was about grew into a crowd, I sidestepped her and scarpered.

Various comments filtered through. One was from Lenny Henry, via a friend: 'Phil should never have left the BBC.'

Around the time of making *Cool Head*, I had finally succumbed and agreed to do a commercial for 'CentroCard'. This was something you could buy that allowed the holder to travel anywhere in the West Midlands, within a certain radius, by bus or train and thereby reduce traffic numbers. That could only be good in my book, so I said yes. The offer came via Judith Holder, whose husband worked for the outfit who'd conceived it. The video was shot by an Oldham-based firm called Catalyst Pictures Ltd, whose artistic director was a guy called Julian Kronfli. Julian and I got along great. I found him easy to work with and was at ease under his direction. The ad was made against a 'blue screen', allowing a background to be added later. The finished 'Busmaster' commercial had me standing wearily at a bus stop, waiting. Several buses go by without stopping and the draughts from them make me sway. This I achieved by employing my miming skills and actually swaying, getting maximum effect by taking the sway to the extreme. When this was speeded up, technically, it had a nice comic look to it. After the fourth bus passed without stopping, I mimed the body language of despair... drooping head, bent knees,

The Tale Continues...

a huge sigh and such when, out of thin air comes the CentroCard to the rescue. I grab hold of it and am whisked off through the town and country, riding by magic of the blue screen to anywhere I please. Giggling like a gremlin and looking so pleased with myself I end up doing a Rik Mayall face to camera as a voiceover gives all the details. My face then ends with a 'freeze frame'. The commercial won the Roses award for the best ad made outside of London.

Julian was keen to work with me again and said he'd had an idea for a TV show using the technique. Les organised a meeting where he, I, Julian and his business partner, Ed Duliba, could get together and discuss it. Julian described a concept he reckoned would be like no other. It was called 'The Motorist', a story with no spoken word in which all the characters would be different driving types, played by myself. There'd be the dimwit type, synonymous with the Morris Minor. The aggressive powerful car type (think BMW or Audi). The truckdriver type. The Hooray Henry open-top sports car type. The difference, though, lay in how they would all be suspended in their relative seating positions in mid-air. In other words, they'd have their vehicles stripped away by the wonders of the blue screen so we could see them in their nakedness, so to speak. I'd already seen what Julian had achieved with this method for CentroCard, which for its time had been impressive. So I was up for it 100 per cent. I thought, 'Yeah, bring on 'The Motorist', especially after Les persuaded Central TV to shell out the money for the development of a pilot. It was shot over a few weeks and the money ran out after we'd got three minutes' worth of material on screen. That was enough, though, to present the idea to the new people at the head of Central TV. 'They' didn't like what they 'saw', apparently. I'd be very surprised if they 'saw' anything. To this day, I don't even know who 'they' were/are, but whoever 'they' were 'they' didn't want to finance it. 'The Motorist' was therefore consigned to the ideas graveyard with a million others.

However, Les informed me that 'they' wanted to stick with Phil Cool at Central and wanted me to meet their new Head of Comedy, a chap called Paul Spencer. Les also told them I'd an idea for a drama/sitcom and would like a typist to knock out some screenplays I'd

Stand-up Chameleon

written. Could I go into the Central offices in Nottingham to dictate them to a typist over a few days? Maybe I could meet Paul too? Subsequently, I was invited over to do just that.

Duplicates International was the title of the sitcom I'd written, though the budget it needed was more in the drama league. I had for years wondered – still do – about why impressionists had never been written for in the form of a story, so aimed to do that myself. I'd driven alone to the Druidstone Hotel, a place I'd stayed at above St Brides Bay in Pembrokeshire National Park, on the west coast of Wales, while touring. It was there that I'd written the first episode, during a couple of days holed up in one of their peaceful Cliffside stone chalets. With this first one done and the concept of the whole series thought through, I came home and wrote another three, all in long hand, with brackets, arrows and countless corrections. Only I could understand the scribbled instructions here and there due to the terrible rushed handwriting. And, before long, I found myself at Central TV to get it all typed up so people could read the damn stuff.

Eileen, the typist, was great fun. We had many a laugh as I read the scripts in the voices of all the characters out loud and in about four weeks we'd got it done. *Duplicate International* is a lookalike agency of that name in London, run by an impressionist always on the brink of retirement but still running the agency with the help of a junior partner and other employees. This guy is nicknamed Bogey because he lives his life in the guise of Humphrey Bogart, his all-time hero. His junior partner is gorgeous Molly Blondell, a genius make-up artiste. Bogey has hundreds of lookalikes on his books ... five Jack Nicholsons ... nine Popes ... ten Marilyn Monroes ... several Robert Redfords ... six Elton Johns and so on. Occasionally he'd coach a lookalike to be more accurate; the more convincing they are the more he can charge hiring them out. He might tell 'Rolf Harris' that the voice should have more raspiness, then demonstrate this for the 'student' before him. In the first episode, we see a lot of this sort thing to establish the idea, before, out of the blue, agency secretary Miss Carson tells Bogey that Paul McCartney has been in touch and wants to meet him urgently. Soon after, Macca visits the premises

The Tale Continues...

and asks for help. The viewer never sees Paul straight on, only in fleeting distorted glimpses in reflections from rippled windows etc, or from the back, thus creating the illusion. I'd pre-record his 'voice' and the actor would mime it. 'What can I do for ya, Paul?' drawls Bogey as he offers him veggie juice. 'Well,' says Paul, 'I've been told by a reliable source that when I do my charity concert for the anti-fur people in Hyde Park next week, just before my encore I'm gonna get kidnapped and held to ransom.' 'So,' says Bogey, offering him a slice of veggie nut crumble cake, 'where do I come in?' 'I want you to do me,' says the former Beatle. 'Just for the encore like, you know, then get kidnapped in my place. I know you can do it. I once saw you take me off real good. Even I thought you were me.'

So a deal is struck and Bogey, with the help of Molly, pulls it off. Everybody's happy. Bogey's reputation travels in the celebrity world and the phone starts ringing again. I wrote another three – one with Sean Connery, one with Prince Charles, as he was then, the other with Bob Geldof, Bogey and Molly solving more problems. And it was then that I met Paul Spencer during a break one day at Central's soulless offices in a less attractive bit of Nottingham. He walked in, introduced himself, said he was dead keen to produce my new shows and admitted he was a fan. We'd have fun working together and should meet soon with Les to discuss the format of the next series and any other ideas I might have.

However, over future meetings it was decided that 'The Motorist' and *Duplicates International* would be put on the 'backburner', i.e. never see the light of day. Les said he didn't think *Duplicates* was written well enough, pointing out there was no subplot and the whole thing was too elaborate for the realistic budget. So I conceded, consigning the thing to the 'Room 101' in my mind. After all those weeks spent writing it, that was disappointing. It had amounted to nothing and left me disillusioned with the idea of writing scripts for concepts. I told myself 'stick to stand-up and songs'. However the outcome of the meetings, at least, was that a new series was definitely going to be made. Paul said it would be called *Phil Cool*, which must have took some thinking of. I requested that it be made in a theatre

Stand-up Chameleon

to give it a different look to my previous series. We were to keep the stand-up but do sketches in between, pausing cameras and stand-up for several minutes while big guys set the scene for the sketch with furniture, beds, equipment or whatever. Geordie comic Keith Donnelly would be on hand to keep the audience amused with his unique crazy humour while all this was going on. Then when all was in place the cameras would roll again, I'd re-do my last lines of stand-up, put on a garment, at the side of the stage, relevant to the sketch about to be performed and walk over to the set and other actors to perform it. That done, I'd do the reverse and go back to stand-up.

Paul chose two writers who worked together yet were different in style. One was outrageous and quirky, Stuart Silver, and the other slightly more traditional, Malcolm Williamson. In the sketches they wrote, I would be helped out by three actors: Sophie Thompson, Chris Everett and Jon Glover. We rehearsed all the sketches in a building somewhere in London over several weeks. By the time we were ready for shooting, though, it became apparent that I only had enough stand-up material for five. So five it was. The chosen theatre was the Belgrade, in Coventry, hired out for six days by Central TV. Les had the idea to link the shows with a local charity, I forget which, ensuring six enthusiastic audiences who wouldn't mind paying a decent ticket price as the money would go to this worthy hometown cause. It worked. We had six sell-outs and each audience was great, which helps immensely for TV shows.

I wouldn't mind betting that in the history of television no performer has ever done five half-hour stand-up shows over five consecutive nights with a sixth as a safety net to re-shoot mistakes from the previous five, but that's what happened. That week, I felt as if I hadn't had a minute's rest it was so intense and, by the end, was completely drained and glad it was over.

One inevitability in shows comprised of sketches and stand-up is that when they overrun, which every one of ours did, to justify the time, expense and effort that goes into them with actors, props and scenery etc, something's got to be cut. And it's the stand-up every time. Quite a lot of it ended up on the cutting room floor, lost for all

The Tale Continues...

time. Despite this, clever editing by the director, Alistair Clarke, left it still highly watchable. So, was *Phil Cool* a success? There were mixed reviews. At the time it was shown, I began to wonder what Central TV executives thought of it as it didn't have a constant slot in the schedules. Being aired at random times is always a bad sign. By this time, though, I was passed caring. I'd had a bellyful of TV.

There were some memorable moments and it was a nice and rewarding experience to work with actors Chris, Jon and particularly Sophie, little sister of Emma Thompson. In one sketch we were in bed together and I did the 'Elephant Man'. Before we were about to make love she slipped a paper bag over my head. Ah, how sweet.

All formats run their course and so did the *Phil Cool* shows. When Les gave me the news over the phone that Central didn't want to 'go' with more of the same and renew the contract, I had mixed feelings. There was, I admit, a flicker of the last dying embers of ego somewhere deep inside me. It was though extinguished by a sense of relief that the circus was over. I'm not saying I never wanted to do TV ever again. I just wanted a long rest from it.

※

When I look back over my telly appearances these days, they've been quite varied. My own series stand out in my mind as most significant obviously, but others have been memorable too.

Like *The Secret Policeman's Third Ball*, which was staged at the London Palladium and televised in 1987, six years after first running from 1979 to 1981 as *The Secret Policeman's Ball*, a series of benefit shows founded by John Cleese and Peter Luff that raised funds for Amnesty International, the human rights organisation. I performed my motorway routine in it, which worked fantastically well.

I also wrote a sketch to perform over the two nights we did there. On the first night, I had Richard Branson to perform it with me and the sketch would again be used years later in the *Cool It* special. You may recall that I performed it as Terry Wogan with the little weather man Ian McCaskill. When Richard Branson did it with me, though,

Stand-up Chameleon

on that big stage at the Palladium in front of a huge audience, he was so nervous and on the brink of hysterics I thought he might bust a blood vessel. As Wogan, I questioned him about crossing the Atlantic in his big pointed boat to promote the Virgin Empire. He went redder and redder, struggling to hold his composure, until his stifled laughter finally got the better of him. When his turn came to speak, I slapped my hand over his face to prevent him doing so, tears rolling down his cheeks. The audience went with it, in convulsions at poor Richard being silenced so 'Wogan' could soak up more limelight and wallow in his famous blarney. When the sketch was over, I made my exit through the stage curtain and fumbled my way in the dark heading for the wings before colliding with a gable end of a man in the blackness. 'You're doing well for yourself, Mr Cool,' he said. 'Oh, thanks,' I replied, not realising who I was speaking to. Only when he walked on stage seconds later did the penny drop. For the first – and so far last – time, I'd just met John Cleese.

The night after, I did my 'motorway' stand-up routine again, but this time did the Wogan sketch with Jonathan Ross. It didn't work. Unlike Branson, he wasn't nervous at all and so matter of fact and cool about what was required that the audience were unmoved.

A few years later, I did the Palladium again, this time for the Prince's Trust. A young Steve Coogan was one of many on the bill. Before the show, as always, the artists lined up to meet the royals, Prince Charles accompanied by his then wife, Princess Diana. I stood next to Carol Decker, the singer with T'Pau, and we had a laugh as we waited to be greeted by the Royal couple. When they finally arrived at the beginning of the line, they were escorted by the best James Bond ever, Sean Connery. It seemed to me as though they had 007 protecting them as they moved up, exchanging a word or two with each entertainer. I can't remember what either of them said to me, so it couldn't have amounted to much, probably a quick 'good luck' or similar. Sean didn't speak, just hovered silently a yard or two away. I was transfixed and couldn't stop looking at him, there, like Bond, ready to spring into action, licensed to kill. I was fantasising that he'd take Nigel Havers out, because he was hogging the royals

The Tale Continues...

like he was desperate for their prolonged attention. Connery then looked my way for a few seconds, rested his gaze on me, and his eyes were peering directly into mine. Before it could turn into a staring contest, the big man winked, looked away, and moved on.

The material in my set that night didn't work too well. At the last minute (always fatal) I decided, following Les's suggestion, to do an impression of the American comic Steve Wright, the act on directly before me. It fell flat and was a big mistake, embarrassing. However, I soon moved on into my space creature routine, but with Ronald Reagan transforming into the alien rather than Terry Wogan. My instructions to the technical people, after reassurance from them that all my requirements would be in place on the night, were, 'Don't forget to turn on the green light.' It was that which illuminated my face as I morphed into the creature. Also: 'Don't forget to turn on the harmoniser,' a special voice effect just before the creature speaks, simple enough for a chimp to take on board, but not these people. They missed the cue and only switched on the green light halfway through, when it was too late, and forgot the harmoniser altogether. When I complained afterwards they said, apologetically, that they would edit it into the programme before it was aired on television, so the viewers heard it. But by then the audience in the theatre hadn't and that had ruined my confidence because I couldn't hear it while performing. I don't know if it was this alone or that my performance in general wasn't up to scratch, but the outcome was that when the show was eventually transmitted my entire set had been edited out.

Surprisingly, though, at the end of the night in the Palladium Cinderella bar, where everyone gathered for drinks, several people I spoke to including Ben Elton and Dawn French said they'd spoken to the Prince and all he 'went on about' was Phil Cool. Eventually, our now King came over and spoke to me for a while, saying he was astonished by my space creature piece, and by how original the whole thing was. I just accepted his praise and said nothing but 'thanks', while thinking 'you should see me on a good night.'

After that final *Phil Cool* TV series in 1992, despite not being invited to do another, I appeared as a guest on numerous television

Stand-up Chameleon

shows, most of which I have long forgotten. Still, it kept me in the public eye for a couple of years and so the smaller theatres up and down the land remained full. The occasional big one, though, wasn't. Still I was doing what I enjoyed ... clowning around on stage and making people laugh with the crazy new ideas that challenged me to try them out ... so was happy. I realised that if I never got another television series of my own audiences would gradually get smaller but, for now, felt easy in that knowledge.

One nice thing that spiced up those post-series years was that Jasper decided he wanted to go on the road with the work-in-progress tour that led to our pre-election night in Wales, mentioned earlier, playing at smallish theatres and thrashing out new material for his TV and theatre shows. He asked if I was interested in joining him on a shared bill. This appealed immensely, as I would share the stage with a friend whose work I admired and after all these years working and travelling alone it would make a pleasant change. So I said: 'Let's do it.' This became the first of several *Carrott and Cool* tours and, after we'd finished it, not only had we worked out some decent new material but people were saying how they'd enjoyed our two different styles brought together. We'd alternate, fifteen minutes each for a two-hour show, interval in the middle. After doing the last quarter of an hour on stage he would call me back on to join him and we'd do a question and answer session. More often than not someone would ask: 'Can Phil do an impression of Jasper?' Carrott would then look at me and say: 'Don't you dare, Cool.' I would then oblige the questioner with a rendition of Carrott doing the first lines of his 'Mole' sketch. 'I got this mole, right? It's making a hell of a mess of my garden,' with my best Jasper face in my best Jasper voice. The audience would explode with delight, Jasper and I would do our bows and get off the stage sharpish.

Glowing reports, kind comments from friends and brilliant reviews prompted Jasper to consider taking the *Carrott and Cool* shows on a tour of the big theatres. When he put it to me, I was all for it. Between 1992 and 1996 we notched up around two hundred-plus shows together.

The Tale Continues...

During that time, Jasper had made the transition from sitting on a stool and talking into a line mic, as he'd done for years on TV and on stage, to using a small clip-on mic and doing animated material, thereby using the whole space. In my estimation he was a lot funnier for doing that, rather than just sitting there on that chrome stool he took everywhere with him. You see, legs can be funny.

Some time during the *Carrott and Cool* touring days several big changes came about. Jasper broke from his manager, John Starkey. Why? It was none of my business, so I kept quiet. It still isn't, so I'll continue to keep quiet. For me, too, it was a turbulent time because all was not well at home. Home being a house out in the countryside of Lancashire that my first wife, Julie, and I moved into in 1987.

We'd lived there for five-and-a-half years, after leaving Leyland with our two daughters. Julie and I had been together since 1975 but now, in 1992, our once happy marriage had gone cold. Any flame of attraction between the pair of us seemed to have died with no hope of re-ignition. Eventually, we split and went our separate ways, dividing our estate in half. She moved out with our girls after buying a nice house locally. I remained in the house we'd shared, alone. I kept working and took things one day at a time.

Months passed and I continued to do theatres with Jasper and on my own. John, still half of Starward with my manager Les, wasn't entirely out of the picture although he and Jasper were finished business-wise. Now, however, only Les took the bookings for *Carrott and Cool* and my solo dates. Steve Hutt, whom Les had delegated to tour manage and organise things, used to travel with me a lot and so I saw more of him. On one occasion we spoke, though, Les said he wanted me to do more TV and arranged for Celador – the production company Jasper was director of that would eventually be famous for producing the global phenomenon *Who Wants To Be A Millionaire* – to work with me in preparing and making a video of new stand-up material. Celador commissioned several prominent writers to submit scripts and so we ended up with piles of paper to plough through. Jasper offered to help choose the best of the bunch and I would then try them out while we were still touring.

Stand-up Chameleon

It must be said again that I am not enthusiastic when it comes to performing other people's stuff, so found it difficult. In the end, none of it was ever honed to perfection or used, just tried out on audiences over a few nights and then given up as a bad job. I remember one by a well known comedian about Billy Connolly rambling on about how he loved the simple things in life, like travelling on concorde, snorkelling in Bermuda and noticing how barnacles on the bottom of the yacht remind him of Beluga caviar, before repeatedly saying to the audience 'Y'know what I mean?' The sketch was designed to illustrate how Billy had fallen for all the trappings of wealth and fame and forgotten his roots, oblivious to the fact as he extolled the high life of a multi-millionaire. In other words, a real heavy piss-take. Jasper thought the routine very clever and wildly funny. 'I've tried it out around the dinner table among friends and they've been in stitches Phil, honest,' he reassured me. I thought it was too complex. 'It's working on different levels,' I was reassured. 'Too many levels,' I thought. Anyway, I gave it the benefit of the doubt and agreed to do it as best I could in wig, beard, 'Billy mannerisms', voice and so on. Yet each night the theatre audience seemed to perceive it as out of order for one comic to do an axe job on another. Especially one who is revered and loved by audiences worldwide. So after six goes at making it work and making a fool of myself I declined to continue.

The pile of scripts supplied to me cost Celador six grand. None were used. They were not pleased, but stuck with me and agreed to let me make a pilot show totally of my own stand-up. A great friend of mine who I'd met scriptwriting for the *Stayback* shows in 1982 now occasionally wrote brief quips and gags for presenters of some Celador shows. His name is Tony Nicholson and he was asked by Paul Smith, Celador's main man, if he wanted to be involved in a new Phil Cool project. Tony was up for it and so was his co-writing partner in comedy Sean Carson (Frank Carson's nephew).

They were commissioned to enhance and expand my material and got to work. Tony and Sean came to my house for several script meetings, then off we'd go on the road, do small theatres, see if the material flew. After it had bedded in and was proven to be funny in

The Tale Continues...

front of audiences, we chose what we thought were the best bits. A theatre was then booked to shoot the video, no doubt on the strength of cost and availability. It was in some obscure place in Norwich, a four- hundred seater. I'd done a theatre the night before in Burton-on-Trent and then driven, with Tony and Sean, to East Anglia through the night, a long and tiring journey. We arrived at the hotel in the early hours half-dead and having only stayed awake by playing memory games like spot the tune of the old TV programmes. We must have hummed every tune from *I Love Lucy* to *Highway Patrol*.

A long lie-in was the order of the next day before doing the shoot and come the evening I did two houses. The first I saw as a bit of a warm-up. The second had the best audience and performance and so was chosen for submission. The material was about schooldays and kids in general, before branching off into films and the movie business. There were plenty of impressions, movement and visual gags, but no music. I was pleased with the result but time moves on, tastes and perceptions change. I look at it nowadays and it's not as good as I once thought it to be.

Celador tried, after topping and tailing the video, to persuade the BBC to take it as a one-off, or the first of a proposed series. The BBC turned Celador down. That's where the whole TV adventure for Phil Cool seemed to come to an end. Les had no 'Plan B'. Neither did I.

Guest appearances on various shows followed, but the writing was on the wall. Still, I was happy with what I'd achieved and content just to go with the flow until the whole Phil Cool story wound down.

There is, after all, life beyond television.

Gone Fishing
– in Ireland

The first time I went to Ireland was in 1974 on a fishing holiday with two mates, Dennis Almond and Kevin Stringfellow. We borrowed a brand new car from another mate who was supposed to come with us, but when we went to pick him up he had such a bad hangover from the night before he just handed us the keys, said: 'See you when you get back,' and crawled off back to bed.

So, the three of us set off in this pristine blue Triumph 1500. Once on the Emerald Isle, we ended up doing more drinking of the old Guinness than fishing as the whole trip was unplanned; typical of lads in their early 20s. We certainly saw lots of scenery, though, as we drove around the place, forever following tips as to where best to fish. We'd got it into our heads – or rather I had – that fishing in Ireland was free and it wasn't. There were reservoirs and lochs you just couldn't fish without permission, as we would discover after driving fifty miles one day and then forty miles the next. Once, in Leinster, we passed a little river called the Inny and I said: 'Come on, let's just stop here and have a fish for God's sake.' So I parked up at the side of the road and we walked about 300 yards downstream with no bait in our tackle baskets and set up the tackle. I'd chosen a place where some small flat-leaved plants grew in the river, dug a worm out of the bank with my hands as my friends looked on, mounted it on my hook and cast just beyond

Gone Fishing – in Ireland

said plants. I was ledger fishing and waiting for a bite to register on my rod tip. After a few seconds the rod nodded and I was into a good-sized perch of about a pound weight. My two mates, who both copied my method, didn't get a bite and came to fish nearer me (where the fish were) but still didn't get any. So off they trotted again, further downstream. After my fifteenth or so perch, my rod nodded once more. As I lifted into a fish I expected to be another perch, a sea trout of about six pounds in weight leapt out of the water like a bar of gleaming silver, only to snap my line in two seconds flat.

We saw the insides of lots of pubs on our travels and overheard many conversations between locals. One was between two guys, one offering the other a favour. They both stood at the back of a pub that overlooked some forlorn building probably treasured in the past but now neglected and dilapidated. It stood in the bright sunshine as these two old Irishman discussed its fate. Both gesticulated and looked over towards the structure, finishing the conversation with one telling the other: 'And I promise it won't be costing you any-ting at all, it won't. The demolition I'll do for free, to be sure. I'll knock it down just for the love of de old place.'

Now the Irish are different from the English in that they don't carry the same psychological baggage, more simple and straightforward. I like their no-nonsense approach. They'll say what they think and you can take or leave it, like or lump it. Once, we dined in a restaurant where I said to the waiter: 'Excuse me, what's the soup of the day?'

'Da soup of da day, sir, is vegetable,' he replied, 'and the vegetable today is mushroom.'

I didn't want to cause any embarrassment so, just said: 'Okay, I'll have the mushroom soup.' Then, pointing at the menu I was holding, I ordered a main course. He left with my order and about half an hour later returned with my soup, which would have been fine had he not brought the main course at the same time and put them both on the table. When I pointed this out to him, he said something I will take with me to my grave. Pointing to the main course I said, sternly, as he was about to walk away: 'Hang on a minute. I'm not ready for this yet.'

At which, he turned, pointed at the plate and replied: 'Oh! Well when you are, there it is.' There's nothing you could say back is there?

We also stopped at a few peculiar guesthouses along the way and got the feeling we'd been transported back in time; the quaintness of the place felt good. The fishing though never really took off being totally

Stand-up Chameleon

unprepared and all, like the idiots we were. Just going on spec without a plan and trusting to luck was bound to be unproductive.

The day before we returned to England we did however fish Lough Sheelin. We were told – by the folk who ran the guesthouse at which we stayed one night – that we'd be able to fish it if we first asked the bailiff at the centre, which was there with regard to all matters boating and fishing etc. So off we went the following morning and were told by this official-looking guy that it was actually game fishing only (trout and salmon), but he'd overlook the fact we were coarse fishing and could go out on our hired boat if we promised not to fish for game fish. He added that should we catch any by accident we must put them carefully back in the water – except for pike.

'Catch any pike, lads, and be sure to chuck dem horrible tings on the bank alright, as they gobble up all da game fish would ya know and affect da profits so they do.' To this we agreed and off we went onto the massive lough in a rowing boat. Results? One trout on worm float fished. I caught it and it went in my bag. It was served up as part of breakfast the next morning. And so concluded the fishing trip. Driving homeward I never imagined that I'd be returning in another thirteen years to the land of my ancestors and be fishing not for fish but laughs.

※

Les Ward, Steve Hutt and I were greeted at the airport by an Irish promoter, Pat Dunn. We were taken to the centre of Dublin so I could talk to the waiting press at some big fancy hotel, which was not far from the venue I was about to play.

Pat had told us that U2 were in the building, but that didn't generate much excitement for us, as U2 were a fairly new band in 1987 and still on the ascent. Even so, when I saw the number of press people there I assumed it was for Bono and the boys (who we'd caught a fleeting glimpse of as they darted about the place), but no, these people were gathered for me. There must have been twenty or more. Rather than doing it conference style they all insisted on a 'one-to-one'.

Among them was a tall dark-haired young woman at the back of the queue. As I got through each interview I could see this gorgeous girl getting nearer and nearer. So the anticipation of finally speaking to her made the task along the way less tedious. When she finally sat

Gone Fishing – in Ireland

down, she was smoking. She hardly ever looked at me and seemed on edge (not Bono's friend), as though eager to get it over with. She asked the dumbest questions and it was glaringly apparent she'd never heard of Phil Cool and couldn't care less about him anyway. She'd obviously been sent by her editor and, obeying orders, had reluctantly gone along. I'm no good at remembering names but made an exception in her case. Lauren MacMillan. Not put off by her indifference, I offered her a complimentary ticket for my show, to be left on the door of this 'sold out' venue that same night. Did she turn up? What do you think? You've seen the cover photo on this book, haven't you?

With the press out of the way Les, Steve, Pat Dunn and me went over the road to check out the venue. To our horror it was practically derelict. What was worse was the discovery that it was actually an old cinema and still in use as one. Due to that, anyone sitting in the first ten rows of the balcony couldn't see a person on stage if that person moved forward slightly from the screen at the back. I would have to perform right up against the screen, wander so much as a yard forward and I would disappear. I tried it out while the others sat up there and shouted: 'That's your limit, right there.' I'd practically have to touch the screen with my back throughout, to remind me not to walk forward and vanish from the sight of around two hundred people.

The crew at this place also provided me with fond memories. Les and Pat went back to the hotel to check us in while Steve and I instructed the crew that for my show the big white screen would have to be covered with black cloth. We then wandered backstage to see if there was anywhere to get changed and prepare. It was very dark, no lights worked, so we stumbled over rubble, bricks, shards of glass and all manner of crap like broken tubular chairs with dirty canvas backs, planks of wood with nails in, the lot. There was a glimmer of light somewhere towards the rear of this black hole and cautiously making my way forward I banged into a three-legged table covered in shite, my ankle then going over on a half a house brick. At last we stood at the foot of a cast iron spiral staircase that we'd been told led up to a dressing room, a dirty skylight window somewhere above providing just enough photons to illuminate our ascent.

When we went inside, this 'dressing room' was in keeping with the rest of this dysfunctional erection. Stifling cries of disappointment that turned into mutant laughter, Steve and I surveyed what should be an artist's sanctum. Smashed mirror ... cracked washbasin ... any hot water?

Stand-up Chameleon

Diversification: In 1994, I did a fishing video — in English, not Gaelic

Forget water. For there to be water, first there has to be taps! We made our way back to the stage via the obstacle course we came by.

On arriving back we found the crew had covered the white screen with huge black cloths. 'Is dat alright for yas, now?' said one, proudly trying to smooth a huge ripple out of the great length of black linen.

'Yeah, it's perfect,' said Steve, 'but you'll have to take it down again'.

'What on eart would we be needin to do dat fer be jabus?' the guy halfway up the ladder replied.

'Well ... you're screening a film later this afternoon aren't you?'

'Oh, feck! So we are,' groaned the stagehand. 'We forgot all about dat. Just give us another while and we'll have it down again to be sure'.

'Do remember to put it back after the film's finished,' added Steve.

'Don't be worryin yourself, we'll have it back in no time,' said the guy. 'And if ders anything else you be wantin, don't be afraid to ask'.

'Well there is one thing you can do for us,' Steve began to explain. 'Would you kindly clear a path with a brush from the bottom of the spiral staircase all the way to where Phil will be walking out on stage, then get a roll of tape and make arrows with it and stick them on the

Gone Fishing – in Ireland

floor? Make sure they're all pointing the way along the path so he can follow them and find his way in the gloom to the audience.'

'To be sure, dat's a marvellous idea, so it is. I've got a fine roll of tape right here. I'll do it in plenty of time for da show alright.'

On hearing this, Steve and I checked out the sound system and my mic and everything was fine, so we left.

On our return, just before the audience came in, I made my way to the spiral staircase, banging into obstacles all the way. I dropped my stage clothes as my ankle went over on a brick. No sign of any arrows in reverse, so it was going to be the same coming back out. 'The bastards forgot,' I said to myself out loud. Five minutes before the show was supposed to start, I'd somehow made my way back and was now waiting to go on, the audience humming like a high-voltage generator. With seconds to go I heard some Irish voice in the crowd shout 'Come on out, Philip. Don't be shy now'. The audience cracked up at this and I walked on.

The show went brilliantly. Even though I felt like I was escaping from Colditz, followed by spotlights with my back up against the screen all the way through it. Thankfully they had put the cloth back up but what of the arrows? Afterwards, we quizzed the guy who said he'd stick arrows of tape down. 'You forgot to do it, didn't you' we said.

'Oh no,' he replied. 'I got a roll of tape alright and made lots of lovely big arrows out of it and stuck 'em all on da floor leading to the stage, just like you said. I did for sure alright. Don't believe me go and look.'

'Show us', we demanded and all went backstage.

'There,' he said, pointing to the floor. 'That's one of de arrows.'

We still couldn't see it, so got down on our hands and knees in the dimness, faces inches away from the deck, and there it was – an arrow shaped out of tape. Black tape!

The other gig I did on that trip was Connolly Hall in Cork.

It wasn't full and was a largely uneventful night, though all went well. As we said farewell to Pat Dunn, who'd kept us well entertained with the old blarney, he handed Les an envelope. Les opened it. It was empty. 'Oh, did I not put the cheque in it now? Well, would ye know, deez tings do happen alright. I've got it right here in my pocket, so I have.'

Les took the cheque and we soon departed from the hotel and headed for home.

I've been to Ireland loads of time since, southern and northern, alone and with Jasper. I did a road trip once with my Bev too, in 1993,

Stand-up Chameleon

which was not good. We'd chosen the first week in August national holiday week and the quaint little roads were congested with traffic. The weather was bad and we both had colds and spent a lot of the time in bed, sharing a bottle of rum.

Once I went over with John Brown, my sound engineer, to do some gigs in the north at festival time. We were out walking in a town one day and came upon an art shop with Waterford Crystal in the window. We stopped to look and John said how he loved Waterford Crystal, thought it was beautiful, and said: 'Let's go in and have a closer look at it.' Reluctantly, I agreed, and in we went to discover the place was stuffed with original paintings by local artists and others from around the world. After an hour or three we came out of the place. John? He never bought a thing. Me? On impulse I bought about two thousand quids' worth of paintings to fill up my wall space at home. Thanks John.

Ireland is a magical place and over the years, whether marvelling at the Giant's Causeway or wandering through the enchanted grounds of Blarney Castle, I've developed a fondness for all things Irish. Though when Bev and I were there we both passed on kissing the Blarney Stone, as we didn't wish either to leave, or pick up, a dose of herpes.

I've sensed too a certain belonging towards the place, knowing that my ancestors on my father's side were from over on the west of the island; Galway I think. They then moved to a little headland on the east coast between Dublin and Dundalk and a town called Clogherhead, eventually crossing the Irish Sea and settling in a small Irish community that became part of my hometown Chorley, in Lancashire.

I will one day return to Ireland, I hope, and have a proper long relaxed look at the place, take the fishing rods again even.

I'll leave Ireland now with the last image I have of it, which was also the last gig I played there. It wasn't a Phil Cool or *Carrott and Cool* show. It was the *Jasper Carrott Show,* with special guest Phil Cool. My name was printed on the poster in the smallest possible print. I couldn't do theatres there any more as I was by then not a big enough draw.

The theatre in question was the Gaiety in Dublin. We were staying at some hotel nearby belonging to Bono & Co. where it cost around £3.75 for a bottle of Lucozade in about 2005. What it would cost now boggles the mind. Its capacity was around 1,000 and the front of house people said it would be packed I knew the audience were going to be fantastic, Jasper's audiences always were, especially Irish ones. He'd asked if I wouldn't mind alternating with fifteen minutes each as we

Gone Fishing – in Ireland

did of old. This surprised me, as I was expecting just to do a short first half of the show on my own before he did a long second-half, as you might expect when billed as special guest. So, I said 'yes, why not,' eager to get more time in front of this full house.

We walked on to raptures of applause and screams of delight and had a marvellous time throughout. The highlight of my part was when I did what I call my 'Irish piece', which contains among many other things a mention of Gerry Adams and Sinn Fein, which you might think very unsafe to do under the circumstances. Here we were, two Englishmen before a Southern Irish crowd.

Jasper and Steve looked out at me from the wings and, to their horror, this lunatic Phil Cool, out there on stage, had started the first line of the gag. Both Steve and Jasper told me later they'd had their head in their hands at the prospect of me blowing the entire show for the sake of one gag. 'And then there's the bearded one,' I continued, no props needed, 'who strikes terror into the hearts of men.'

Nervous laughter from the crowd, Jasper in the wings groaning, he knows the piece and what's coming next.

Gerry Adams thunders on: 'The Sinn Fein executive has disbanded and formed a sixties revival band with me as lead singer... (*more nervous laughter*). Listen out for Gerry and the Peacemakers (*the audience erupts in an almighty explosion of laughter, I pause, waiting for it to subside, then deliver the cruncher*) with You'll Never Walk ...Again!'

Off went the roof of the Gaiety, much to Jasper's relief.

Back at 'Hotel U2' that night, we analysed that particular piece over a pint of Guinness or two and concluded that Irish audiences take to you even more if you dare to be brave.

The Tale Continues...

By now I was remarried, to a lovely woman named Bev. We met through Les Ward, she was a friend of a friend of his, and I'd spoken to her briefly backstage. Occasionally, gigging in the Manchester-Oldham-Rochdale area, where Bev lived, Les would take up an invite to visit her at home for a few drinks and a laugh with mates. I too would call in, have one beer, unwind, and then go home.

Six months or so after my divorce, Bev asked Les if I would do a charity event for a local hospital's 'Silver Heart' appeal at the Gracie Fields Theatre, in Rochdale. Bev's brother-in-law was a manager there. I agreed to do the show for nothing and it was a big success. The place was full, made good money, and so everybody was happy. Bev and I started dating after that and hit it off. She has a great sense of humour and captivates everyone telling a tale, including myself. Especially about her amazing experiences working for the NHS.

In 1994, Bev gave birth to our son Joseph and we married in July 1995. At the time of writing, Joe is in his late-20s and well on his way to being a success in the music industry. As he's very interested and talented, I've told him: 'Forget any inclinations of being a comic and just concentrate on being a serious singer/songwriter.' For,

The Tale Continues...

behold, if the comedy genie gets out of the bottle it will surely destroy any credibility you have as a musician. The two are like oil and water. Hopefully, Joe will fulfil the dream I once had.

In the end, Les Ward acted as my manager from 1984 until 1995. When the TV interest in Phil Cool dried up I told him one day, while on tour with Jasper, that I thought that we should go our separate ways and stay friends because our artist management relationship had run its course. My career didn't seem to be going too well. It felt directionless and I thought some new management that was more in the loop – and could network on my behalf in the capital among showbiz agents and managers – might do the trick. Les was very unhappy and adamant he was doing all that could be done. I was equally adamant that we should split up. Even If I didn't get myself on anyone else's books, I would at least have a sense of freedom and make some kind of fresh start unrepresented. Scaling things down and I would still be happier than in the present situation. I pointed out to Les that we'd been together for ten years and I'd be prepared to give him six more months. He argued that if we were to split he'd need twelve and in that time I must work as much as I could so he could 'go out' with as much money as possible. I thought this made sense for the both of us, so agreed. Twelve months it was.

Shortly after this agreement, my tour manager, Steve Hutt, urged me (in front of Les) to let him take over and give him two years and he'd get my career 'back on track'. He was always good at insisting, I didn't think he could for one minute, but I conceded. Sure enough, after two years I was still doing the same old gigs. By then, though, any fire of ambition had gone out and I'd had a change of heart about trying to rebuild my profile and enduring all the hassle that goes with it. I became content with our ever decreasing workload and my diminishing celebrity status.

And, hey! There was one big bonus. I could walk down the street again without being mobbed. Hallelujah! Alas, Steve Hutt's two years became ten, during which time innumerable unsuitable offers came in. Still, the business has a way of its own and a few did appeal, so in that decade I did play all kinds of obscure yet interesting gigs.

Stand-up Chameleon

Like the one at the Laugh Factory, a comedy club on Sunset Boulevard, Los Angeles, that I did for no fee just the experience. Yes, you guessed it, Steve's idea. We travelled over there with a producer and publicist called Richard Brecker who had several contacts in the USA. He got us into the audience of the top two TV talk shows and then a backstage studio pass to meet both Jay Leno and a guy named Howie Mandel, whose own talk show was also syndicated but lasted one year, unlike Jay's *The Tonight Show* that went from 1992 to 2009. Nothing came of either meeting. The Phil Cool video we left behind would most likely have been used to wedge the door open I'd think.

I 'warmed-up' for my five nights at the Laugh Factory with a spot at the Ice House in Pasadena, Jim Carrey's old haunt that had also played host to such legends as Bob Newhart, George Carlin, Robin Williams, David Letterman and Leno in its time. I also gigged at the Comedy Store in La Jolla, the original one, and was soon itching to get at the Laugh Factory audience. I had of late grown curious as to whether my humour would work in the States and it did, to a certain extent. The Bill Clinton/space creature routine certainly impressed some of the other comics. One remarked in an LA drawl to someone on the other end of his cell phone: 'Hey, man! You gotta see this Phil Cool guy; he's even weirder than I am!'

A few months later, I was in London doing a Jongleurs comedy club recording for ITV's *Live At Jongleurs* that went out in 1997 and did the same set, introduced by Rick Wakeman. It went down great and a few American comics were on that bill too. One congratulated me on it. I told him I'd done it fairly recently in Los Angeles, but hadn't had any offers. 'Yeah,' he said. 'The audience out there are too parochial, everything just revolves around the LA scene. If you'd done the same set in New York, where everyone's a lot sharper, it would have been a different story. Keep tryin' fella.'

The trip out there *had* been amazing and only cost me twenty-two thousand quid! So any New York aspirations were short-lived and I just got back into my UK touring groove.

I also amazed myself by agreeing to a gig in the remote expanse of the North Sea on the Brent Charlie oil platform that with Alpha,

The Tale Continues...

Bravo and Delta was one of the four biggest at the time. For that, I did a warm-up gig in Shetland, at a theatre in Lerwick. Steve and I then flew out from Sumburgh with the workers by helicopter. Before climbing aboard, we underwent safety and emergency drills in case we went down in the drink. I performed twice, first to the day shift at 8.00pm, then the night shift at 8.00am. Needless to say, 8.00pm went best. Morning and shows just don't mix. Two memorable gags:

1. Recounting the flight out, the helicopter pilot nervously saying over the tannoy: 'Sumburgh! We have a problem!'

2. When the only woman on board with five hundred men, a brave lady called Nova, came up on stage to hold the raffle ticket bucket so I could pick out winners at the end, I said, as Sean Connery: 'Here's Nova, isn't she something special? I've heard she's called Super Nova, because she's one great bang.' Boy, was she a hard case! Didn't even flinch!

I also played in the south- and mid-Atlantic islands, the Falklands and Ascension. My folk singer pals Keith Donnelly and Gilly Derby supported me. They'd done the trip several times previously and had to travel in a Hercules transport aircraft, using a bucket for a toilet. I went on a proper commercial airliner with all the trimmings, hired by the RAF, and we worked the first night in Stanley Town Hall. The second was on top of Mount Kent, then Bryon Heights, Mount Alice and three nights in the big gym at Mount Pleasant. Except for the gig at Stanley, the audiences were all military personnel and, as you can imagine, gagging for a bit of entertainment, so very responsive.

While there, I even managed to fish for sea trout on the mouths of the rivers estuaries. I only caught one fish, though, a two-and-a-half pound brown trout. On another day my sound engineer John Brown and I took a trip out on the Atlantic in a small boat with our St Helenian skipper. We went about a mile offshore and John landed a sixty-five pound tuna! I'd have congratulated him but was busy at the time with my head over the side returning my breakfast of

Stand-up Chameleon

kippers to the ocean. The sea down there is very very cold, even more reason for Keith to dive in several times.

Heading back north with two shows to do on Ascension Island, the captain of the plane invited me into the cockpit, where I sat in the pilot seat and was served a meal that I ate from my lap. I was gazing at thunderstorms on the radar panel that were way out ahead of us in the distance for a while until, looking around, realising I was on my own. The plane was on autopilot. As we rode above the clouds illuminated by the moon, and with the dark Atlantic waters far below, I felt a surreal sense of wonder that was surpassed by a feeling of 'Am I dreaming?' Or 'Am I the star of a new *Twilight Zone* series?'

On his return, the captain handed me the mic and I made an announcement to the passengers as Rolf Harris. 'This is Bomber Harris at the controls. We are just about to arrive over Dresden...' The two Ascension nights were incredible, the first of them all RAF. Keith and Gilly got a standing ovation. 'Jeez,' I thought. 'I'm never gonna follow that.' But I did, and got a standing ovation myself, one of the very few I've had in my career. It made me wonder if everyone got them here. Maybe that's why it's called Ascension Island.

※

I could go on forever about the weird and wonderful adventures my career has given me over the years, but this book is too long as it is. So, to cut a long story even longer, I'll just add that I spent a good deal of my own money on pilot shows of various bird-brained ideas.

One was a children's story I called *Stories From The Face* where I would tell a tale (shades of *Jackanory*) and do all the characters. The story was set in Ireland and shot in Manchester and featured a giant – the builder of the famous causeway in County Antrim. I portrayed him like Ian Paisley, the loud loyalist politician and Protestant leader. Other characters included a little Leprechaun; a space traveller called Sbgnew; and a snail. The backgrounds were lit with gobo projectors to give the effect of forest or clifftop scenes, all enhanced by a lovely musical score. Kronfli Duliba Productions made it and it looked and

The Tale Continues...

On Ascension Island showing off captain John Brown's 65lb Yellowfin Tuna

sounded great, but the story and script were over-complicated. It was too wordy and needed to be delivered at a pace that left the viewers straining to follow. Another six grand down the bog!

Another one I dreamed up involved an arms dealer with a broad Lancashire accent, based on a 'take off' of my next door neighbour, who sold everything from rocket launchers to plutonium and used a shelving business as a 'front'. It also had a creepy head of children's TV called Maurice Krudd. He liked spaghetti hoops and fish fingers and had the mental apparatus of a five-year-old. My favourite was a character named Angus MacIntosh, host of a series called *Holiday Britain*, who would talk to camera in the great outdoors, endorsing and enthusiastically praising the merits of holidaying in Britain as opposed to travelling abroad. As he walked and picnicked in beauty spots or sat in the beer garden of English pubs with a pint and meal, it rained, rained and then rained some more, never stopping. Angus, though, just kept on smiling and talking as he got wetter and wetter. By the end of the piece he was soaked to the skin. For this to work I had to hire the local fire brigade to create the rain. Very expensive

Stand-up Chameleon

pilot that was. All the crew needed paying too and had to be found accommodation in local hotels and so on. Steve Hutt assured me (he was always good at assuring) that our pilot had landed on the desks of comedy TV producers, but they'd said it wasn't good enough. So that became another waste of time, effort and this time twenty-one thousand quid. What was I thinking of, for God's sake? I swore I'd never venture on another homemade pilot and told Steve to keep his suggestions to himself from now on.

Towards the end of the Steve Hutt era I no longer had any urge to get back on television – not even a slight one. I did though appear on *The Des O'Connor Show* several times because '*Des*' was easy to do. That, though, also resulted in sweet nothing elsewhere. As I left the set of the last show I did, its producer said: 'Thanks for a brilliant bit of TV. Goodbye.'

Eventually (shame on me), I succumbed to doing a 'proper' TV commercial for Müller yogurt, mainly as an obligation I felt toward Julian Kronfli, who made it in conjunction with another ad firm. He dearly wanted me to do it, so I agreed, feeling that I owed him one for financial favours they'd given me while making *Stories From The Face* etc. Thus my heart got the better of my head. It was for Müller Crunch Corner and Naomi Campbell and Joanna Lumley had done their ads before me, which made me think their choice of actors was getting prettier and prettier. Hugh Laurie did the voiceover, while I wandered on screen like a mischievous little devil with a desire to taste these nuts in the corner of the carton and super smooth yogurt in the main tub. I had no script, just did plenty of facial expressions to illustrate the contrast between the smooth and the crunchy.

At some point in the middle of the Steve Hutt years, 1996-2007, I was crazy enough to let him persuade me to go on a long trip that started with him, me and Keith Donnelly flying to Capetown, South Africa, to perform at a theatre there. Then, after a few days relaxing, we would hop on a cruise liner and sail the Indian Ocean.

Sounds good, eh? And a simple enough job? Well no, not simple. In fact, insane! I am feeling seasick just thinking about it.

But here it comes anyway...

Death on the Ocean Wave

It began with Pam Ayres, whose husband was Steve's business partner in Hutt Russell Productions, with an office at Dudley and Pam's home.

Steve and I were there to drop something off before he, me and Keith Donnelly were due to head for Cape Town after having returned to Steve's place to pack. Pam wasn't at home but she was on the phone to Dudley, talking about some cruise liner work she had been booked for, but for which she'd been forced to pull out at the last minute for some reason. On hearing this, Steve suggested I replace her. After giving it a bit of thought, I agreed, not knowing what I was letting myself in for. As we were halfway out of the door, Dudley paused the rest of his conversation with his wife and shouted: 'Bye, Steve. Bye, Phil. Oh... Pam says: "Phil, will you give my regards to the knitting circle?"'

This should have been a clue and was, in a way, but the little shiver it sent down my spine I shrugged off. Even now 'knitting circle' and 'old' somehow equate with each other and 'old' and I don't mix, sense of humour wise. Perhaps, deep down, I thought there would only be a few oldies; I mean how big *is* a knitting circle? I was going to find out.

The one theatre show we had to do in Cape Town went well and once it was out of the way (we took a trip to the Cape of Good Hope and had a day out up Table Mountain too) we were ready to set sail for and on the Indian Ocean. Amazingly though, shortly before we left,

Stand-up Chameleon

we had a brief encounter with Eamonn Holmes, who just happened to be in South Africa presenting a live show from one of its lovely beaches. We chatted to him on air and sneaked in a wave to the folks back home. Soon, however, the time came for Steve, Keith and myself to leave the quayside and climb aboard what turned out to be a colossal-sized cruise ship. It seemed endlessly long and so high it made you feel as if you were going to collapse backwards looking up at it.

The three of us went up the gangplank, after showing our papers, and stepped aboard this floating city. The ship's entertainment officer didn't look like a happy soul as he greeted us and said he would send someone to escort us to our individual cabins. We caught a glimpse of the captain welcoming everyone aboard as we waited for our escort. Captain Campbell he was called, if I remember correctly.

I was fascinated by how tiny he was. I mean *really* tiny and yet in charge of this gargantuan, state of the art liner. He could have stretched out his arms and legs and would've only spanned one of its portholes. What fascinated me more, though, was his uncanny resemblance to Sir John Mills, who, as we all know, starred in many a wartime sea adventure, *In Which We Serve, We Dive At Dawn* and *Above Us The Waves* among them. So this sort of made up for his lack of size and rebalanced my doubts. I couldn't take my eyes off him and wondered if he might one day make a film with Hayley Mills called *Honey, I've Shrunk Your Dad*.

At this point, Keith broke my train of thought and, in his Geordie twang, said: 'Look at the state of what's comin' aboard, like.' He was referring to all the people being helped aboard in wheelchairs and on zimmer frames by people who were ancient themselves. They kept on coming too, in their droves, with an average age of ninety-something. 'You're not gonna be able to entertain these lot, like,' Keith said, 'not unless you do impressions of Douglas Fairbanks Sr, Bela Lu-bloomingosi and Rudolph Valen-flippin-tino.' He was right. I could tell there and then that I'd got a shipful of people who wouldn't understand a word I said, or any references or impressions in my repertoire. No, these were folks from another age, another dimension even, whom I figured had all come on this voyage for the same thing – a free burial at sea.

Eventually, we set sail and, after eighteen miles out to sea, swung north east, heading for the straits between Africa and Madagascar. It was then we got word that we were to turn around and go back. A passenger had died. I had visions of Captain Campbell putting his little foot down on the ship's accelerator while struggling with the giant

Death on the Ocean Wave

steering wheel at the same time. Whatever he did, it got us back to Cape Town before you could say 'I'm not feeling too good myself.'

The corpse was removed from the ship and we were soon back on course, full steam ahead, trying to make up for lost time. Once we were out on the Indian Ocean, the entertainment officer briefed me on what to expect, enquiring as to the kind of material I had to offer on the two show nights I was contracted for, both of them Thursdays. I went through a list of stuff, explaining: 'Well, I open up with my *Star Trek* routine, which ends up with my space creature... then I do a Rolf Harris thing... etc, etc.' And the more I went on the more he shook his head and moaned in despair. 'They won't show any interest in that,' he said. 'They only want something they don't have to think about, but just look at. Something easy on the eye, like pretty young scantily-clad dancers with ostrich feathers, glitter, and an occasional good clean easy to understand joke, like what we provide before you go on.'

Briefing over, Steve said, 'It'll either work or it won't' and we left it at that. But as the first show day approached my stomach was in knots. Steve and I asked the entertainments officer if we could go do a sound check in the theatre with my small clip on radio mic, make friends with the room. He said: 'Follow me. It's a beautiful place, you'll love it, seven hundred seats.' It was indeed a gorgeous theatre with a wide gap between the stage and front row that must have been an orchestra pit, although seldom used, I should think. It also transpired that when they put on their little camp show, before the main act, they always used recorded music. Steve and I, after trying to get my mic to work, began to wish we had our own sound engineer, as our efforts to get the damn thing to work were hopeless. It just howled with feedback caused, perhaps, by the fact that we were surrounded everywhere by the ship's metal structure. No amount of adjustment made it behave and we had in the end to settle for the ship's mic.

So there I was, having to revert back to a mic on a stand, which I'd not done for years. This would compromise my movements and timing, so affect the quality of a show only a short time away. I felt decidedly nervous, imagining all those ancient critters staring at me from a dark auditorium in bewilderment as I waffled about *Star Trek* in a language that might as well have been Vulcan. I tried to convince myself that this was a temporary lapse of confidence and just pre-show nerves. These seven hundred old dears would just be fine on the night.

Meanwhile, news broke that someone else had died and as we were

Stand-up Chameleon

so far out to sea, and unable to turn around again, a helicopter was on its way to pick up the body and take it to the mainland. Sure enough, the chopper arrived and then off it went with this poor departed soul.

My thoughts, however, were selfish, pondering the prospect of an ever decreasing audience: 'If we get them down to just three, I might not have to play.' On the eve of the show Keith and I, both meant to be writing new stand-up material, somehow acquired writers' block which, when you think about it, is a bit like constipation in that you can sit for hours on end just staring at a blank piece of paper.

So, bored and down with cabin fever, we decided to visit the ship's 'Charlie Chaplin' cinema. An action-packed Bruce Willis blockbuster was showing and, while we were watching it, it dawned on me that the film had been specially edited and overdubbed, so as not to have the slightest chance of offending anyone. Any swear words in my own show would go down like a cup of cold puke. The overdub that stands out as I look back was when Bruce's lips moved with the line 'You son of a bitch.' It was replaced by a voice that said: 'You son of a female dog.'

'God,' I thought. 'If these people can't handle 'bitch' I'm in trouble, because I've got several bastards, five bloodys and a piss.'

The rest of the time before the show was just spent walking around the decks dreaming up what the letters P&O might stand for. The answer, I now know, is Peninsular and Oriental, but among those that came to mind were Pathetic Organisation and Passengers Overboard.

News soon spread among P&O workers that another person had died, then another, and then another, until the morgue was full. When that happens they store them in the banana hold. 'You can always tell when someone else has gone,' went the whispers on the soft tropical breeze, 'because a glut of bananas suddenly appear on deck.' From then on, whenever I saw a bunch, I'd stand by them in a two-minute silence. Eventually, they ceased to appear, which also unnerved me. 'Oh dear,' I thought. 'The banana hold must be full. What are they going to do with them now, then? Use them for fuel?' Walking the decks, I would regularly look up to check if the funnel smoke had changed colour. It never did so there were obviously still plenty of people left which, unfortunately for me, meant the show must go on.

'Good evening, ladies and gentlemen. Would you welcome on stage, Phil Cool,' said Steve, from a mic in the wings. Following which, I walked out to enthusiastic applause that quickly died off to silence. It's so long ago now that I can't recall exactly what material I used in my set, but

Death on the Ocean Wave

'How do you mean, you've never heard of Star Trek? Wake up at the back!'

I do remember feeling ill at ease after the opening lines. Completely blanked by ninety-five per cent of what was a full house, I got a few laughs early on from the remaining five per cent (presumably only in their eighties) which, as the show progressed disappeared altogether, probably from the embarrassment at finding themselves laughing alone.

My *Star Trek* routine was an absolute killer in normal circumstances, but here? Zilch. I began to wonder, as I went through it on automatic pilot, how could *Star Trek*, a programme that had been on TV for forty years and shown in every country on Earth, not be related to in any way by these people? In between bits and stories that usually brought applause and laughter of the type that fades yet still leaves an air of expectancy, in a kind of rumble as people adjust themselves in their seat, clearing their throats in readiness for the next thing, here there was only silence. Except for peculiar off putting sounds coming through it, like an unnerving clicking noise that I later worked out could only have been seven hundred boiled sweets rattling around seven hundred sets of dentures. Also, I heard what may well have been the sound of walking sticks falling over around the auditorium.

Stand-up Chameleon

By the time I was a quarter way through I was praying for a laugh, *any* laugh. Halfway through, I was praying for an iceberg. Which, when you think about it, is a bit futile crossing the Equator. I figured my cue to wrap the show up early was when several people asked their carers to wheel them out. 'Good evening, thanks for coming to the show,' I said and disappeared behind the side curtain, staying hidden there.

The crowd then vacated the theatre in thirty minutes flat, rumbling as they went in low tones of disapproval.

'I told you so,' said the entertainment officer, seconds later, waiting in the wings and shaking his head. 'It's a specialised field, getting through to these people. They are the oldest ones we ever have and come out here every year to escape the cruel British winters. You've got to know exactly which buttons to press to win them over.' With that, he said I need not go on stage next Thursday as it would be a waste of time. I agreed wholeheartedly and admitted defeat.

The name of the game for the rest of the cruise was to stay out of sight as much as possible. When I ventured out occasionally and walked into a room, say, there'd be a silence. Then, when the chatter resumed, I'd hear snatches of phrases like, 'What is this "Star Trek" thing he was going on about?' Occasionally, I'd open a door and be face-to-face with an unflinching cold gaze that said 'I haven't paid £6000 and travelled all this way to listen to that bloody rubbish.' I avoided drawing attention to myself and would often look at the floor when passing people, any eye contact excruciatingly embarrassing. In the gents once, while using the urinal, I heard the commotion of several antiquated geezers making their way in. So as not to get into a confrontation, I slipped into a big cubicle and locked the door. When they'd all settled at the urinals, not thinking clearly and still in a state of trauma, I unlocked the door as quietly as I could and tried to make a discreet exit, pulling an orange cord as I went, thereby setting off the disabled alarm. It sounded like a submarine about to dive. The old sods clocked me as I limped out awkwardly, leaving this deafening din behind me.

One day, Keith and I wrote one page of script that didn't amount to much and gave it up as a bad job. With all this time on our hands too! To be honest, I was in no mood for writing. So instead we hung around doing nothing much, making casual observations and watching flying fish leap out of the deep blue sea and skim across the surface, as they do. Keith told me how, one day, he saw one ship's officer walk up to passengers at rest in their deckchairs and poke them with a stick

Death on the Ocean Wave

to see if they were breathing. One afternoon, we were approached by the entertainments officer, who we now knew as Paul. I think he had come to check I was still on board and hadn't topped myself in despair. Keith had mentioned that he was bored and wouldn't mind trying to entertain those passengers who ventured into the cabaret lounge, a big oval-shaped room that held about three hundred. Paul sucked in a jet of air through puckered lips, which created a whistling sound, and said: 'I'm not sure you'll do any better than Phil, after all these are some of the same people.'

'I'll give it me best shot, like,' said Keith, all optimistic in his infectious Geordie singsong way.

'Okay,' said Paul, 'but we can't pay you, of course...'

'Doesn't matter, man,' interrupted Keith. 'I just want something to do, like, y'know?'

'Fair enough,' said Paul. 'I'm willing to give you a chance; you can get up in there tomorrow night and we'll see how you do.' At which Paul left our company and went on his way, doing whatever it was he did.

I sat in the audience that night and watched the pre-show, ie the on-board entertainment that was indeed scantily-clad girls and boy dancers in tight trousers camping it up with song and dance, corny jokes and a sketch that involved Paul doing a 'drunk' routine, complete with included audience participation. I sat watching all this, but mainly the punters, who clapped in all the right places but that was it. No uproarious laughter. No signs of joy or pleasure, just a tired response. Eventually, Keith came on and probably had the worst reaction of his career. The expression on some of those ancient faces never moved. They just stared, never made a sound. Keith went into overdrive and pulled his best piece out of the bag, his impression of a slice of bacon. In it, he lies on his back on stage and makes a sizzling noise, twitching, to emulate the bacon slice spluttering in its own fat in the frying pan. Then, he suddenly flips his entire body over so he is laying face down. The audience must have thought he'd escaped from the ship's asylum and a few began to leave. I counted at least three people who were actually asleep, heard snoring in the silent vacuum Keith had left.

'Good night, like,' he said, softly, as he mercifully made his exit.

※

Stand-up Chameleon

My next show in this theatre would have been a few days away, had I been doing it, that is. When Thursday arrived I was assured by Paul that it was just going to be the on-board cabaret again because I was still out of favour big style. My name wasn't 'Cool', it was 'mud'.

Apparently, passengers were still talking about how dreadful I'd been so I continued to keep as low a profile as possible. I didn't walk around so much as creep. An old newspaper came in handy. It went up in front of my face every time a bunch of old cruisers came along, muttering my name. The ship docked at Réunion Island, east of Madagascar and about one hundred miles south of Mauritius, where Steve, Keith and I hired a car to explore the place for a few hours. It had a volcano, Piton de la Fournaise, that I now know is one of the most active in the world. We drove to the summit and had a look in the crater, thinking it was dormant. Apart from that, driver Steve almost mowed a stray dog down.

Another welcome break from the dark mood aboard came when we reached Mauritius, hired another car, and had a quick look around there too. We'd taken our trunks and towels and saw a gorgeous hotel with its own beach. Steve suggested we gatecrash it, so we went for a swim in the warm waters of a bay extending out to a headland. On returning to our towels by some sun loungers, we sat to dry off and were approached by a member of hotel staff. We thought for a second that we were going to be confronted over our absolute cheek at being there, but no. This lady, dressed so colourfully in what seemed like national dress, offered us refreshments of local fruits and juices. It was hard to contain our laughter.

Before long, Keith and I waved goodbye to Steve on the quayside. He would be staying on the island to take a week's holiday with his wife, who'd fly in shortly from Heathrow. Back aboard and out to sea, Keith and I were soon back to watching flying fish until, to break the monotony, I went for a haircut in the barbershop. Fortunately the staff hadn't seen the show. Had they done so, a razor might have slipped.

One night I was having a drink in one of the many bars when I got into conversation with one of the crew, a guy who said that I shouldn't have signed up for the winter cruise because it's always the same, British senior citizens getting away from the awful weather. 'You should come out in summer,' he enthused. 'It's mainly younger people, so your stuff would go down a storm and at night, out on deck, under the big tropical moon, there's orgies going on.'

I gleaned more interesting things. One of the crew told me that on

Death on the Ocean Wave

the last winter cruise there had almost been a mutiny instigated by a gang of old dears carrying placards and shouting and chanting slogans about 'staff disobedience'. Upon investigation, it turned out their big grudge was that the ship had run out of Horlicks and, in order to quell the uprising, the captain had a consignment flown in by chopper.

Another intriguing story surrounded a passenger who had taken advantage of a chance to go ashore, to one of the islands, for a few hours and died just before re-embarking. He was left on the quayside in his wheelchair, the gangplank was lifted and the ship got the hell out of there, which apparently saved the ship's company the arduous task of filling in all the necessary paperwork and shuffling bananas.

When Thursday arrived, Paul approached me and said: 'You may as well go back on again tonight. A week has gone by now and it's likely most passengers won't even remember you.' So that's what I did.

By the time we reached Singapore, our destination, I was the only person on board who died twice. I never did bump into the knitting circle, although, had I done so, I'd have kept my mouth shut so as not to tarnish Pam's image by association. Keith was scheduled to fly back to England from Singapore and Steve was scheduled to fly from Mauritius to Singapore to meet me. After a day, we then caught a flight to Hong Kong to do a show there.

On the last day aboard, I got diarrhoea, how's that for bad luck?

Keith? He felt fine.

Now we had two new additions to our silly P&O game: Perilous Organisms and Plagueship Oriana. The medical officer sold me a £2.50 pack of Imodium for fifty quid – which was nice of him. So, when I finally hooked up with Steve again, in Singapore, I was forever on the bog – any bog I could get to quick enough.

While in Hong Kong over the following days we spent most of our time looking for chemists. In the end, however, I decided against taking drugs, against the medical officer's orders, and chose to starve the bugs instead. This was difficult, Steve cheerfully gorging on chinese banquets while I looked on pitifully with a glass of water.

When, eventually, I got home I continued to be ill for a month. 'One day,' I told myself, 'I'll look back on all this and cry.'

So, what did I learn from this? Mainly, that I am no lover of the sea. I wouldn't care if I never set foot on it again.

The Tale Concludeth

Like I said earlier, things have a way of turning up in showbusiness and they certainly did for me. Throughout the Steve Hutt years I was never out of work and even kept going despite having had what seemed at the time to be a heart attack.

It happened in August 2000 and I was hospitalised for eight days, under observation. It transpired that it was more of a 'warning' than an attack, though, and the results of an angiogram – the process of creating a picture of the heart's inner workings and arteries by means of releasing a special dye into it – showed that mine were narrowed but didn't need urgent surgery. The pain, my specialist assured me, was most likely caused by a small and insignificant vein that had completely disintegrated, but was not in the least life threatening.

However, the tests had also revealed that narrowing, caused no doubt by all those long years of quaking with stage fright in the dressing rooms of merciless venues. Yeah! That's what had done me in, along with all the smoke that hung like smog over the audience and onto the stage precisely at the level of the artist's mouth.

My specialist assured me, though, that if I exercised regularly I would find that my heart would improve by itself. So this is what I

The Tale Concludeth...

did. I'd walk the hills, near home, with my new friend, a black and white springer spaniel pup Bev brought from a local dog sanctuary. Our son, Joe, wanted to call him Elvis, but I said: 'No way am I shouting Elvis when I want him to come back to me. People would think I'd totally flipped. I chose Dylan instead and both Bev and Joe agreed. The only time it had repercussions was when we were out one day and a woman with a black labrador descended, as we walked up and passed them. Dylan ran off uphill and her dog followed him, at which its owner shouted for it to come back.

'Bob!' she yelled.

'Dylan!' I hollered. And so it went on.

For a good few minutes, actually.

'Bob!'

'Dylan!'

'Bob!'

'Dylan!'

I realised straight away, of course, and was having a bit of fun with it, but this woman didn't spot the absurdity at all, remaining straight faced. Perhaps she had never heard of one of the greatest songwriters of all time and, eventually, they went their own way.

After ten years of walking those hills with my beloved Dylan, I sensed that my 'warm-up' angina had worsened. One day, out of the blue, I felt a slight chest pain when I wasn't even walking, a dull ache that was present while sitting still. I thought perhaps it could be a viral infection affecting the old ticker, but that I'd best report it on my next visit to the specialist, which was imminent anyway. During our appointment, upon my mentioning this 'new' twinge he peeled off the ECG electrodes from my torso and said: 'Well, it is ten years since your angiogram so it would be wise to have another one to see if your arteries have narrowed even more over that time.'

This latest look went ahead shortly after and the results revealed that they had indeed become slightly narrower. 'I'll put you in touch with a surgeon,' he said, in a matter of fact sort of way. 'Go and have a talk with him and I'm sure he'll put you at ease, so you may not be so uncomfortable with the idea of the operation.'

Stand-up Chameleon

I had, a decade before, expressed my dread of being opened up like a rack of lamb on a slab to have my innards tampered with, but the first thought in my mind as I came around from the anaesthetic was: 'It's over.' The second was: 'The pain is not as bad as it was after my third umbilical hernia op'. Boy, that had been painful.

I'd struggled with that since being twenty years old and developed it either by coughing my eyeballs out or throwing my guts up, who knows? An umbilical hernia: the wages of tobacco and alcohol over indulgence. Back then, I was told by my doctor in Chorley that if I didn't have it fixed pronto I'd have trouble with it in later life. He was right! Situated just slightly over the navel, it was just a small lump at first, but got worse over the years. If you put two fingers tips on it and shoved, it would pop back in. And then, before long, pop back out again. It was damn sore too. As the years rolled by, the more strenuous and animated my stage performances were, the more aggravated the hernia became.

In. Out. In. Out. I became a walking cuckoo clock – some might say with a bent pendulum, forever shoving the thing back in. It got bigger. It got painful. It got me down. I'd get relief from the wretched thing during performances and before the show by placing a Perrier water bottle top (sharp end out, flat end in) strategically over the lump, then fix a short flat piece of wood on top with gaffer tape. This had to go around my torso like a belt, after taking in a deep breath, to help hold my belly in and bear pressure onto the wood and bottle top on breathing out again. It became a ritual every night before each performance. Needless to say, eventually the idea of an operation to fix the problem became more attractive than the agony I was going through before every time I played a gig.

It still took until I was forty years old, however, to visit a local hospital, after a consultation with a private surgeon. And the bloke fixed it. To start with. I was okay for two years before the cuckoo reappeared. Not in exactly the same spot it must be said, half an inch from the old scar. Back to the surgeon I went. 'Oh, it's not my stitches that have broken through,' he explained. 'I always sink them deep into the surrounding flesh exactly for that reason.' So I went back

The Tale Concludeth...

into hospital and let this guy have another go. 'At last,' I said to myself as I lay in bed back home, recuperating on pain-killers. 'The job has been done properly.'

Two days into my convalescence, I was affording myself a little stretch to ease my weary immobile limbs when, to my horror – the cuckoo! I felt the bastard reappear somewhere else. Slightly down and to the left. I had a good long think about this, during which time two years went by, me having reverted back to bottle top and wood.

By then, though, I'd graduated from the gaffer tape to borrowing a weightlifter's belt to help me through performances and in the end thought: 'Ought I to give this private surgeon a third go? Or maybe get another surgeon? Should I get it done on the NHS? Or continue to suffer with this crazy ritual every night?'

Eventually, I chose to go back to the one who had done the job.

'Yes,' he said, in a rugged Scots accent, after prodding my navel region. 'They do that sometimes. It's gone in yet another place from last time; surprisingly as my stitches went even deeper than before.'

Dappled light danced across framed diplomas and family photos on the wall of his consultation room while, through the bay window of this fine Victorian house, fingers of sunshine and a gentle breeze infiltrated the branches and yellow leaves of a trembling beech tree near the park outside. Sitting back behind his broad oak desk, with no expression on his face, he looked me over through a ten-second silence. 'I can fix it once and for all now,' he eventually said. 'There's a new gauze product on the market. Pity it wasn't out years ago when you first came to me, but it's used successfully in operations such as this'. He paused again, tossing an admiring glance towards a picture of his yacht, harboured in Saint-Tropez. 'I'd open you up real wide this time and put a patch of this special gauze, as big as your hand, in. What happens is, the flesh grows though the gauze and when the whole thing has healed it's like having armour plating in there.'

Upon waking from this third private operation I was in pain and as the effects of the anaesthetic faded it advanced and intensified for the next day or so. Forever pleading for more diamorphine, I was a wreck. I'm no mardy arse, not by a long way, but I cried. When you

Stand-up Chameleon

contemplate a navel, it must have the highest concentration of nerve endings in the body. Well, mine had been sliced through vertically, the cut was six-and-a-half inches long, and now it was swollen and covered in prickly stitches.

It took a long time to subside did that intense agony, burning away in my solar plexus. What remains is a wide scar growing paler with every passing year. The cuckoo still hasn't shown its head. The gauze held, like the man said. If anyone ever asks when I have my midriff bare: 'What the hell is that?' I always romanticise a bit.

'Oh, a chainsaw accident,' I say, which is actually believable given the state of the damn thing. Or, pointing at it: 'Oh, this? Twelve foot thresher! Great Barrier Reef, 1988!'

The worst jibe back was: 'Caesarean difficult, was it, Phil?'

Since that final umbilical hernia operation I've likened private medical treatment to being mugged. When you come to think about it, it is much the same thing. You end up surrounded by people in masks, one of whom opens you up with a blade and takes loads of money off you. Nowadays, I have no navel, as such, just a slight indentation where it once was and the whole area is numb. I do have a photograph of it, though, and often take a nostalgic look at it.

✳

So, as I said, coming out of the quadruple heart bypass operation, on the NHS this time, I didn't feel anywhere near as bad. Which is not to say it wasn't painful. It was, but in a different sort of way.

After my recuperation in 'The Vic', Blackpool Victoria Hospital, I came home on the fifth day – my birthday. It was a bright, warm and lovely spring afternoon. Bev made me a nice healthy salad, as I sat outside soaking up the sun. Dylan was ready to take me on long walks again. This, though, would only be after three months, the recommended convalescence period, although I did do a gig in a small theatre in Lincolnshire after nine weeks at a much gentler pace.

The surgeon who did my operation was Mr Russell Milner. And he must have done a good job because I have felt no angina pains

The Tale Concludeth...

whatsoever since. All the staff at Blackpool were magnificent, so caring and professional. They and Mr Milner received my eternal thanks. Thanks also went to my wife, Bev, and lad Joe, for being so well-behaved and mature beyond his years. He is still well-behaved, as far as I am aware anyway, some ten years later.

What though has happened in the intervening period and how do I see things shaping up in future?

Well, I'm 76 as I complete this book and since recording it in my mid-sixties, now have an album to boast about, produced with ace guitarist and songwriter Ken Nicol. Our joint-CD, *Nicol & Cool*, has nine of my songs on it and four of Ken's. We toured Britain with folk band Fairport Convention to sell it and wowed a huge crowd at Cropredy Festival. So, I have at last, after a lifetime of dithering, been up on stage performing my own serious songs. It feels as though I've come full circle on that one.

I am still doing it too, in smaller venues mainly and sometimes in tandem with Joe, who is a professional musician in his own right – look him up at *www.joemartinmusic.com*. Described as a modern day troubadour, he is always playing somewhere, whether in the UK, Europe or even Nashville, Tennessee. We are very proud of him.

Once a songwriter always a songwriter, I suppose. These days I am a member of performing rights society too.

※

When my first attempt at writing this book was completed in Spring 2013, it was the same year I had planned to retire. At that point, I'd intended to do lots of fishing, a bit more writing of songs, gags, short stories, even a novel maybe, purely for pleasure. Dream on, Philip!

Life won't let you retire. It always has a surprise around the corner. And now here we are, over a decade on, and I'm still occasionally on stage, albeit mainly with music these days if you don't count the chat between songs, and continuing to feel nervous in green rooms!

Before I go, I would like to express my thanks to all those people who have helped to shape my career down the years, be it those who

Stand-up Chameleon

have given me encouragement as I've gone along, or those who have given me chance to prove myself when I have been written off as too different and obscure, perhaps with a flippant 'You might be good in yer own way, lad, but where are we gonna put ya?'

A number of people in these pages are no longer with us, sadly. It's the price you pay, I suppose, for a long and generally happy lifespan. I must mention Bob Johnson, though, a lifelong friend who was best man at my and Bev's wedding. Bob passed away on 7 May 2011, but I feel I should express gratitude for all the encouragement he gave me over the years. Les Ward left us too, in late 2013; Owen Hughes a year or so ago. And Steve Weddle, who died on 5 March 2020. He truly was the instigator of the whole Phil Cool success story.

Thanks too to my once agent, Pete Gill, who encouraged me to write this book in the first place, and an extra special thanks to Steve Hutt for all his many suggestions and persuasions, without which I wouldn't have remembered enough wild and crazy experiences to put in it. I must also say how much I appreciated the way in which my great sound engineer/tour manager Martin Mitchell took good care of me over my latter years of being out on the road.

Special mentions for Keith Donnelly, who supported me with his contributions and additional material on my stage and TV shows, and my son, Joe, for helping me out with all things digital.

Many thanks also to Tony Hannan, Phil Caplan and Ros Caplan from Scratching Shed, for taking on this project and making it a physical, tangible reality. Especially to Tony for his patience with me and editing skills; I would highly recommend them to any author. A thank you, too, to Peter Barton for putting me in touch with Tony and Phil and getting the ball rolling.

Thanks are also due to John Brown, for taking care of me on my early touring days, and the wonderful impressionists Jon Culshaw, John Thomson and Stephen Merchant for their kind words on the back of this book. Also, Bev Bevan for his brilliant forward.

Lastly, a big thank you to all my fans (Coolies) who turned up at theatres to watch me strut my stuff – and to anyone who helped me with just a kind word here and there along the way.

Encore

Throughout this memoir I've tried to be honest, so why change now? The truth is, although I've not lost my sense of humour, I'm not really into comedy anymore. You have to be in the mood for it, don't you, and having not done it for a while it's gone a bit dormant in me. Besides, you don't see many impressionists on TV nowadays. Why? Because they're all being treated for multiple personality disorder.

I do sometimes wonder, though, whether I'd have been so successful in getting my act on television today.

Back in the day, one reporter – I won't name her or her publication – made a comment, during an interview, that made me think. 'Seeing your show,' she said, 'I don't know if you're a brilliant impressionist or a brilliant hypnotist who made the audience *believe* the impressions were brilliant.'

'Hmm,' I thought. 'She could be on to something there...'

Some of my impressions... I look at them now and think they're not that good. It's the mentality behind them that gets the laughs, and the set-up as well, because I tried to weave them into stories.

There are practical things to consider too.

Firstly, when I started there were only four television channels to aim for and no internet. You might think it would be harder to be seen then than it is on the hundreds bombarding us now, but the pie was less divided. If you did break through, more people saw or heard you.

Stand-up Chameleon

So there is that element. And then there is luck. If and when your chance comes, you've got to be ready. If not, you'll blow it. You have to be like an athlete, constantly fit, on your game, so when opportunity knocks you are fully prepared to seize it.

Plus there is my style of humour, which – in terms of why you don't see clips or repeats of my shows today, even with streaming and loads of channels – isn't just about political correctness but how a lot of the cultural references I poked fun at have vanished into telly history.

If young people happened on one of my shows, I doubt they'd have a clue what I was on about sometimes. I might be riffing on the Bible, John Wayne as Jesus at the sermon on the mount or some such, and who would get those references nowadays? It would be a similar story when I spoofed 1980s adverts. That said, some things from those series would stand up today, which the BBC or ITV, if they had the inclination, could turn into a nostalgic special or two, leaving in all the stuff that hasn't dated and there's plenty of it.

But what if I was young comic doing the same sort of material now, just starting out? Well, that's a different story. If I had the guts to get up on stage as an electrician back then, I'm sure I would as a youngster in this day and age, probably doing impressions of the Kardashians or whoever. Working people – even entertainers – are products of their time, so why would I be different? Also, I clearly had the fight in me.

Making working class blokes laugh on building sites is one thing; dealing with all the banter there and dishing it out myself was decent preparation. Yet going from that to doing comedy on stage, for people who have paid to get in, is an entirely different proposition. Even as an electrician myself I struggled like mad in working men's clubs. Now and then audiences were astounded by my originality, but more often thought me the worst thing ever. One line did go well: 'The only thing I liked about being an electrician was watching the houses I wired burn down.'

Who knows, maybe I would have my own YouTube channel or, as my son Joe puts it, be pulling faces on TikTok. I would certainly have had the will-power, sense of ownership and creative drive to do it for myself. As hinted at earlier, being asked to perform material by someone else drives me up the wall; a sort of resentment builds inside me. I want to do my own stuff, material dreamt up by myself, otherwise what's the point? It's just my temperament, I suppose.

The comedians I tend to like most are comic actor types, people

Encore

able to create characters and worlds and inhabit them completely, like Paul Whitehouse, Harry Enfield and Ricky Gervais. Although, while understanding Ricky's brilliance, I do think his extreme sexual material can be like a race to the bottom.

Peter Kay? Well, he doesn't cover the range I went for, like talking about American presidents, obscure subjects, and what have you. He concentrates on funny things in life everyone can relate to. Domestic stuff; behaviour we all take for granted, pointing out how ridiculous we are, but with affection. And since I first saw his act in Edinburgh, he's developed a shorthand in delivery that is very effective. Where anyone else might say 'then she said this' or 'and then she walked into the room' ... using linking words ... he doesn't, just enacts it as an actor would, because he is an actor really, isn't he? And a very good one too.

Another thing Peter is apparently very good at is organising himself and his career, which I'm not. Terrible, in fact, especially when it comes to embracing internet technology, where I am still a Luddite really. That's why our Joe is looking after the promotion of this book!

Of the older comedians? Like I said earlier, my favourites were the story-telling greats like Connolly, Carrott, Harding, Tony Capstick, Malc Stent, Shep Woolley and Derek Brimstone. All these guys had a flare for music too, that's how they got started, singing, playing and joking in the folk venues.

When it comes to comedy actors, though, Steve Coogan is my favourite, who, as with Peter Kay, I first saw on the way up. The way his Alan Partridge has evolved from humble beginnings is genius and completely relatable in and out of showbusiness. Being ostracised and sent to Norwich was something I found hilarious; nobody else could have done it as well. Steve is very astute and inhabits the character he is playing absolutely. It's been a while since we last met, back in 1996 at Bill Wyman's Sticky Fingers restaurant in London.

Bill once called me his favourite comedian, probably because he and his band, the Rhythm Kings, used to crack up at my Jagger take-off while watching the *Cool It* series on their tour bus. He had asked Steve Coogan and myself to do a short set each at his forthcoming charity evening, hosted at Sticky Fingers. Musicians Paul Young and Tony Hadley finished off the evening's entertainment with a set of their own.

The first time I saw Steve was years earlier at the London Palladium Princes Trust event. By his own admission, he isn't very good at stand-up and had been mediocre that night, but his potential was obvious. I

Stand-up Chameleon

knew he was great. He was staying at the same hotel as my manager and me and, after the show, we were in the bar and he came up to share a few words. There was no sign then that he was destined for greatness. He's got to where he is now through sheer ingenuity, with his acting skills and long list of crazy characters, but Partridge is still the all-time champion.

I was also a big admirer of Caroline Aherne, before she died, in 2016. There was something about her, a wonderful comedic spirit. I never met her in person, although I nearly did, and once again that was at Sticky Fingers but this time in Manchester, on its opening night there. I had been meaning to meet her later on, after the meal had finished, but before I could a fight broke out between her husband, the musician Peter 'Hooky' Hook of Joy Division and New Order, and her television producer boyfriend. To Caroline's obvious distress they began to throw punches on the dancefloor, a row about a divorce settlement or something. Of course, the papers made a huge deal out of it, the tabloids really had it in for her at times, but even then she was able to make light out of it, on the surface at least. 'It was a heated debate that got out of hand,' was the quote attributed to her, making reference to her famous *The Mrs Merton Show*, no doubt.

When I was starting out, Caroline did a character on stage, a nun called Sister Mary Immaculate. It was mildly funny, I remember, but very enjoyable because of her naturalness, without doubt her best quality. And as her later appearances on *The Fast Show* and *The Royle Family* proved, she was also a wonderful actor.

Victoria Wood, who also died way too young in 2016, was different. As a live performer, she was really disciplined with material and a style of delivery that served her well in acting roles too, honed to perfection. Like Peter Kay, she dwelt on a mixture of domesticity ... coat hangers, wardrobes, bed quilts ... and everyday behaviour mixed up in a funny way. Is that a very northern thing? I'm not sure. It's certainly popular everywhere... a down-to-earth people kind of thing maybe.

Those aren't the only sorts of comedians I've liked and enjoyed down the years. Jeremy Hardy, for example, who died in 2019, was a very witty favourite of mine and so was lovely Norman Lovett, still with us last time I looked, who stayed at our house a few times. Norman's humour was very gentle and he even used the tale in the last chapter about our dog, Dylan, and his fellow runaway, Bob.

In fact, mentioning that now reminds me that something similar has

Encore

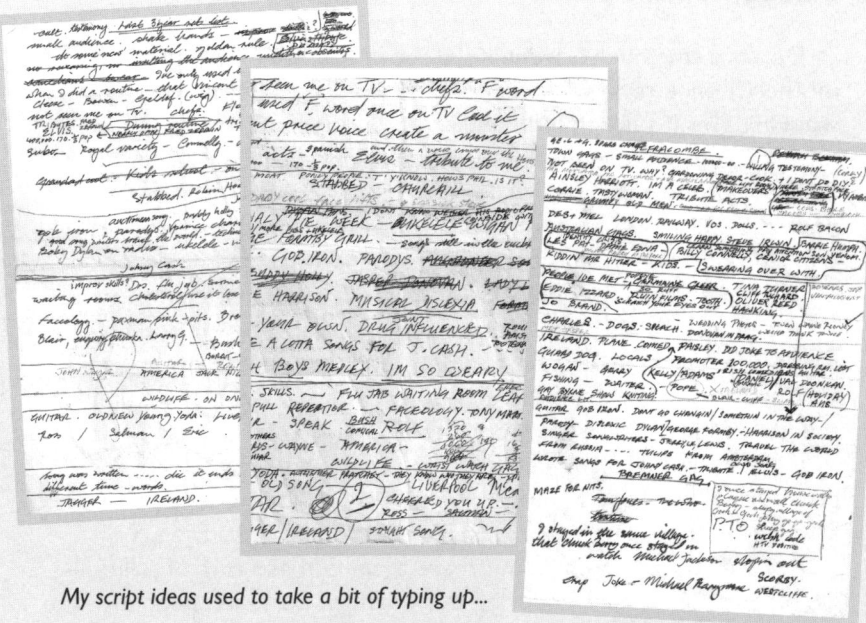

My script ideas used to take a bit of typing up...

happened since with our new dog, Beau (pronounced '*Boe*', obviously), when it met a dog called Alfie, and off we went again.

'Here, Alfie!'
'Here, Boe!'
'Alfie!'
'Boe!'
'Alfie!'
'Boe!'

Increasingly, though, the comics I admired coming up tend to have slipped under the radar nowadays. I did a show with Malcolm Hardee and compadres once that my manager put together in Milton Keynes. It had and a little comedian on the bill who seems to have disappeared now. Ian Macpherson was his name, Irish lad. He was wonderful. And Dominic Holland, who won the 1993 Perrier Best Newcomer Award in Edinburgh, was great as well, these days the father of Spider-Man.

Dylan Moran, I like him ... a romantic Irish comic. He was in the sitcom *Black Books* with Tamsin Greig and Bill Bailey and I've always felt that there's a bit of Bailey in me; we've the same comedic mentality and I do a lot of musical jokes as well. My reviews haven't always been as good as his, though, even when written by fellow showbiz types.

Stand-up Chameleon

Do you remember Gorden Kaye out of *'Allo 'Allo!*? Well, him and his mother(!) once reviewed a video of mine – I can't recall where (and wouldn't give it publicity if I could). It concluded: 'Once you've seen one face, you've seen 'em all.' Boy, that stung. I thought, well, they don't really know me, because that René Artois fellow couldn't do a two-hour show like I do. An hour, then a break, then another hour. In that time, the face-pulling aspect is five minutes, so what am I doing for the other hour and fifty-five? Mimes, stories, caricatures, impressions, music ... Wogan turning into a space creature and such. Anyway, soon after Kaye's damning opinion went to print, part of an advertising hoarding smashed through the windscreen of his Honda CRX and hit him in the head. Mmm, makes you wonder, eh?

If I do respond to comedy these days, it's most likely to those rare gems that arise spontaneously in normal conversation, as opposed to listening to anyone up there on stage doing a planned stage act.

I wouldn't relish walking out there again in these days of political-correctness-gone-mad, enduring the wrath of obsessed people who take offence at anything that doesn't suit their opinion or philosophy.

I'd sooner go fishing.

Looking back, I probably could have been more outrageous, but I was never interested in heading into more dangerous territory. I held back, where Connolly wouldn't. If you go there, the critics latch on and are soon on your back. I just wanted a quiet life, always have done, and especially now I'm retired!

Here's a strange thing, but I thought I would shoehorn it into the book somewhere. It's a true story of what happened to me as a kid. It has lain deep in my mind for 70 years, but resurfaces every blue moon.

In 1954, aged six, I was walking to school on my own and reached a T-junction. In the road, a car was waiting, ready to turn left.

On the opposite side of the street, two women stood engrossed in conversation. One had a toddler by her side, around two-and-a-half-years old. As they chatted, a piece of bright pink tissue paper, the kind you see in a hat box, suddenly appeared in the air from out of a back-street. It looked like a dancing spirit on the wind, floating and swirling in a long trail. The child saw it too and, entranced, ran into the road to

Encore

chase it just as the driver of the waiting car started to turned left. He was looking the opposite way, right, at some distraction instead of the direction he was going and ran over this little girl in front of my eyes.

I hung around a while, in shock, as you would be. The woman, her mother I assume, was going hysterical. They got a chemist out of his shop, who phoned the ambulance. After a while, I just went on my way to school and did my lessons thinking about the three people I felt were to blame for killing this child. 1) The person who dropped the litter, or didn't put it in the bin properly. 2) The woman, for not paying proper attention to her child. 3) The bloke in the car for not looking where he was going.

Whenever this memory surfaces, I still ponder it. Nowadays, a kid would get counselling. In fact I can picture it really vividly ... the old-fashioned car ... the colour of the paper ... and have come to realise that women probably didn't give much significance to cars in the 1950s because there weren't many around. She probably didn't think she needed to grasp her child tightly.

It was demonic, that little bit of dancing paper.

And strangely I've drawn on it as a kind of metaphor for when temptation might try to lure me astray. And I say to myself: 'Don't go after it,' because of that awful incident.

✻

At the age of 29, after having smoked for twenty-two years, I stopped.

It was a habit I'd had since the age of seven, going through all sorts... dog ends, rope, homemade pipes, cigars ... and inhaled all the time as well. Including on a proper pipe filled with St Bruno, which is crazy and probably why I sound like I do nowadays.

I wanted desperately to stop because, for one thing, I was always after doing a great Elvis impression, but when I reached a high note I would hear my lungs crackling, all because of smoking.

Another reason was that my wife-to-be became pregnant and said she would stop smoking from then on, so we quit together. That was New Year's Eve, 1976. Neither of us have smoked since. Still, I didn't get away with it fully. It left me with emphysema. But only just enough of it to leave my lungs pitted and give me a voice with all the qualities of an old Stradivarius violin that's been stood on by a cow.

Stand-up Chameleon

Of course, now that I'm no longer in the media limelight, I've got a lot more time to ponder alternative viewpoints, whether in print or on TV. Not that I'm quite ready to buy David Icke's theory of western 'democracy' being run by a genetically modified hybrid race of reptilian shape-shifters, mind – been there, done that!

Less stressfully, during the last ten years, along with all my other health issues I've also had my prostate yanked out. So, as well as spend more time strumming my guitar, from hereonin I'd like to get back to angling and do more of it.

What do I love about fishing?

Well, apart from catching fish(!), the tranquility of escaping to the country mainly. I live in the countryside and that's why: to go where the fishing is. I love going to rivers and still waters. I'm close to the Ribble and have caught some fabulous barbel.

As for my biggest catch, that happened on a trip with Martin James, the famous fisherman, who took me down to a river down south near Newbury, the Kennet. I got a lovely barbel there too, on a bait and rigg prepared by Martin's friend and excellent angler Will Carson. If you'd put your finger on the scale it would have weighed 15lb. I once got a 13.5lb salmon from the Spey, in the north east of Scotland. I can sit on a riverbank for hours – writing a song in my head, maybe, if I've got a line I can't quite get right. I'm like a dog with a bone, but mainly it's the tranquility.

There's also a bit of nostalgia in it, going back to my childhood.

One of the most exciting things that happened to me fishing was at this pond, near to where I lived as a lad. It was free in those days and I'd done it many a time. This particular evening, it would have been about quarter to seven, my float wasn't cocking properly. It wouldn't stay upright, just lean. Anyway, I left it. I was catching roach, about seven inches long, beautiful. A fellow called Mr Monks who lived just up the road from our council estate came along. He used to walk the fields, I'd see him many a time, popping around to see if anyone had caught anything. 'Hello lad,' he said. 'How are you doing?'

'I've had a couple of roach,' I replied and had no sooner done so than I got another on the hook.

'Eeh, that's a nice fish, lad,' he said, a really nice bloke. 'But bloody hell. One night I was fishing t'other side and hooked this tench. It were massive. Rod nearly snapped, bent right over. This fish was on for quite a while, but got off. Oh, I was so disappointed, but it was a big bugger.

Encore

My personal best fish – a 14lb 15oz barbel...

I bet its still in here. Anyway, I'm off now. Good luck,' and he wandered off a bit further up, to the snigg – or eel pit.

Anyway, after he'd gone my float moved again. 'Aye, aye, another roach,' I thought, but no. I'd only gone and hit this exact same fish he'd just been talking about – a tench, and really massive. I'd no landing net or anything – just this cane rod hand-me-down from my brother that was creaking like mad. And rather than play the fish, as I'd have done if I'd been more skilled, I just tried to drag the bugger in and beach it up the sandbank. The line snapped, though, and it got back in the water. I remember struggling to grab hold of it with my hands but tench are very slippery and it just slithered out of my hands... and away, having fought ferociously. The surface of the pond was now full of bubbles and I had to pack in for the day because I'd run out of tackle. I went back and was literally jumping up and down, telling everybody about the huge tench I'd lost. I'd have been about 12 at the time, pulling my hair out, like kids do.

Stand-up Chameleon

That's the thrill of fishing, you never know what you'll get.

But lately, I'm not fishing as much as I'd like to, having a dodgy knee, an old injury fishing on the Spey, made worse by arthritis. I'm booked in for a knee replacement operation shortly, so hopefully I will be back on the banks of the Ribble soon. I have done a bit of armchair fishing though, watching a few angling programmes on television.

There's an ITV show on at the moment called *Monster Carp* in which three of four young blokes travel to exotic places to catch ridiculously big fish. It has departed from the ways fishing shows have traditionally been presented; the emphasis is on competition between the guys with lots of boyish banter. That stuff doesn't appeal to me much, but that's just my taste. I will say though that its visuals have improved lately, new tech, cameras and lenses giving the show a more 'lush' look. And that obviously interests young anglers because, having just looked it up, I now learn it's being distributed to over eighty countries worldwide.

Monster Carp though, for me, still has a long way to go before it catches up with the quality and style of *A Passion for Angling*, the old BBC2 fishing show from the early 1990s and best ever in my opinion. It took many years and a whole lot of ingenuity, patience and, as it says in the title, 'passion' to produce what is without doubt a work of art in every way. Every shot, whether of a misty dawn, with spiders' webs adorned in dew drops, a sleepy sunset or lazy hot afternoon, together with scenes of winter frost on river foliage, is breathtakingly beautiful. The gentle music almost completes this masterpiece until the voice of narrator Bernard Cribbins is added to the mixture, slipping in so hypnotically it draws you, via an inspired script, into this secret world. And behold, there it is, finished and perfect.

Another delight which may lie somewhere between *Monster Carp* and *A Passion for Angling* is *Gone Fishing*, featuring fellow comedians Paul Whitehouse and Bob Mortimer. Over six series now – and counting – they've developed a great formula, having gone from a mundane situation of two old codgers grumbling about their aches and pains, to then losing themselves and forgetting their troubles in the pursuit of angling. I've heard plenty of people who don't even fish praise the programme to high heaven.

On my longer tours, I would sometimes take my tackle along and try to find time to cast a line on free afternoons. My friend Steve Fairclough suggested that I should make a programme out of these expeditions, mixing in my stand-up and comedy routines, for which I

Encore

had the working title *Fishing For Laughs*. It never transpired however. It seems Paul and Bob beat me to it. Good on 'em!

※

On television, I also watched a few Mike Yarwood repeats when they got an airing on his death in September 2023 and enjoyed them very much, both for nostalgic reasons and because Mike was so brilliant. Which raises the question, I suppose, of which other impressionists I admire. Well, Jon Culshaw obviously, he is deadly accurate, and I've remained a friend of Alistair McGowan, star of *The Big Impression* and much else, and went to see him perform a great set not so long ago in Chorley. John Thomson and Steve Nallon I admire too.

Growing up, the first impersonator I liked was Peter Goodwright, who was on the ITV show *Who Do You Do?* in the 1970s with the likes of Russ Abbot, Janet Brown, Les Dennis, Freddie Starr, Aiden J Harvey, Paul Melba and many others. Yarwood was the biggest ever, though, because it was the golden era of television. They did all the old showbiz stuff though that I came in on the back of, with all the 'new' comedy.

So, why I have I now written this book?

Well, mainly because I wanted to put my experience of what I now see as a remarkable time that will never come back in black and white.

When I initially met my last agent, Pete Gill, he asked if I had any ideas for a new project, or material. I told him I had the idea of writing a book with a format similar to my favourite film, *The Thief of Bagdad*, which starts in the middle of the story, flashes back to the past, catches up to the middle where the reader started, before continuing to the end. 'That sounds good,' he said. 'Get on with it then!'

Having raised the possibility, I then couldn't say no, actually, I can't be bothered, so got stuck in and started writing. The result, around ten years ago now, was an ebook that was available online that sank, without promotion or fanfare, pretty quickly. Oh well, I thought, at least if any young comedians read it, it might give them inspiration and assure them that dedication, getting your head down and generally keeping going can pay off. You do need to have talent in whatever your chosen field is, obviously, but they are among the golden ingredients.

Anyway, I hoped my words might help somebody.

And now here we are, in July 2024 as I write, the book finally about

Stand-up Chameleon

to be published in paperback – updated, revised and professionally produced.

One of the hardest bits about penning an autobiography or memoir is trying to remember the names, places, dates and details of everything that went on all those years ago. I think I've got most of the facts right, especially the major ones, although apologies in advance for any mis-rememberings. It occurs to me now, for example, that when I mention in the Prince's Trust chapter that Nigel Havers was hovering around (now King) Charles, I am no longer one hundred per cent certain that he was the culprit. Well, it was either Nigel or Lionel Blair.

With an ebook, you couldn't include images, which left it looking impoverished, I thought. I wanted nice pictures spread throughout because I'm a visual comic and that has now been put right.

Even on first publication, I knew not so deep down that my comedy career was over. I'd got out of the habit of making people laugh on stage. Nowadays I just sing and play guitar, but am still nervous as hell before I start.

Sometimes, when doing interviews, you get asked how you'd wish to be remembered. Well, I wish to be remembered as the comedian everybody forgot.

At which, somebody might quip, you've already got your wish.

Some comics may want to be remembered as the comedians' comedian; in fact most would probably say that. Me? Well, maybe the musicians' comedian, because I always felt I made a greater impression on musicians with my musical gags and obscure approach to comedy, which is typical, I guess, of the frustrated musician that I am.

As I write these final words, I am getting pestered by the springer spaniel I mentioned earlier, Beau. He is giving me that piercing *'take me walkingziz'* look. So I will oblige my big furry angel and be off with him up the fell, gammy knee and all...

I hope you've enjoyed my tale of adventure, fun and woe. Now that we've reached its end, here is how – in one word – I would describe all the memories: Priceless.

PHIL COOL

the story so far...

> 'He's a joy to behold. But, most of all, that face..! It's remarkable'
> — Jasper Carrott

.... it's the impressions that have converted Cool's career into big business. They are uncanny, almost unnerving.
— Time Out

TONY'S CHOICE
COOL IT (BBC-2, 10.0). Do have a look at the clever comedy impressionist Phil Cool — I reckon he's something of a gem. He scarcely uses a prop, but has the most remarkable ability to transform his face into likenesses of his victims. His script is good too, and I'm sure we're going to see a lot more of him.
— The Mirror

Cool — my hot tip

TELEVISION comedian of the year has to be the outrageous Phil Cool. His repertoire of impressions ranges from Hans and Lotte Haas to Prince Charles, Mick Jagger, E.T. — and even Quasimodo as a folk singer. He's the funniest man I've seen in years. What makes him really different is that his impressions are contemporary; his gags reflect what's going on NOW.
— The Mirror

PHIL COOL is the freshest, funniest new comic to hit the TV screen since Rowan Atkinson. You don't have to take my word for it — just catch his Friday night BBC2 show tonight and prove it yourself.
— Westminster Press

Hot Stuff from Cool

COMEDY impersonator Phil Cool has the hallmark of genius.

His range of characters, without props, is varied and unmistakeable — and uproariously funny.

Where has he been hiding?
— Daily Star

If you've missed it so far, catch the final show next Friday, because he's the most refreshing face for some time.
— Sunday People

COOL'S HOT ON COMEDY

★ THE BBC has found a great new talent in Phil Cool, a Northern impressionist whose underwater spoof of Hans and Lotte Haas was marvellously inventive. Mr Cool knows it is not enough simply to imitate. His material is hilariously first class.
— Daily Express

 PHIL COOL is a remarkable new talent. His three shows were a delight to watch.

Anyone who can take the mickey so brilliantly out of people like Rolf Harris, Mike Harding and Roger Whittaker deserves to succeed in a big way on TV.

Let's see some more of him soon, please.
— The Star

It's a mystery Phil hasn't been snapped up before. Second-rate impressionists are two a penny. Talented funny ones are rare. And Phil is very funny.
— Daily News

Impressive Cool...

— Broadcast

Phil Cool's face is his fortune. Like a large piece of plasticine in an imaginative child's hands, it can reform into 1,001 different poses in a split second.
— Evening Mail

There's a hot rumour that a new team is about to wrest the 'Kings of Comedy' mantle from the Comedy Strip squad. The new team includes President Reagan, Rolf Harris, David Bellamy, a VW Beetle, a Morris Minor and Quasimodo.

Not such a motley crew as they sound, because in fact they're all one man.

Phil Cool is a unique comedy sketchist, with an elastic face and a sharp line in grotesque impersonations — a *Spitting Image* puppet brought to life.
— HIT Magazine

Phil Cool, star of **Cool It** (BBC-2), is a long, lanky, former electrician from Chorley (Lancs.) who looks as if he might have been assembled by an absent-minded mechanic. His impressions of Quasimodo and Rolf Harris repainting the Sistine Chapel are brilliant.

Pebble Mill must feel it is promoting the new Jasper Carrott. In fact, it has got something even better.
— The Daily Telegraph